Scientist as Subject:
The Psychological
Imperative

Scientist as Subject: The Psychological Imperative

Michael J. Mahoney
Pennsylvania State University

1976

Ballinger Publishing Company ● Cambridge, Massachusetts
A Subsidiary of J.B. Lippincott Company

This book is printed on recycled paper.

International Standard Book Number: 0-88410-505-9
Library of Congress Catalog Card Number:

Printed in the United States of America

Library of Congress Cataloging in Publication Data

Mahoney, Michael J.
  The scientist.

  Bibliography: p.
  Includes index.
  1. Scientists. I. Title.
Q147.M33   502'.3   76-5878
ISBN 0-88410-505-9

To those who will read this,
   and to the few who may act upon it . . .
Your fantasized existence has been my prime incentive.

Contents

Foreword

Science is often viewed as a highly efficient inquiry system. The tangible evidence of its awesome power is a daily theme in the mass media. We can now predict and control the movements of subatomic particles with an accuracy that virtually defies human comprehension. We can miniaturize electronic circuits to the point of near invisibility and have even begun to explore our neighboring planets with extraterrestrial craft. Geoscientists have unraveled many of the mysteries of our own planet's infancy, and medical researchers are continually challenging the restrictions of our mortality.

Any way you look at it, science has been productive; Francis Bacon's maxim that "knowledge is power" has been amply illustrated. Although some of the products are unquestionably frightening, one can hardly deny that the frontiers of knowledge have been expanding at an amazing pace. Relative to the last century—or even the last decade—today's scientists know quite a bit about virtually everything on our planet—with one ironic exception. The exception, of course, *is* the scientist. He remains a mysteriously unexamined inhabitant of our planet. In his relentless analysis of everything under (and including) the sun, he has remained curiously self-exempt from the scrutiny which is the creed of his vocation. This book is an invitation to remove that exemption.

It is estimated that there are over 40,000 current scientific journals and that over 90 percent of all scientists ever alive are alive today. There are over half a million scientists in the United States alone. Nevertheless, although our libraries and classrooms are filled with hundreds of thousands of volumes on the *sciences*, one can find very little information about *scientists*. A small minority of historians, philosophers, and sociologists have provided us with our only insights into the mysterious inquisitor. Unfortunately, the glimpses they offer are predominantly based on biographies and social systems analyses, so that we are still left with a very meager understanding of the *psychology* of the scientist.

Our relative ignorance about *homo scientus* is not, in my opinion, a harmless omission which simply disturbs the esthetic balance of our current knowledge. The oversight is not benign. Our continued neglect of the scientist could well be the most costly blunder in the history of empiricism. We can hardly hope to have much confidence in the products of science if we choose to remain ignorant of the limitations imposed by its human imbodiment. The contents of this book are aimed at expanding and illustrating that assertion. I will argue that the conventional image of the scientist is not just a myth—but perhaps a malignant one. He is not the paragon of objective reason; the saintly purveyor of truth. On the contrary, he is a thoroughly fallible human being—capable of bigotry, ambition, and political expedience. Far from his mythical image, he is probably the most passionate of professionals. His research and reasoning skills are easily seduced by Procrustean desires—bending the evidence to fit his hypotheses. In short, he is more often a paradox than a paragon.

This book is intended to be a heuristic illustration of the scientist's fallibilities. Its goal, of course, is to stimulate interest in empirical research on the processes and parameters of scientific behavior. I make no pretense to its being a scientific documentary. As a matter of fact, in those areas where I had a choice, I have tried to avoid encyclopedic documentation of supporting evidence. This was motivated by both stylistic and philosophical considerations (the latter will become clear late in the book). Rather than handicap my delusions of prose with parenthetical references and footnotes, resources are briefly noted at the end of each chapter and compiled in their entirety in the back of the book.

I should point out that my treatise and its illustrations are necessarily influenced by my own restricted professional exposure. As an academic psychologist, many of the examples I employ derive from my own profession. I have largely portrayed the *academic* scientist—not because he is more fallible than other breeds, but only because he is more familiar. With slight variations, I think the portrait can be easily generalized. Likewise, although I like to consider myself a supporter of sexual equality, I repeatedly refer to the scientist as a man. This is because the vast majority of scientists have been male and the research which I shall describe has predominantly involved *men* of science. I, for one, will be glad to see the day when male gender is no longer a prerequisite for genius.

There are those who may view this book as an exercise in muck-raking or perhaps even iconoclasm. For them, my efforts may seem motivated more by sensationalism than by a dedication to the constructive appraisal of a profession which I deeply respect. The lingering shadow of such a misinterpretation was a recurrent concern throughout my writing. Hopefully, my convictions about the continuation and improvement of rational inquiry will be readily discernible. Pursuant to those convictions, all of the proceeds from this book will accrue to the Foundation for Applied Inquiry, an organization devoted to encouraging research on the processes and products of science.

Those who have read any of my previous writings may detect more than a few rather sweeping shifts of position in the present manuscript. My perspectives on epistemology and philosophy of science have recently undergone a veritable overhaul. As a matter of fact, I was most eager to finish writing this book so that I could discover where I stood on several key issues. I often entered the arena from a very different door than that which marked my exit, and I often did not know what I believed until after I had read what I had written. Now that (I think) I know where I hover, I realize that some of my current actions may appear to contradict my arguments. For example, even though I am very critical of statistical inference in several chapters, I shall probably continue to pay homage to "tests of significance" in the papers I submit to psychological journals. My rationale for this admitted hypocrisy is straightforward: until the rules of the science game are changed, one must abide by at least some of the old rules or drop out of the game. While some of my colleagues might encourage me to opt for the latter, I shall continue my expedience for two reasons—(1) I value my opportunity to participate in science, and (2) reforms, if they are to have much chance of survival, are more powerful when they are initiated from *within* a perspective. Thus, until the reforms gain strength or I am convinced of their waywardness, I shall abide by at least some of the old rules and work to encourage their critical scrutiny by my colleagues.

I am indebted to a number of colleagues and prior writers. The works of Thomas S. Kuhn, Ian I. Mitroff, Warren O. Hagstrom, Bernard Barber, and Walter B. Weimer have been particularly important in suggesting and illustrating many of the themes pursued in this book. Several friends and colleagues have also shared valuable time, information, and support. I consider myself privileged in the assistance I received from Walt Weimer, Jake Lesswing, and Lynn Carpenter. For their comments and suggestions on the manuscript, I thank Diane Arnkoff, Rus Bauer, Anne Boedecker, Alan Kazdin, Marty Kenigsberg, Kitty Mahoney, Ian Mitroff, and Todd Rogers.

In the writing of this book and the conduct of the research it reports, I have learned to appreciate the need for some degree of autonomy in scientific endeavors. The person who takes an unconventional path is often faced with isolation, and occasionally with persecution. This was underscored by repeated signs of disapproval from my colleagues—three indictments to the American Psychological Association, two attempts to have me fired, and eighteen rejections from journals and publishing companies. There were times when I felt the oppression of that disapproval, and many moments when I wondered whether my handful of friends were aware of their own deviance in supporting me. Without their encouragement, a difficult task might have been impossible. As the months wore on and the professional isolation continued, I found myself frequently whistling a song written by Kris Kristofferson. In it he describes a conversation between a young idealistic singer and a weathered veteran of hard times. The old man warns the youngster that his songs are futile and his hopes unreal, that the world will never listen to his pleas for reform. But the penniless young singer remains undaunted by this advice and uses it to re-kindle his motivation to sing. I must have identified with that singer, and particularly with the final line in defense of his idealism: "I don't believe that no one wants to know." There were many times when I owed at least some of my perseverance to that song, and that line. I shall soon discover whether my whistling was truly in the dark.

Finally, I would like to express my appreciation to the persons who were most intimately connected with the actual production of this work. Sandy Ranio transformed my scribblings into occasionally coherent sentences. Her superhuman deeds were supplemented by those of several Ballinger personnel. And, if I may paraphrase a line from Daryl Bem, I am ultimately indebted to Kitty, Benjamin, Sean, and Duffy—without whom this book would have been finished months ago.

MJM
March, 1976

There is something fascinating about science. One gets such whole-sale returns of conjecture out of such a trifling investment of fact.

Mark Twain

Idolatry is the necessary product of static dogmas.

Alfred North Whitehead

To be boosted by an illusion is not to live better than to live in harmony with the truth.

Santayana

No society is safe in the hands of so few clever people (scientists).

Lancelot Hogben

It is common to men to err; but it is only a fool that perseveres in his error.

W.R. Alger

Certain features of the mental life of the scientist . . . affect the trustworthiness of his product, and in particular make the findings of science subject to weakness and passion like other human constructions.

D.L. Watson

The scientific establishment is gravely inadequate to its professed aims, commits injustices as a matter of course, and is badly in need of research and reform.

Alfred de Grazia

Science . . . is nothing but a confident expectation that relevant thoughts will occasionally occur.

Alfred North Whitehead

Chapter 1

Illusions and Idols

Science is a prestigious profession. Although its specific disciplines may wax and wane in their public image, there can be little doubt that being a "scientist" carries more social status than the majority of occupations. It is equally clear that our culture worships knowledge. The glorification of truth is so pervasive that it is almost imperceptible—our thinking is imbued with a respect for knowledge. This worship of *truth* may partially explain the popular worship of the truth seeker. The scientist is the high priest of knowledge. He is our capable and mysterious liason with reality, our ambassador to wisdom. Moreover, the stereotyped image of the scientist portrays him as a superhuman organism. He is viewed as the paragon of reason and objectivity, an impartial genius whose visionary insights are matched only by his quiet humility. He combines the wisdom of a prophet with the dedication of a martyr.

THE STORYBOOK IMAGE
OF THE SCIENTIST

Robert K. Merton and Ian I. Mitroff have pointed out that the popular stereotype of the scientist is reminiscent of character portrayals in children's storybooks. This public adulation of the scientist is perhaps not surprising—adulation is a frequent element in our culture. The popular image of the scientist, however, places him in a more demure category of heroes—where he is joined by some (e.g., physicians) but set apart from others (e.g., movie stars and popular singers). More startling, perhaps, is the realization that scientists are sometimes just as adulating as the public in their self-image. Although somewhat more restrained in his self-portrait, the scientist tends to paint himself generously in hues of objectivity, humility and rationality. He accepts the saintly prestige accorded him by the public and eagerly welcomes the title of Paragon of Inquiry.

This self-perception will occupy many pages in this book. In my opinion the scientist's image of himself is a critical component in his research. The average scientist tends to be complacently confident about his rationality and expertise, his objectivity and insight. I shall argue at length that this complacency is naive, unfounded and potentially disastrous to the pursuit of knowledge. In a sense, the remainder of this book is devoted to redressing that fallacious self-image.

Before embarking on that campaign, however, let us take a closer look at the storybook image. What are these virtuous characteristics of the scientist? They are more often described as professional "norms" rather than "virtues" and they are implicit, if not explicit, in most introductory textbooks. Capsulized summaries have been offered by a number of writers (e.g., Barber, West, Diederich, and Mitroff). With generous paraphrasing and integration, the list goes somewhat as follows.

Storybook Characteristics of the Scientist

1. *Intelligence*, occasionally spiced with creativity;
2. Faith and expertise in *logical reasoning*;
3. *Experimental skills* which insure the optimal collection of accurate data;
4. *Objectivity* and emotional neutrality, with a loyalty only to truth;
5. *Flexibility* reflected in a willingness to change one's opinion;
6. *Humility* and personal disinterest in fame or recognition;
7. *Communality* reflected in an open sharing of knowledge and active cooperation with colleagues; and
8. *Suspension of judgment* when scientific evidence is insufficient or unclear.

Numerous scientific volumes document the pervasiveness of this self-image. The following are representative selections.

> The scientific attitude of mind produces many . . . virtues . . . . Patience, endurance, humility, teachableness, honesty, accuracy—without these it is impossible for a scientist to work. And the history of science is as inspiring in its human values as are the legends of the saints. Contemplate

the heroism of a Galileo, the patience of a Darwin, the humility of a
Pasteur; a modern eleventh chapter of *Hebrews* might be written listing
the names of all those men of faith who by quiet work, unremitting in
their zeal, one by one discovered facts which made man's lot easier and
happier in what was otherwise to him a hostile and unhappy universe
(Knickerbocker, 1927, p. vii).

Such generous praise and reverence is not a thing of the past—it has
endured and flourished in more contemporary times:

(Scientists') actions and thoughts, being more free from the influence of
passion than those of other men, are all the better materials for the study
of the calmer parts of human nature .... By aspiring to noble ends ..,
(these men) have risen above the region of storms into a clearer atmosphere, where there is no misrepresentation of opinion, nor ambiguity of
expression, but where one mind comes into closest contact with another
at the point where both approach nearest to the truth (Maxwell, 1960,
pp. vii–viii).

And similarly:

Willingness to change opinions .... A scientist ... is more willing than
most to alter an opinion, once he sees reliable evidence to the contrary,
because he knows that, every time he does so, he has learned something
....
Humility .... A scientist realizes how little is known with any certainty; he commonly looks for little truths that the unscientific would
consider not worth the trouble.
Loyalty to truth. A scientist is sometimes subjected to humiliation as his
findings shift and invalidate some conclusion to which he has previously
committed himself; but his loyalty to truth is such that he would rather
cut off his right arm than suppress the new data. The general picture is of
lofty and even noble devotion to the facts, however they may affect one
personally.
An objective attitude. A scientist has a high regard for facts and tries to
behave in accordance with them; while an unscientific person tends to see
only the facts he wishes to see and to react emotionally against others.
Suspended judgment. A scientist tries hard not to form an opinion on a
given issue until he has investigated it (Diederich, 1967, pp. 23-24).

Thus, even in modern times, the scientist is viewed as the passionless
purveyor of truth. Intelligence—even genius—is considered a prerequisite for his pursuits, and his emotional neutrality is often assumed
to pervade even his personal life. "It is therefore not surprising that
he is believed to have a relatively unhappy home life and a wife who
is not pretty " (Beardslee & O'Dowd, 1961, p. 998).

HOMO SCIENTUS: THE BIASED AND
PASSIONATE TRUTH SPINNER

Committed to truth, unbiased by emotion, open to new ideas, professionally and personally unselfish—the scientist thus described *deserves* sainthood! It is little wonder that we have built a shrine to science and canonized its clergy. If the foregoing attributes are actually displayed by scientists, we have good reason to place them on a pedestal. Judging from their own reports, these virtuous accolades are not seen as scientist fiction. Interviews with members of a variety of disciplines suggest that this sacrosanct image is a frequent one among scientists. Although self-awareness of some fallibility may be increasing, it seems safe to say that the storybook image is alive and well (and it is certainly not hiding). Scientists continue to "keep the faith" by nourishing a public and self-image of human transcendence.

As I have already noted, the basic goal of this book is to critically examine and hopefully refine this prevalent image. By way of contrast to the previous list of scientific virtues, I should perhaps preview some of the things we will find:

1. Superior intelligence is neither a prerequisite nor a correlate of scientific contribution;
2. The scientist is often saliently illogical in his work, particularly when he is defending a preferred view or attacking a rival one;
3. In his experimental research, he is often selective, expedient, and not immune to distorting the data;
4. The scientist is probably the most passionate of professionals; his theoretical and personal biases often color his alleged "openness" to the data;
5. He is often dogmatically tenacious in his opinions, even when the contrary evidence is overwhelming;
6. He is not the paragon of humility or disinterest but is, instead, often a selfish, ambitious, and petulant defender of personal recognition and territoriality;
7. The scientist often behaves in ways which are diametrically opposite to communal sharing of knowledge—he is frequently secretive and occasionally suppresses data for personal reasons; and
8. Far from being a "suspender of judgment," the scientist is often an impetuous truth spinner who rushes to hypotheses and theories long before the data would warrant.

Our survey will take us into the human side of science, documenting its subjectivity and its pervasive limitations. We will find that Knickerbocker's dispassionate "saints" were often involved in fierce personal battles over the "ownership" of an idea. We will encounter great men blatantly plagiarizing the work of others, and no less eminent scientists than Newton, Galileo and Mendel apparently "doctoring" their data to fit their theories. We will find bigoted intolerance of new ideas, intense commitment to personal opinions, blatant refusals to examine "alien" data, and prejudicial inequities in publication and professional recognition. In short, we will see the scientist as a thoroughly fallible organism.

As I mentioned in the foreword, the present undertaking is intentionally critical. This does not mean that it is misrepresentative, nor do I intend it to be destructive. In my opinion, the portrait I shall paint is probably not far off the mark. My emphasis on the liabilities rather than the assets of the scientist stems from two considerations. First, I think that the "virtuous" side of *homo scientus* has already received too much publicity. I do not wish to contribute any further to the myth by extolling or reiterating prevalent misconceptions. Second, by highlighting the human frailties of the scientist, I hope to stimulate both self-examination and empirical inquiry. Our own technical skills have too long remained neglected by our technical skills. The quality and pace of our scientific knowledge is critically dependent upon our scientific behavior. It is high time that we look at ourselves with the same critical inquisitiveness which has characterized our quest for worldly knowledge. We must stop exempting ourselves from the well-documented limitations of human information processing and start nourishing *scientalysis*—a critical, constructive, and enduring study of the scientist. This viewpoint will be a recurrent one in the pages that follow.

My campaign for scientific self-appraisal is hardly revolutionary. As early as 1621, Francis Bacon was warning his peers about the "idols" which often beset rational inquiry:

> The human understanding is like a false mirror, which, receiving rays irregularly, distorts and discolors the nature of things by mingling it own nature with it (p. 48).
> The cause and root of nearly all evils in the sciences is this—that while we falsely admire and extol the powers of the human mind we neglect to seek for its true helps (p. 40).

Bacon's foresight, however, was not heeded; and although phenomenology and the pervasive subjectivity of experience became bywords in philosophy, these realizations were seldom acknowledged or explored in the scientist. A more explicit protest and entreaty was voiced by D.L. Watson in a timely volume titled *Scientists Are Human*:

> Central to any estimate of the nature of scientific truth and of its value
> for humanity are: (1) an understanding of the psychological constitution
> of the investigator, and (2) an understanding of the social forces which
> produce him, encourage or oppose him, and transmit or ignore his work
> (1938, p. 3).

Despite his assertion that *"The chief problem of science is the scientist"* (p. 45), Watson's statements apparently fell on deaf ears, for his book remains obscure and his proposals have stimulated scant research.

There have, of course, been a number of philosophical works extending phenomenology and subjectivism to epistemology (theory of knowledge) such as those by Polanyi, Bartley, Turner, and Weimer. Naive realism (or the doctrine of immaculate perception) has been only one of the many principles attacked in these writings. While a few individuals have defended the objectivity of science (e.g., Scheffler), the bulk of the arguments and evidence seems to rest clearly with the "fallibilists." But, again, these works have been philosophical in nature and—as we will see in a later chapter—the scientist seldom invokes or even acknowledges philosophy unless he is in a theoretical crisis. For the majority of scientists, philosophy is a hack —to be tolerated when necessary and reluctantly consulted only when internal problems or theoretical rivals force apologetic defense.

A more direct and contemporary treatise on subjectivity in science is offered by Ian I. Mitroff in a stimulating volume which describes his research with 42 geoscientists. Prior to the lunar landing of Apollo 11, Mitroff realized that the Apollo missions offered a unique opportunity for the examination of scientist behavior, attitudes, and emotions. Some of the most eminent geophysicists in the world had been recruited by NASA (the National Aeronautics and Space Administration) to design and evaluate experiments on such issues as the nature and origin of the moon. Many of these scientists had publicly committed themselves to various lunar hypotheses. The Apollo missions would be returning "hard data"—samples of the lunar soil— which would bear directly on these hypotheses. How would our eminent lunar rock scientists react to the data returns? Would they live up to the storybook image by exhibiting dispassionate objectivity and a willingness to change opinion? Through a series of interviews spanning five of the Apollo missions, Mitroff was able to offer some startling answers to these questions. Excerpts and illustrations from this significant piece of research will be found sprinkled through-out the present text. By way of preview, however, it can be said that Mitroff's data clearly reflect the biases of the scientist. His scientist-subjects were often prejudicial and dogmatic, refusing to alter their beliefs and eager to discredit data which contradicted their hypotheses.

It might be worth commenting here on the possible desirability of a dispassionate scientist. Three questions are appropriate: *Is* the scientist objective and emotionally neutral? If not, *could* he be? If so, *should* he be? The answer to the first question is resoundingly negative. As we shall see in this book, objectivity and emotional neutrality are not characteristic of the scientist. Could these features be attained? Perhaps, but it is doubtful. The reward system of science and our cultural worship of knowledge make it almost impossible for truth-seeking to be an austere and aseptic endeavor. In addition to the unfeasibility of emotional neutrality, it is impossible for any human being to be "objective" in the technical sense of that term. As processors of information we are inherently biased. More important, the desirability of passionless science has been seriously questioned. Mitroff and others have argued that the scientist's emotions facilitate his perseverance and motivate his queries. From this perspective, emotionalism is a necessary prerequisite for science. My own opinion on this matter (cf. chapter 6) invokes a delicate balance of emotions—sufficient intensity to provide research incentive but simultaneous constraints from their unduly threatening objectivity, integrity, and flexibility. In other words, I will argue that the scientist's passion for his theories should be adequate to sustain a courtship or even a marriage—but inadequate to prevent divorce. This metaphor introduces an alternate image of science, and one which deserves at least brief consideration.

ALTERNATE IMAGES: SCIENCE AS A ROMANCE, A RELIGION AND A GAME

I have already previewed our finding that the saintly image of the scientist is patently untenable. In this section I would like to examine briefly some alternate metaphors. My reason for this is simple —throughout the remainder of this book these metaphors will frequently be invoked. I shall not digress here on my stylistic preferences for alliteration and metaphorical description. There are, I think, several features which make these practices communicatively powerful. Metaphors, for example, are highly condensed messages which invoke numerous unspoken attributes by tapping semantic associations. They rely on a conceptual shorthand which is forceful in its density. Their power will, I think, be apparent after our brief survey of science metaphors. Needless to say, all metaphors are limited in their accuracy. However, for our purposes, a "good" metaphor will be one which yields maximal portrayal and minimal distortion.

One delightfully suggestive metaphor portrays science as a love affair. Thus, Agnew and Pyke write:

> Research is like a love affair. The ingredients include: (1) your image of the girl; (2) the real girl as she would appear if you . . . had access to all information about her; and (3) the bits, pieces, or samples of information you have, some of it clear, some of it vague, some of it twisted by memory or biased senses . . . . Changing a once-loved picture is a very painful process, and we know the degrees to which a lover will go to ignore twist, and blink away negative data . . . (1969, p. 128).
>
> The rejection of a theory once accepted is like the rejection of a girl friend once loved—it takes more than a bit of negative evidence. In fact, the rest of the community can shake their collective heads in amazement at your blindness, your utter failure to recognize the glaring array of differences between your picture of the world, or the girl, and the data.
>
> • • •
>
> We suspect that there are those who would disagree violently with this love affair model of research. They will say that the researchers must be completely dedicated to objectivity, that he is only interested in the truth. Perhaps there are researchers like that. We haven't met enough to fill a phone booth (p. 162).

As we shall see in the chapters that follow, the love affair metaphor beautifully captures many of the correlates of scientific behavior—passionate enchantment, tenacity, defensiveness, and a very biased filtration of the data. Unfortunately, our rapidly changing cultural mores have begun to stretch the tenability of the metaphor. Having an "affair" in contemporary times has acquired connotations of brevity and even superficiality. The scientist's romances, however, are seldom fleeting. As Agnew and Pyke note, courtship often leads to marriage and, as we shall see in chapters 6 and 8, the average scientist is violently opposed to divorce. Even when the grounds for dissolution are overwhelming, he often remains faithful to his theories until his death. (What he does after that might be better addressed by the next metaphor.)

A second metaphor portrays science as a religious cult with varying degrees of fanaticism. I have already invoked this descriptor in my use of religious adjectives ("saintly," "clergy," etc.). Knickerbocker, among others, has contended that the metaphor is justified by the saintly virtues of scientists. My defense of its appropriateness draws on very different features. While I do not agree with Standen (*Science Is a Sacred Cow*) or Andreski (*Social Sciences as Sorcery*) in their extreme and often irrational attacks on science, I do think that the religious metaphor conveys several significant aspects of scientist behavior. Science does involve worship (e.g., of knowledge) and various forms of ritualistic behavior designed to serve that worship (e.g., publication, research, and convention attendance). It has dogmas and a hierarchy of clergy ranging from prophets (e.g., Nobelists) and gate-keepers of truth (journal editors) to the more mundane occupants of the pulpit (college instructors). It collects its memorabilia and enshrines them in museums as sacred reminders of our fight against ignorance. Moreover, science is a thoroughly persuasive enterprise. Like religions, it makes ambitious claims about both the nature of reality (ontology) and the appropriate methods of gaining access to that reality (epistemology). While its pulpits are a bit more subtle than those of organized religion, its attempts at proselytization are no less energetic. Its temple is often the classroom and its persuasion is often transmitted in the form of textbooks, popular magazines and the mass media (on any morning but Sunday).

The foregoing remarks should be viewed as descriptive, not evaluative. There are, I think, many striking parallels between organized religion and organized science. Both are populated by passionate and often dogmatic adherents who work diligently toward system-specific goals. In the appendix we will expand the parallels even further and discuss what appear to be common themes in almost all forms of human belief. For the time being, suffice it that I consider the religious metaphor a viable one in communicating at least some aspects of science.

A third metaphor portrays science as a game. Admittedly, the object of the science game is not to win but to continue playing (which has also been said of the game of life). Advocates of the science game metaphor have often provided enlightening parallels to buttress this image (e.g., Cowan, Agnew & Pyke and McCain & Segal). In my opinion the features described by Mitroff offer lucid illustration. With abridgement and some embellishments of my own, the characteristics of games may be paraphrased as follows:

1. individual players;
2. teams (replete with coaches and division of labor among the players);
3. designation of "home teams" and rivals;

4. a sanctioned field of play (with "out-of-bounds" and "foul" territory);
5. regulation equipment and sanctioned plays;
6. prerequisite skills for players;
7. recruitment and training of talented players;
8. major and minor leagues;
9. public performances and social gatherings, sometimes viewed as tournaments;
10. game rules which specify objectives as well as sanctioned methods for attaining those objectives;
11. a scoring system which allows quantification of the competition (among both players and teams);
12. umpires, scorekeepers, and commentators;
13. eminent players and heroes;
14. trophies and special awards—such as enshrinement in the game's "hall of fame";
15. preservers of game tradition (e.g., historians) who record great moments in the game and collect game memorabilia and lore;
16. fans and supporters;
17. extensive bartering and mobility in promising young players;
18. a "grapevine" of personal and professional gossip, often nourished by game writers;
19. periodicals and books which describe various aspects of the game; and
20. intense emotional involvement and personal competitiveness—the "thrill of victory and agony of defeat."

I can't imagine many scientists reading the above list without some emotional response (hopefully, a self-conscious smile)—the parallels to science are so vivid that one can hardly call it a metaphor. We have our umpires and our heroes, our trophies and our game rules. As a matter of fact, I think all 20 features can be readily identified in academic science. The next few chapters will be devoted to that task.

Bear in mind in what follows that the various metaphors are not being employed as degrading portrayals or sarcastic caricatures. They are condensed descriptors which may facilitate our taking alternative views of scientific behavior. Their intended purpose is expository, not theatrical.

The purpose of this book is not simply to challenge an erroneous image or to chide scientists for their naive self-appraisals. The storybook image is not just a vain and flattering distortion of reality. It is my contention that *popular misconceptions of the scientist significantly threaten the very foundations of scientific knowledge.* To the extent that he sees himself as a rational and unbiased truth-seeker, the scientist will be complacent, overly confident, and tenaciously committed to his theories and hypotheses. The problem does not reside only with theoretical scientists, however. As we shall see in chapter 8, the quality of allegedly "raw" data is often influenced by the scientist. His biases are not only reflected in how he interprets the data, but also in the data themselves. Scientific evidence is not some pure glimpse of reality to be fit into a grand jigsaw puzzle. Rather, it is an inevitably biased and sometimes grossly distorted shadow of a reality which will never be completely fathomable. The raw data of science are raw only in the sense of their crudeness, not their purity.

Contrary to the popular adage in introductory textbooks, *our theories often generate rather than reflect the data.* Science is not a magnificent display of inductive logic where the accumulating data fall together into higher-order maxims and theories. There is now ample documentation of the frequent priority of hypotheses over evidence. When forced to choose between conceptual models and the data, many scientists will choose the former. Such instances of a direct showdown between theory and data are probably rare. However, the interactions and interdependence of these two cohorts are unmistakable. Our theories often lead to selective and distorted data which, in turn, serve to maintain a distorted view of reality.

But theories and conceptual models are not the only culprits in our quest for knowledge. There are numerous aspects of the scientific culture which work to impair both the accuracy and the rate of our successive approximations to reality. In many cases scientific progress is made *in spite of* our graduate schools and institutions of higher learning. Likewise, I shall argue that many scientific journals have seriously retarded our progress by absurd, inefficient, and often prejudicial policies. The list is a long one—academic tenure, territoriality of ideas, secretiveness in research—these are but a handful of the influences which often mitigate against the optimal growth of knowledge.

The major premise of this book is a very simple one—namely, he is most deceived who is self-deceived. So long as we honor the implicit norm to avoid studying scientists, we will remain self-deceived. So long as we ignore the psychological and social factors which influence our investigative behaviors, we can go on spinning our truths without too much fear of challenge. After all, if the data agree with our theory, what does it matter that the theory may have generated them? Were I not so committed to this nebulous endeavor called science, I might be able to defer to these alluring locutions. However, as I stated earlier, it is my opinion that our continuing neglect of the scientist may well be the most expensive oversight in the history of empiricism. Obviously, it is *not* my contention that science is ill conceived or predominantly impotent. I would hardly be advocating a "science of science" unless I considered empirical inquiry an indispensable component in our approach to knowledge. My contention is that our methods of knowledge gathering—even though they have demonstrated unquestionable power—remain relatively crude and unrefined *because* of our failure to critically scrutinize their human embodiment. How can we be confident in our knowledge when we have so little assurance of the credibility of its source? How can we legitimately exempt the scientist—of all organisms—from the critical scrutiny which is deemed befitting of every other animate and inanimate occupant of our planet? Can we afford to glibly accept the truths of science without gauging the limitations of its primary instrument?

In my opinion, we cannot. But again, my contention is not simply critical—it is intended to be constructive. By systematically studying the scientist, we may not only develop an overdue appreciation of his very human limitations, but we may also begin to develop means for improving his skills. By examining the factors which influence objectivity and conceptual flexibility, we may hope to refine our inquiry skills well beyond their current state. Notwithstanding our neglect of this area, there can be little doubt that science has evidenced awesomely tangible progress in the last century. What additional benefits can be expected when we begin to "bootstrap" our queries with a science of science? The answer can, I think, be partially gauged by the salience of our current limitations and crudity. These are the topics of the next few chapters. They belie a consensus with Whately's apt maxim that "He who is unaware of his ignorance will be misled by his knowledge."

REFERENCES

4, 7, 19, 24, 26, 31, 32, 33, 38, 70, 105, 121, 158, 232, 273, 286, 287, 294, 305, 316, 323, 351, 352, 398, 425, 447, 461, 466, 467, 468, 469, 473, 476.

Science should not presuppose what it is yet to discover.

David Bakan

There is no source of deception in the investigation of nature which can compare with a fixed belief that certain kinds of phenomena are impossible.

William James

The Law of the Instrument: Give a small boy a hammer, and he will find that everything he encounters needs pounding.

Abraham Kaplan

False facts are highly injurious to the progress of science for they often endure long; but false views, if supported by some evidence, do little harm, for everyone takes salutory pleasure in proving their falseness.

Charles Darwin

Chance favors the prepared mind.

Louis Pasteur

In this poor world we talk by aggregates and think by systems.

Elizabeth Barrett Browning

Man's mind stretched to a new idea never goes back to its original dimensions.

Oliver Wendell Holmes

What science deals with is an *imagined* world.

D.O. Hebb

It is theory which decides what we can observe.

Albert Einstein

Many shrewd blows may be received by the unfortunate custodian of new truth.

Oliver Lodge

Chapter 2

The Science Game: an Overview

To date, our relatively meager understanding of *homo scientus* has been gleaned from two generally disparate fields. The first is primarily a subdivision of philosophy. Within that nebulous arena called "philosophy of science" a handful of workers have specialized in analyzing historical factors in the growth of knowledge. These individuals have offered substantial contributions toward understanding some of the forces and patterns which seem to be perpetually reflected in science. Their efforts have been supplemented by another group of workers who hail from the discipline of sociology. Although its origins are very recent, the sociology of science appears to be a rapidly growing discipline.

Were it not for this small group of renegade inquirers, our knowledge about the behavior of scientists would be almost nil rather than simply meager. The contributions of these philosophers and sociologists will be very apparent in the chapters which follow. For the time being, let us take a brief look at some of the general themes which have emerged from their efforts.

CULTURES, PARADIGMS
AND REVOLUTIONS

Fields of inquiry are often dominated by a small number of "classic" works or perspectives. This is undoubtedly the case in the historical analysis of science, where Thomas S. Kuhn's *The Structure of Scientific Revolutions* has monopolized both thought and controversy.

Kuhn's analysis of the historical processes in the growth of scientific knowledge has remained dominant for over a decade. Although it has not totally escaped criticism, its relatively rapid and unilateral acceptance can hardly be challenged.

Kuhn's theory of scientific progress is unusually comprehensive in both content and perspective. Although it emerges primarily from a historical viewpoint, it integrates elements spawned by a number of disciplines—sociology, epistemology, political science, and psychology. And herein lies at least part of its relevance for our exploration of *homo scientus*. Kuhn's theory offers a molar view with which our forthcoming molecular analyses will be very compatible. His descriptions of broader cultural forces converge symbiotically with the detailed individual portraits contained in the chapters to follow. Kuhn offers a lucid and revealing "big picture" within which to place our more intense and personal scrutinies. It is for this reason that we take a moment here to outline the structure of Kuhn's perspective. Since the following rendition is undoubtedly filtered and frequently embellished by my own conceptual biases, I would urge consultation of the original source.

One of the major themes in Kuhn's classic study was simply that science is not "truth by accretion." Contrary to the popular image conveyed by introductory textbooks, our knowledge is not a smooth accumulation of scientific evidence. According to Kuhn, historians of science and textbook authors have perpetrated this myth by *reconstructing* rather than *reporting* the actual growth process in science. Like public relations writers, they have often chosen to put forth a very distorted public image of science—one which portrays it as an elegant and awesomely efficient approach to knowledge. In popular mythology, science is a well-tuned truth machine whose relentless march on ignorance is strategic, well coordinated, and inevitable. This image, according to Kuhn, could hardly be less accurate. In his brief treatise on the growth of knowledge, Kuhn shows that scientific progress would be more aptly described as a series of frequently uncoordinated fits and seizures. Moreover, as subsequent writers have agreed (e.g., Weimer) the accretion theory is repeatedly contradicted in the history of science. We are not piling up "facts" in constructing our scientific theories. Our "facts" are just as fickle as our theories. Today's facts are yesterday's science fiction and tomorrow's myths. More important, yesterday's facts are expediently reclassified when so demanded by contemporary theory. The long-acknowledged "facts" of a flat earth, a permeating ether, and an indestructible atom can hardly be called foundation stones of contemporary science. These errant bricks were purged from the superstructure when their truth tolerance was questioned by subsequent architects. Since our facts change almost as readily as our theories, one can hardly describe science as their progressive accumulation.

In addition to his attack on the accretion model, Kuhn proposed that the growth of scientific knowledge could be portrayed as a repetitive cycle of static and dynamic phases. According to the theory, these phases are *normal science, crisis,* and *revolution,* with the revolution being followed by the development of a new normal science.

The normal science phase is basically that which is emphasized in popular and textbook portrayals of science. It is imbued with a complacent confidence that the current theories are valid, supporting data are pouring in, and—in short—all is right with the world. The most salient feature of normal science is the *paradigm,* which is a set of generally accepted assumptions and rules regarding the nature of problems in a given discipline and the appropriate means for addressing them (e.g., "where" to look, with what instruments, and so on). The paradigm is the conceptual and methodological world of the scientist. For any given specialty or sub-specialty, the paradigm embodies the contemporary creed of its adherents. As a system of beliefs and practical guidelines, it endorses an *ontology* (theory of reality; the nature of things) and an *epistemology* (theory of knowledge; the methods of appropriate inquiry).

There is a paradox in paradigms. Almost singlehandedly, Kuhn has rendered the term "paradigm" a household word in science. Contemporary texts often introduce the student to science by talking about its various paradigms. The paradox stems from the fact that Kuhn's critics have been most upset by his use of this term. Masterman, for example, has suggested that Kuhn used the term "paradigm" in no less than 21 different ways, thereby obscuring its intended theoretical meaning. By way of partial concession and reclarification, Kuhn refined his use of the term in 1970 and responded to some of its critics. Although these terminological subleties are philosophically important, they must be considered tangential to our present overview of Kuhn's theory. The interested reader is urged to consult Lakatos and Musgrave for an excellent series of exchanges on this and related issues.

For any given field of research, the development of a paradigm is a sign of maturity. It indicates that the discipline has "made it" as a speciality or even a dominant molar theme. By establishing its own creeds of knowledge and inquiry, a renegade or revolutionary stream of research and theory can become integrated into the larger family of science. As with most elitist groups, however, entrance into the country club of science requires credentials, and many of these are embodied in the paradigm. For example, even though there were several excursions into natural selection and physical relativity prior to Darwin or Einstein, these perspectives were not accepted until they could present elaborate conceptual credentials.

The development or maturation of a paradigm is often marked by events supplementary to a conceptual system. For example, specialized journals will emerge and a society devoted to the paradigm may develop. A technical jargon often follows, along with specialized instruments. One unequivocal sign of an emerging paradigm is its appearance in the college curriculum. With introductory texts, specialized courses, and perhaps the beginnings of a new college department, the paradigm has taken strong roots and a phase of "normal science" has begun.

In one sense normal science could be described as a communal exercise in "keeping the faith." Its primary goal is the "legitimation" of the paradigm—that is, its confirmation, refinement, and expansion. Adherents of the paradigm are busily grinding out theoretical and technological details. Kuhn refers to much of this normal science activity as "mopping up" operations. As we will see in a later chapter, a shovel may often be more useful than a mop.

During normal science phases, researchers are not actively looking for new phenomena. Indeed, they are often blind to them when they do appear. Unanticipated or discrepant data are often overlooked or actively suppressed at this stage of inquiry. Moreover, the prevailing paradigm not only affects what the scientist may look for or see, but also *how* he sees it. Kuhn emphasizes the pervasive conceptual and perceptual biases thus imposed. He likens them to several phenomena in visual perception. For example, look at the Necker cube in figure 2-1. If you look at it long enough, you will experience a dramatic perceptual shift. For example, you may have first seen the shaded side as the front of the cube only to find later that you can also view it as the back. Notice that the "data" (i.e., the cube) in this situation do not change—it is your perception of them that changes. Also note that you cannot view the cube from two perspectives at once. Kuhn suggests that this kind of perceptual exercise conveys some of the elements of paradigms and paradigm shifts. A change in perspective often forces a new interpretation of old data. Moreover, when the researcher has adopted one way of viewing things it often restricts his conceptual vision. He can seldom see alternative ways of viewing the cube.

Up until this point it may sound as though the normal scientist is a bigoted and deleterious element in the growth of knowledge.

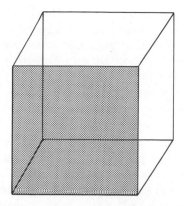

Figure 2-1. The Necker cube.

However, Kuhn has strongly argued that normal science is not only valuable but essential in the progress of inquiry. Again, the critics have often thought otherwise.[a] According to Kuhn, normal science performs a critical function in setting the stage for paradigm crisis and subsequent revolution. Because of their relatively intense and myopic cultivation of their paradigm, normal scientists engage in a degree of research scrutiny which would otherwise be impossible. That is, in their often enthusiastic efforts to legitimate the paradigm, they develop instruments and perform experiments involving very minute technical details. Ironically, in so doing, they often uncover the seeds of the paradigm's demise. In their painstaking and sometimes obtuse efforts to promote the paradigm, they discover its deficiencies—places where it doesn't hold up and data which contradict it. These anomalies might well have gone unnoticed were it not for the technical precision encouraged by normal science. Moreover, as Kuhn points out, "Anomaly appears only against the background provided by the paradigm" (p. 65). That is, by setting up a strong counterexpectancy, the paradigm actually highlights the anomaly. I think it was David Hume who pointed out that ignorance and surprise are incompatible. In the case of paradigm anomalies, the surprise is caused by a contrast with the accepted model.

Normal science is primarily an exercise in problem solving—an attempt to increase the precision and power of the paradigm. Bear in mind, however, that the paradigm often defines *which* problems are legitimate topics of research. Generally, the paradigm concentrates

[a]The role of normal science in knowledge growth is addressed in the aforementioned volume edited by Imre Lakatos and Alan Musgrave. There, Kuhn's views are contrasted with Popper's invitation to "Revolutions in Permanence!" and Feyerabend's "philosophy of proliferation."

on problems it can solve and avoids or rationalizes those it cannot (e.g., as being irrelevant, less important, or the domain of another discipline). As mentioned above, the resulting focus on technical sub-issues often results in anomalies—observations which do not "fit" paradigm expectations.

With the appearance of anomalies, the stage is set for a "crisis" phase. However, the crisis is seldom induced by scattered or infrequent anomalies. As a matter of fact, Kuhn argues that all paradigms are colored by some forms of anomaly at almost all points in their development. Thus, the prognosis of the paradigm depends partly upon the *nature* and *extent* of its anomalies. Moreover, as we shall see in a moment, it is also dramatically influenced by the availability of alternative paradigms.

When an anomaly first appears, it is often overlooked or rationalized. Kuhn notes that these early discrepancies between theory and data are frequently thought to reflect the inadequacy of the researcher rather than of the paradigm. With continued documentation or the endorsement of authority, however, the anomaly becomes "legitimate" and soon dominates the research efforts of paradigm adherents. This period is often marked by signs of insecurity and frustration as the inadequacy of the prevailing model becomes more and more apparent. There are often frenzied attempts to salvage the paradigm, either by discrediting the anomaly via experimentation or by patching up the model with qualifiers and "fudge factors." During these system-saving efforts, competition frequently becomes keen and passionate—there are immense professional prizes awaiting the paradigm saviour. It is noteworthy that recourse to philosophy and methodological issues are most pronounced during times of anomaly and crisis. The problem is often subjected to a fine grain semantical analysis, and the limitations of human knowledge are sometimes invoked as a rationalization. These reactions and several others will be expanded in later chapters.

Kuhn argues that anomalies and paradigm crises are critical elements in the growth of knowledge. As Humphreys has put it, "The logical structure of scientific theories and their historical evolution are organized around the identification and explanation of anomalies (1968, p. 12). Anomalies do not always lead to crisis, however, and crises are not inevitably followed by revolutions. As will be documented shortly, resistance to anomalies is often strong and tenacious.

According to Kuhn, a prerequisite for scientific revolution is the existence of an alternate competing paradigm:

A scientific theory is declared invalid only if an alternate candidate is available to take its place. . . . The decision to reject one paradigm is always simultaneously the decision to accept another (p. 77).

It should not be assumed, however, that the crisis was a prerequisite for the emergence of the new paradigm. It is sometimes the case that the new model appeared before the crisis and then rapidly rose to visibility or popular acceptance when the former paradigm started to falter. Also note that the competition may extend to several other contenders. These alternate models must compete not only with the old paradigm, but with the numerous theoretical attempts at salvation which have proliferated during the crisis. Thus, in its battle with radical behaviorism, contemporary cognitive psychology has had to vie with such hybrids as neobehaviorism and social behaviorism.

The personal and epistemological aspects of paradigm competition are both complex and intriguing. For example, as Kuhn aptly points out, each paradigm evaluates its competitors on the basis of its own criteria. This results in considerable miscommunication and, of course, intolerance. Moreover, as the adherents of the incumbent paradigm are quick to point out, the challenging paradigm usually has anomalies of its own. According to Kuhn, the ultimate victor is not necessarily that model with the best contemporary data fit or the least number of anomalies. Relative to other factors, the data often appear to play a somewhat nominal role in the final choice of a paradigm. The conceptual features of the new model, for example, seem to weigh more heavily in this evaluation.

The revolutionary phase of scientific growth is often long and fitful. When the new paradigm has ascended to some degree of popularity, this does not automatically result in the concession of the old guard. Paradigm clashes may continue for centuries—with cold wars, frequent skirmishes, and occasional head-on confrontation. In one sense, then, old paradigms seldom die a quiet, dignified death—their demise is often marked by prolonged groans of atrophy and unmistakable conceptual sclerosis.

In my opinion, it is somewhat ironic that some of the same social forces appear to nourish both theoretical dogmatism and radical innovation. In the face of oppression or competition, the common reaction seems to be one of affiliation and stubborn resistance rather than concession or resignation. The old guard are incensed by the revolutionaries. While they remain in power, they oppress the young upstarts on every possible front—in research funding, journal publication and professional employment. This oppression, in turn, encourages the revolutionaries to "hang together lest they hang separately." A truly intense revolutionary spirit develops, born of oppression and an almost missionary zeal to edify. After the revolution has succeeded, cohesiveness among the revolutionaries declines and there is rapid development of factions. Former solidarity and *esprit de corps* are replaced by subschools and arguments over who contributed most to the revolution. Meanwhile, the declining old guard huddle together in embittered resentment, lamenting the frivolity of youth and predicting their own ultimate reascension.

The contrast I have painted between the old guard and the young revolutionaries is more than figurative. Kuhn points out that the central figures in most scientific revolutions are young or new to the field. Not having yet become entrenched in the prevailing paradigm, they are able to see the field through alternate models. Likewise, their radical views are much more readily received by youthful rather than aged scientists. This resistance to conversion is aptly captured in the autobiography of Max Planck:

> A new scientific truth does not triumph by convincing its opponents and making them see the light, but rather because its opponents eventually die, and a new generation grows up that is familiar with it (1949, pp. 33–34).

However, as Kuhn and others have argued, this tenacity can be viewed as an asset rather than a liability. Frequent and impulsive paradigm shifts might not allow the intense research which seems to be a prerequisite for knowledge growth. Kuhn argues that resistance to revolutions is an integral part of the whole pattern:

> The transfer of allegiance from paradigm to paradigm is a conversion experience that cannot be forced. Lifelong resistance, particularly from those whose productive careers have committed them to an older tradition of normal science, is not a violation of scientific standards but an index to the nature of scientific research itself. The source of resistance is the assurance that the older paradigm will ultimately solve all its problems, that nature can be shoved into the box that the paradigm provides. Inevitably, at times of revolution, that assurance seems stubborn and pigheaded as indeed it sometimes becomes. But it is also something more. That same assurance is what makes normal or puzzle-solving science possible (pp. 151–152).

When a paradigm change has occurred, the scientist's world changes dramatically. The new model is fit to the old data, usually accommodating those which were anomalous. Things that were consistent with the former paradigm are now fit to the new one, and there is often a sense of exhilaration as the pieces are fit into the new puzzle board. With sweeping changes in conceptualization, changes in perception are inevitable. The data do not "look" the way they used to. Anal-

ogous to our earlier demonstration of the Necker cube, the world
may take on a very different configuration. Not only are old data
viewed differently, but new data often begin to pour in. The paradigm shift has obscured or altered the former boundaries of fair
play in the science game. Researchers start to look in areas which
were previously out-of-bounds or inconceivable. Moreover, they begin to report new data from within their old playing field. That is,
phenomena which had been overlooked or suppressed by the previous paradigm are now discovered and scrutinized. Kuhn thus reminds us of the rash of new observations in astronomy during the
first half-century after the appearance of Copernicus' revolutionary
theory.

Once accepted, of course, the new paradigm tools up for its own
enthusiastic problem solving. Technical instruments and specialized
journals develop, and the adherents of the new model settle down
to a phase of normal science. In so doing, they lay the groundwork
for the powerful and intense scrutiny which leads to anomalies,
crises, and another revolution.

This brief rendition and embellishment of Kuhn's theory provides a valuable paradigm in itself. As will be repeatedly apparent in
the chapters which follow, the molar configuration offered by Kuhn-
ian theory is one to which my molecular analyses can be comfortably
fitted. Lest there be any doubt, however, about the limitations and
problems of this paradigm of paradigms, I would again urge reference
to the volumes by Weimer and Lakatos and Musgrave.

THE SOCIOLOGY OF SCIENCE

A second major effort toward understanding some of the molar
aspects of science has its primary roots in the discipline of sociology.
Although its parentage and gestation can be traced back to the turn
of the century, its rise to visibility is extremely recent. In the 1930s
this effort was restricted to a sociological interpretation of the history of science. After three decades of maturation, however, this
"sociology of knowledge" has spawned a discipline which is appropriately termed the sociology of science. Its interests are no longer
restrictively historical and its growth curve in the 1960s and 1970s
has been nothing short of awesome.

As we will see in a later chapter, the assignment of parentage for a
given theory or discipline is often frought with historical vagaries as
well as intense personal reactions. Contributions to the fertilization
of a sociology of science can be traced to a number of early scholars,
including Emile Durkheim, Pitirim Sorokin, Alfred North Whitehead,
Talcott Parsons, and George Sarton. However, at least one contem-

porary worker in this area has ventured to grant primary paternity to sociologist Robert K. Merton:

> If Robert K. Merton has not yet been publicly described as a founding father of the sociology of science, there is at least substantial agreement among those who know the field that its present strength and vitality are largely the result of his labors over the past forty years (Storer, 1973, p. xi).

There can be little doubt that Merton's work has dominated both early and contemporary themes in the discipline. Beginning with his early writings in the sociology of knowledge, Merton has prolificly analyzed and stimulated the field. Moreover, a number of his students have become primary contributors to contemporary sociology of science.

This is not to deny that other individuals have lent considerable theoretical and empirical impetus to the discipline. The classic works of Bernard Barber, Derek J. DeSolla Price, Warren O. Hagstrom, and Norman W. Storer are cases in point. However, as Storer's comment certifies, Merton's ideas and analyses have offered both precedent and invitation for many of these efforts.

In addition to these fundamental volumes, the proliferation of both conceptual and empirical endeavors in the sociology of science can be readily documented by a partial list of other books it has stimulated in the last two decades. Ranging from theoretical and experimental studies to the mushrooming collections of readings in this area, their growth rate suggests an equally expansive audience:

1955	De Gre	*Science as a Social Institution*
1960	Marcson	*The Scientist in American Industry*
1961	Price	*Science since Babylon*
1962	Barber & Hirsch	*The Sociology of Science*
	Obler & Estria	*The New Scientist*
	Kornhauser	*Scientists in Industry*
	Strauss & Rainwater	*The Professional Scientist*
1963	Feuer	*The Scientific Intellectual*
	Hill	*Management of Scientists*
1964	Glaser	*Organizational Scientists*
1965	Goldsmith & Mackay	*The Science of Science*
	Kaplan	*Science and Society*
	Paisley	*The Flow of (Behavioral) Science Information*
1966	Pelz & Andrews	*Scientists in Organizations*

	Perry	*The Human Nature of Science*
1967	Reuck & Knight	*Communication in Science*
	Bernal	*The Social Function of Science*
	Greenberg	*The Politics of Pure Science*
1968	Klaw	*The New Brahmins: Scientific Life in America*
	Hirsch	*Scientists in American Society*
	Zaltman	*Scientific Recognition and Communication Behavior in High Energy Physics*
	Ziman	*Public Knowledge: The Social Dimension of Science*
1969	Rose & Rose	*Science and Society*
	Haberer	*Politics and the Community of Science*
	Greenberg	*The Politics of American Science*
1970	Cotgrove & Box	*Science, Industry and Society*
	Nelson & Pollock	*Communication among Scientists and Engineers*
1971	Ben-David	*The Scientist's Role in Society*
	Krohn	*The Social Shaping of Science*
	Ravetz	*Scientific Knowledge and Its Social Problems*
1972	Blissett	*Politics in Science*
	Shils	*The Intellectuals and the Powers*
	Richter	*Science as a Cultural Process*
	Barnes	*Sociology of Science*
	Crane	*Invisible Colleges: Diffusion of Knowledge in Scientific Communities*
	Halmos	*The Sociology of Science*
	Nagi & Corwin	*The Social Contexts of Research*
	Mulkay	*The Social Process of Innovation*
1973	Gaston	*Originality and Competition in Science*
	Merton	*The Sociology of Science*
	Cole & Cole	*Social Stratification in Science*
	Taylor	*The Scientific Community*
	Jevons	*Science Observed: Science as a Social and Intellectual Activity*
	Dixon	*What is Science For?*
1974	Blume	*Toward A Political Sociology of Science*
	Whiteley	*Social Processes of Scientific Development*
1975	Zuckerman	*Scientific Elite: Studies of Nobel Laureates in the United States*

This partial and rapidly expanding list may explain why I shall not undertake a brief synopsis of the field. Compared to the relatively neat theoretical model offered by Kuhn, the sociology of science presents a much more difficult task of condensation and summary. Although there are unmistakable themes in the discipline, a monolithic or integrative model is not dominant. Among the more popular topics of analysis have been:

1. science as a community or professional culture complete with its own ethos;
2. systems of communication in science, ranging from the "invisible college" to formal professional journals;
3. the reward system of science with its emphasis on priority, territoriality of ideas, and personal competition for recognition;
4. the relationship between science and society; and
5. the politics of professional science.

Since each of these topics will be addressed in later chapters, I shall not here digress on their discussion. Suffice it to say that sociologists of science have contributed invaluably in both theory and research. In many ways, their efforts have laid the groundwork for more of an intense individual analysis—the psychology of the scientist.

IRONIC NEGLECT: THE UNEXAMINED PSYCHOLOGY OF SCIENCE

When compared to the broad and expanding sociological literature cited above, the psychology of science can hardly claim a skeleton let alone some flesh. Notwithstanding their seemingly voracious scrutiny of everything from planaria to the behavior of crowds, psychologists have granted a mysterious research exemption to *homo scientus*. One could speculate almost endlessly on the possible sources of this unspoken convention. Does the psychologist assume that we already know how scientists think, feel, and behave? Or is he reluctant to expose some of the elements he suspects he would find? Is he protecting either the scientist or the public from the destruction of their palliative image of the truth seeker? Or is he simply unwilling to subject these busy and sometimes difficult creatures to intense scrutiny?

I suspect that these and other factors may be at the root of at least some psychologists' reluctance to place the scientist under his own microscope. However, I fear that even more of this neglect stems from an implicit and, I think, dangerous assumption—namely, that the study of the scientist is a less pressing or relevant research priority. After all, we have so many more urgent topics to occupy our limited professional time. We must demonstrate such "mysteries" as the fact that humans will work to obtain rewards and avoid punishment, or that they tend to like people who share their views.

Don't misinterpret my cynicism. With few exceptions, I can readily see the relevance of most contemporary psychological research, particularly in applied and clinical areas. My sarcasm stems from the belief that we are sadly deceived if we think that the psychology of the scientist should be very low on our research priority list. There is a trite adage that a science can never be more precise or powerful than its instruments, and this statement has unquestionable relevance for the human instrument as well. It is *not* a minor and benign oversight that we have neglected the primary instrument of all research, psychological and otherwise. Our capacities for knowledge and its effective use are limited by the characteristics of the primary element in knowledge gathering—*homo scientus*. Without critically examining and hopefully refining the information processing capacities of this mysterious creature, our understanding of this planet and its universe will remain unnecessarily limited and crude. Moreover, in terms of the urgent research topics which have apparently pre-empted the scientist, our abilities to actively affect and responsibly control the betterment of our existence will probably be both detained and diluted because of our misplaced research priorities.

The above passage may sound like a melodramatic sermon on the waywardness of our efforts and the dire consequences we can expect if we fail to change our ways. I obviously do feel strongly about the critical importance of understanding the scientist. However, I do not deny the fact that some sciences seem to have made considerable progress despite our ignorance of their participants. My argument does not contend that we are faced with a dichotomous choice between the heaven of "real" scientific truth and the hell of perpetual ignorance. Rather, the issue is one of optimization. It is my opinion that the pace, validity, and perhaps even the relevance of our scientific knowledge could be substantially improved by a continuing analysis and refinement of scientist behavior. As will be apparent in the chapters to follow, it may be the case that this assertion is somewhat more pertinent in those disciplines where the scientist is a more central and interactive instrument in the given research (e.g., in the social sciences). In any case, I confess to the strong conviction that any appreciation or improvement of *knowledge* requires an understanding of the *knower*.

This being the case, what is the current state of the psychology of science? Two words aptly summarize our knowledge: nominal and fuzzy. Controlled experimental studies of the scientist's thoughts, actions, and emotions are virtually nonexistent. There are, of course, several autobiographical accounts of scientific life and some attempts to trace the origins and personality profiles of eminent scientists. Research on creativity has occasionally recruited scientists and their students as presumed paragons of innovative thought. There have also been a number of theoretical and analytic contributions from philosophy and sociology which have addressed specific aspects of the scientist's psychological make-up (e.g., Maslow, Merton, and Singer). In terms of concentrated scrutinies of *homo scientus*, however, there have been next to none. Psychologist Anne Roe interviewed 64 eminent scientists and collected information on their home life, their upbringing, and selected aspects of their thinking skills and "personality dynamics." Using a similar format, Bernice Eiduson interviewed and administered psychometric tests to 40 scientists. Perhaps reflecting the dominance of psychoanalytic themes in career analyses, both Roe and Eiduson restricted their psychological assessments to the predominantly psychodynamic constraints of Rorschach inkblots and the Thematic Apperception Test. These projective instruments have been notoriously unreliable and questionably relevant to valid personality assessment (see Mischel). Notwithstanding some of their limitations in methodology and scope, however, these studies have contributed toward our understanding of the scientist. Some of their specific findings will be presented in subsequent chapters. Likewise, I shall present data from some preliminary studies conducted with my colleagues at Penn State. By way of preview, however, it should be reiterated that our current empirical bases are extremely limited.

The present text is therefore not a literature review but rather an invitation to research. I begin with *the premise of the turtle—that movement often requires having first stuck your neck out*. It is my hunch that at least some of the inactivity in the psychology of science may stem from the absence of a theoretical reference point—a model from which to begin one's grope in the darkness. Theoretical models are, of course, a sad species—they inevitably invite their own demise, as Kuhn has aptly pointed out.

In the chapters which follow I shall attempt to outline some reference points from which to scrutinize *homo scientus*. My data bases will range from the literatures already citied by my own subjective observations of the science game. At many points I will wax philosophical, and several of my evaluative recommendations for reappraisal and change will be explicitly polemical in the constructive and heuristic sense of that term.

These concessions having hopefully disarmed at least a few critics, let us set off on our journey into the scientific looking glass.

REFERENCES

3, 24, 26, 29, 41, 44, 45, 47, 51, 52, 53, 71, 85, 86, 87, 97, 98, 104, 110, 119, 122, 126, 134, 137, 151, 153, 157, 160, 165, 166, 169, 171, 174, 175, 186, 188, 195, 196, 200, 209, 213, 218, 228, 230, 231, 237, 243, 244, 246, 247, 248, 250, 263, 273, 279, 282, 284, 305, 306, 307, 313, 316, 321, 324, 327, 333, 338, 340, 341, 346, 349, 359, 360, 365, 369, 371, 375, 376, 377, 378, 407, 408, 409, 411, 415, 418, 430, 431, 433, 438, 439, 441, 463, 466, 467, 468, 469, 470, 477, 489, 491, 497.

Academic persons, when they carry on study, not only in youth as a part of education, but as the pursuit of their maturer years, most of them become decidedly queer, not to say rotten; and those who may be considered the best of them are made useless to the world.

Plato

Examinations are formidable even to the best prepared, for the greatest fool may ask more than the wisest man can answer.

Anonymous

In the customs and institutions of schools, academies, colleges, and similar bodies destined for the abode of learned men and the cultivation of learning, everything is found adverse to the progress of science.

Francis Bacon

If you wish to appear agreeable in society, you must consent to be taught many things which you know already.

Talleyrand

The shortest and surest way of arriving at real knowledge is to unlearn the lessons we have been taught, to remount first principles, and to take nobody's word about them.

Bolingbroke

Motivation and endurance seem to count for at least as much as intelligence in producing superior scientific work.

Harriet Zuckerman

If Socrates seemed not reluctant to drink the hemlock, it may be because he realized what he had created: the *genus Academicum*.

Richard Armour

It's what you learn after you know it all that really counts.

Harry S. Truman

Chapter 3

Rites of Passage: Selected Absurdities in Graduate Training

As with most elite societies, acceptance into professional science requires a set of credentials. One must not only be endorsed and sponsored by already established members, but one must demonstrate certain required characteristics and propensities. Most of these are thought to be reflected in admission to (and endurance of) graduate school.

The portrait of graduate training which will be offered in this chapter is neither new nor often publicly acknowledged. It is aired widely in the dungeons of graduate carrels, occasionally touching the outer world in the form of graffiti or an anguished lament at an all-student party. To anyone who has ever been a victim of graduate education or the spouse of such a creature, the description offered by Bernard Dixon may seem extremely benign:

> It is a process which, like education generally, the more able people manage to survive rather than thrive upon (1973, p. 161).

The present chapter will examine some of the performance rites which are usually entailed in that survival.

It should be noted at the outset that the following portrait is both impressionistic and phenomenological. Should the reader think that it is therefore unsubstantiated by data, I recommend perusal of the valuable works of Caplow and McGee, Berelson, Hagstrom, Klaw, and Dixon. To avoid this somewhat cumbersome citation practice, I shall hereafter refer only to primary sources of research or commentary. Again, this is based on a healthy confidence in the representativeness of the portrait which follows.

Perhaps it is unnecessary to note that the forthcoming rendition of graduate life is considered representative, but not universal. I was fortunate enough to enjoy a graduate program which was probably very atypical in its encouragement of independent research, personal tutelage, and professional self-respect. Contrary to the norm, my experience was a stimulating apprenticeship, relatively devoid of hurdles and absurdities. There will always be such exceptions, and it is my hope that today's exceptions will become tomorrow's rule in graduate education.

THE ORIGINS AND PERSONALITY CHARACTERISTICS OF SCIENTISTS

Needless to say, one does not simply decide on a science career and then contact some lucky graduate school. The prerequisites seem to regress in an almost endless series. One cannot get into graduate school without having attained a bachelor's degree and one can seldom become an undergraduate without first having met still other requirements. In meeting each of these successive hurdles certain skills are invaluable. A handful of recent inquiries have attempted to categorize these skills in a manner which might aid the future selection and early encouragement of budding scientists.

The studies cited earlier by Anne Roe and Bernice Eiduson were two attempts to provide a psychological profile of the scientist. Using an *ad hoc* and retrospective approach, they interviewed and tested eminent scientists in an effort to determine their developmental histories and adult personality characteristics. In general, their findings emphasized a heterogeneity of *homo scientus* with extreme variability in skills ranging from social to intellectual. Both researchers commented upon several aspects of early childhood development, such as the frequent absence of one parent (particularly the father) and prolonged intervals of social isolation (often induced by physical handicaps). These early experiences were interpreted as encouraging a precocious independence and a preoccupation with non-social pursuits. Other findings included a very high incidence of being the first or only child. There were, of course, no small number of less profound observations, such as that "social scientists are deeply concerned about human relations" (Roe, 1952, pp. 233–234). Unfortunately, both of these studies suffered from extensive methodological problems and, as they note, their implications for the prediction and selection of scientists must be examined critically. It would be an unfortunate and illogical inference, for example, to use all of the reported characteristics of their sample in evaluating science aspirants, since their most consistent characteristic was their gender—all 104 subjects were male. One would hardly want to conclude from this that masculinity is a necessary prerequisite for significant scientific contribution. In addition to their sampling problems, these two studies also relied almost exclusively on interviews and projective personality tests, both of which have their own share of inadequacies.

There have, of course, been other attempts to trace the origins and developmental experiences of scientists. Their results have generally indicated wide variations around a few main themes. For example, a sizeable percentage of scientists come from the middle and lower socioeconomic classes, thereby questioning Sartre's comment that in the United States a Ph.D. is given as "a reward for having a wealthy father and no opinions." Relative to their respective frequencies in the population, very few scientists have come from Catholic backgrounds while larger proportions have had Jewish upbringing. The most striking finding in these studies, however, has been the relative monopolization of graduate training. A very small number of universities have supplied the bulk of contemporary scientists, and an even smaller elite group of schools has spawned the most eminent of these researchers. This imbalance will be examined critically in a moment.

For the time being let us acknowledge that the developmental origins and psychological make-up of the scientist remain poorly understood and sparsely examined. The meager evidence available suggests more heterogeneity than anything else, and we are tempted to tentatively concur with Eiduson that:

> They are more different than alike . . . . The stereotyped depictions of the scientist as a person given to mood swings, or depressions, or on the other side, overly controlled and logical in his emotional make-up, have not been borne out. On the contrary, in all these respects there is a wide range of reaction pattern, much more so than one might have expected in the light of the long-standing and deep-seated impressions that have existed in the public mind (1962, p. 113).

Aside from the absence of blatant psychopathology, however, the student's personality is seldom considered in decisions regarding admission to either undergraduate or graduate degree programs. Judging from some of the zany antics I have witnessed (and occasionally fostered), one might even say that bizarre actions are often openly tolerated in the science aspirant—providing that other credentials are apparent. And in most admissions decisions, of course, the primary credential is intelligence.

INTELLIGENCE: THE KEY TO GRADUATE ADMISSIONS

Most graduate training programs select their applicants on the basis of one major criterion—intellectual superiority. This is thought to be reflected in a number of general and specialized tests which the applicant must endure prior to even receiving consideration (e.g., the Graduate Record Examination and the Miller Analogies Test). Additional indexes of the student's intellectual promise are considered apparent in (a) his possession of a bachelor's degree, (b) a high grade point average, and (c) strong letters of recommendation. The likelihood of acceptance is almost assured if these credentials are combined with having attended a prestigious school and having been endorsed by one or more eminent sponsors. Factors such as motivation, undergraduate preparation, and—most recently—gender and minority group membership are also considered. However, there can be little doubt that intelligence is the primary credential.

This may not seem surprising what with the generally conceded necessity of superior intelligence in scientific pursuits. As mentioned in chapter 1, the public and self-image of the scientist presupposes above-average intellectual ability. And, indeed, the academic files of current and past scientists suggest that their I.Q.s probably average somewhere near the upper 5 percent of the general population. Those writers who have posthumously estimated the intelligence of deceased luminaries have been very generous to *homo scientus*, sometimes assigning scores over 200 (e.g., Cox). In her interviews with 64 eminent researchers, Roe administered an improvised intelligence test and reported that her subjects did very well. Reflecting the extent to which the premise of brilliance is adopted, Eiduson refrained from testing the I.Q. of her scientists, explaining that "no test has sufficient spread in the top ranges for so superior a group" (pp. 114–115).

Let us concede the well-documented fact that graduate students in both science and non-science have scored above average on intelligence tests. This would suggest that most contemporary scientists are likewise exceptional in this sphere. Does it then follow that superior intelligence is a prerequisite for scientific work? No—at least not logically. The fact that most scientists have high I.Q.'s can be simply accounted for by the fact that *only highly intelligent individuals have been allowed to enter science*! Our graduate admissions policies have restricted their consideration to bright applicants and then justified this practice by pointing to the superior intelligence of past graduates. Were this same logic employed in the consideration of female and minority applicants, neither would be represented in contemporary graduate programs.

What is the relationship between intelligence and scientific performance? This question has been addressed by a few correlational studies *within* groups of scientists. For example, in some of his early research Liam Hudson found that the academic records of famous scientists were no better than those of their less eminent contemporaries. Likewise, Bayer and Folger reported a slight *negative* correlation between intelligence and scientific productivity. Studying 499 academic scientists, Jonathan Cole and Stephen Cole also found no significant relationship between I.Q. and either number or quality of published scientific papers. In a recent comparison of the problem solving skills of scientists and non-scientists, Bob DeMonbreun and I found no significant differences on overall success and some degree of superiority in non-scientists on specific reasoning factors. These studies do not, of course, support James Watson's brash assertion that "a goodly number of scientists are not only narrow-minded and dull, but also just stupid" (pp. 18–19). They do, however, challenge the premise that exceptional intelligence is essential for scientific achievement.

The annals of science seem to have suppressed many of the incidents which contradict the superiority premise. Prior to his revolutionary theory, Einstein was not considered the paragon of intellectual brilliance. As a child he was very slow to develop language skills and his early school performance was subnormal—particularly in mathematics. His first application to graduate school was rejected. Similarly, Andreski reminds us of Isaac Newton's early failure to obtain a Cambridge fellowship and Lobatchevsky's image as a lunatic prior to the acceptance of non-Euclidean geometry. On a more contemporary theme, I know of several relatively eminent psychologists whose scholastic and intellectual records are far from dazzling.

My argument is not that intelligence is irrelevant. A certain minimal degree of cognitive skills would seem to be necessary. However, in view of the current evidence, I tend to concur with Price's conclusion that "general and specific types of intelligence have surprisingly little to do with the incidence of high achievement" (1963, p. 107). In sociology of science, a corollary of this notion has been termed the "Ortega Hypothesis" after one of its early spokesmen, Jose Ortega y Gassett:

Experimental science has progressed thanks in great part to the work of men astoundingly mediocre, and even less than mediocre (1932, pp. 84-85).

Whether or not "mediocre" scientists actually account for the *bulk* of research progress is itself a controversial issue. The point here, however, is that scientific contributions are not restricted to geniuses, and exceptional intelligence may not be a useful recruitment criterion.

Which brings us back to graduate school admissions. Applications are often subjected to a complex regression equation which involves the weighting of various factors such as Graduate Record Examination (GRE) scores and undergraduate grade point average (GPA). How well do these factors predict success during and after graduate school? In a word, poorly. In fact, the evidence for their *poor* predictive powers is so strong that one is amazed at the tenacity of their use in graduate admissions. In over a dozen independent studies on predicting graduate performance, measures of intellectual performance have been consistently weak in their predictive validity. The importance of these predictors has already stimulated such educators as Albert Marston to suggest their omission in future selection policies. I might add that a colleague at a large midwestern university recently informed me that their patient and complex regression analyses had turned up only one significant predictor of successful graduate performance—non-attendance at church. In an analysis of admissions criteria at The Pennsylvania State University, Roger Blashfield found that the length (in inches) of recommendation letters was a significant predictor of acceptance and that successful attainment of the Ph.D. was strongly correlated with the first digit of one's zip code.

Despite the fact that they have shown very little predictive utility, quantitative indexes of intelligence continue to be employed as the major admissions criteria in most graduate programs. With ritualistic simplicity, each applicant's folder is assigned a standardized ("z") score based on his or her various achievements. Then, when final decisions must be made, the admissions committee can escape any feelings of arbitrariness or futility by rationalizing their choices with numbers. Applicant A is selected over applicant B because her score was 1.54 instead of 1.46. If she is aspiring to be a clinical psychologist, who cares whether she can talk to people—her GRE's were outstanding.

An irony in all this is the fact that graduate programs have recently been forced to elevate their admissions criteria because of the growing number of annual applicants. Each year the new aspirants present more awesome credentials, and as the *average* GRE and GPA scores rise, the *minimum* credentials for admissions are increased. This has left us in the delightful predicament that *a sizeable percentage of college professors could not compete in today's admissions race.*

It may appear from the foregoing that the *only* problem or inequity in graduate admissions is that dealing with intellectual criteria. Unfortunately, this is not the case. While academic and intellectual performance are the primary elements, a number of other factors are considered. For example, a lukewarm recommendation letter from an eminent scientist may carry much more weight than strong endorsement by some unknown. Homage to a friend or hero may be paid in this manner. "After all," the rationale goes, "I know what *his* evaluations mean." Likewise, one's undergraduate institution is taken into account. Research by Knapp, Berelson, and others has suggested that having attended the "right" college may substantially enhance one's chances of acceptance.

Finally, in the absence of more salient factors, one's graduate admissions chances may be determined by variables ranging from rhetoric to financial self-sufficiency. For example, a single word or obscure passage in a recommendation letter may destroy an application. If a sponsor labels a student's skills as "adequate" rather than outstanding, this may be interpreted critically. A Rutgers colleague recently commented that letters of recommendation have come to sound like winter ski reports—their only vocabulary is "good," "exceptional," and "outstanding." If the student has had the misfortune to choose a less articulate faculty sponsor, he may have inadvertantly sealed his own graduate fate. A neutral or conservative letter has come to be judged as "negative" amid the barrage of superlatives that usually flow in these endorsements. Since the young faculty member seldom gets any relevant training in "competitive letter writing," it may take him several years to realize that his candidly conservative recommendations have impeded the careers of several dozen students.

Since I will soon be presenting a summary of suggestions for change in graduate training, I shall here reserve my comments. It should hardly need preview that I favor extensive reappraisal of current admissions policies.

LIFE IN GRADUATE SCHOOL: PARANOIA AND DIPLOMA-CY

After having submitted the required forms and anguished over what his faculty sponsors may have written in their letters, the aspirant can usually retire to several months of sleepless anticipation. Each mail delivery produces a state of desperate panic, which is only made worse by the frequent inquiries of friends and family—"Have you heard yet?" By the time the first letter arrives, adrenal atrophy may be so pronounced that the student is simply numb to the news, whatever its content.

Most students apply to a number of graduate schools, thereby increasing their opportunities for both delight and despair. To add insult to injury, applicants are occasionally placed in the limbo status of being an "alternate," which means that they will be accepted if one or more already selected applicants decline the offers made them. Knowing that they were "second choices" is seldom considered a factor in their later reactions to graduate stress.

Occasionally, a student has the mixed blessing of having been accepted by two or more institutions. *He* is in a position to choose, and the outcome of his choice may either help or haunt him for the duration of his professional career. As we will see in the next chapter, the site of one's graduate training exerts substantial influence on later options in the job market, prestige, and even ease of publication. In their classic volume *The Academic Marketplace*, Caplow and McGee summarize their research findings as follows:

> The initial choice of a graduate school sets an indelible mark on the student's career. In many disciplines, men trained at minor universities have virtually no chance of achieving eminence. Even in those disciplines in which the distribution of professional rewards is not tightly controlled by an inner circle of departments, the handicap of initial identification with a department of low prestige is hardly ever completely overcome (1958, p. 225).

Among the benefits of securing admission to a prestigious graduate program are: (a) probable exposure to eminent and influential teachers, (b) superior research facilities and support, (c) sufficient time and encouragement to begin independent research, (d) enhanced opportunities for early publication, perhaps with an eminent co-author, (e) indelible prestige based on the source of one's degree, and (f) substantially greater likelihood of securing postgraduate employment at another prestigious institution. As reflected in the data of

Berelson and Caplow & McGee, the consequences of these differential opportunities may be dramatic. Replicating some of these observations, Cole & Cole have commented on the process of "Accumulative Advantage":

> In graduate school, certain students are labelled as being 'bright' and 'promising.' They usually become the students of the most powerful and eminent professors. As graduate students, they are given access to greater resources and often have the opportunity to publish papers with their mentors. Perhaps even more important, they pick up self-confidence and the belief that they have what it takes. The 'knighted' students of the most eminent professors are also most likely to receive first-job appointments to prestigious academic departments or research laboratories. At these research centers they again have resource advantages and find it easier to publish (1973, p. 237).

Since professional recognition often leads to an increased valuation of one's work, a repetitive cycle may develop in which prestige and recognition cross-fertilize. Some minimal degree of quality and competence is, of course, required; accumulative advantage cannot overcome ineptitude. But given these minimal criteria, the stage is set for differential achievement and recognition. The self-fulfilling prophecy takes hold.

> Science . . . defines some students as 'promising' and others as 'run-of-the-mill' and then systematically sets up the very conditions that produce the expected and predicted consequences (p. 245).

Regardless of institutional prestige, however, graduate life is seldom a bed of roses. It is more often imbued with confusion, anxiety, and a paranoia which is occasionally reinforced by the quirks and injustices of the mysterious "system." Within his department, in the office of the registrar, or somewhere in the graduate college, there lurks a sinister being whose sole purpose is to thwart the student's progress. Lost transcripts, rejected thesis proposals and an endless sequence of "required forms" leave little doubt that the forces of darkness are abundant. Their haunting presence seems all the more salient shortly before landmark events in graduate life—the thesis, evaluation meetings, comprehensive examinations and the dissertation.

The incoming graduate student soon learns to respect the presence of these vague tormentors. In addition to adjusting to a new town, a tight budget, and the usual insanities of moving, he must confront a strange hierarchy of superiors who seem to relish in their secret knowledge of the "real" program requirements. There will be many moments when the ordeal will seem like one of endless imprisonment in which the pain is accentuated by the delusion that someday it will all be over. Rather than provide structured guidelines for the incoming captives, some programs seem to guard their requirements with utmost secrecy. Course and residency requirements are spelled out in half-legible mimeographs which are several years out of date. Moreover, in the social sphere the novitiate is faced with a menagerie of creatures ranging from the anxious assistant professor and the harried associate to the self-assured full professor and, of course, the indomitable chairman. Their reactions may vary from subtle suspicion ("*you're* the guy we accepted?!"), through frantic impatience, to a warm and sincere welcome. Meeting his new mentors, the student is faced with a number of often unspoken questions and concerns—how should one address the instructor ("Doctor, Mister, Professor, or Jim?"); can one ask domestic questions (e.g., where to live); and what about academic intimacies (e.g., whose courses to avoid)? These are often answered only through painful trial and error.

In addition to these multifarious captors, the new student will meet his peers—again, a heterogeneous group spanning the extremes of self-confident extrovert and pale, trembling recluse. In competitive departments, attrition is high and graduate classes are annually trimmed by ousting the less successful students. Here peer interaction is anything but supportive. A cut-throat philosophy often develops—manifested in secretiveness and the mysterious disappearance of required readings from the library. Students compete for the favors of the instructors, and there is a pungent atmosphere of desperation as initiates drive themselves mercilessly just to "keep up." Graduate survival often becomes the core of existence, leaving personal and family priorities to deteriorate.

It seems as though almost every first year student feels that his or her undergraduate background was particularly weak. Their initial months may be spent in anxious and sporadic attempts to "catch up," although the criteria for their self-improvement are seldom clear. These masochistic exercises in remediation are added to an already onerous academic load. Like military boot camp, the first year of graduate school is often devoted to a survival marathon which is intended to separate the weak from the strong. As Berelon has noted,

Graduate schools typically screen students more fully *after* admission than before . . . . The rationale is clear enough: admit by intelligence and screen for other qualities later (p. 58).

During his first nine months as a graduate student, the individual is usually pushed through a relatively inflexible series of "core" courses which, besides spanning the discipline, are often the most difficult in the program. If he survives them, he is usually past the first hurdle of graduate training. This progress is sometimes formalized in a special evaluation meeting whose primary purpose is the expulsion of faltering students (rather than the commendation or repair of survivors).

Survival of the first year often brings some belatedly mature insights into the game. Naive images of graduate school as an environment of intellectual freedom and collaborative growth may be replaced by very different (and sometimes bitter) portraits. The student has often learned that his graduate research experience may never exceed that of a laboratory technician.

Perhaps the most serious thing wrong with graduate education in the sciences is that the student too often is treated as a peon. Instead of being initiated into the art of doing independent research, he is set to work on tedious but essentially trivial tasks whose accomplishment will contribute mainly to the reputation of his professor (Klaw, 1968, p. 35).

This phenomenon is evidently widespread in graduate education. In a secondary analysis of Berelson's data, Hagstrom found that sizeable percentages of recent Ph.D.s felt that "major professors often exploit doctoral candidates." Also noteworthy was the discrepancy between the perspectives of graduate faculty and students. While the former deny that doctoral programs create unnecessary anxiety, recent Ph.D. recipients consistently report just the opposite.

Even when he is pursuing his own research, the contingencies of graduate education often force the student to avoid meaningful problems—risky, lengthy, or ambitious research projects. He is instead urged to pursue conservative, short-term projects with guaranteed results and a higher likelihood of nourishing his vita. Given the extensive reliance on graduate students by many faculty research projects, the nature and execution of a substantial amount of contemporary science may be dictated by factors which are hardly conducive to progress.

A second realization of the veteran graduate student is that *education* is seldom the highest priority of graduate *educators*. Faculty members are also expendable and they, too, are working to meet evaluative criteria. Although they are paid to teach, they are evaluated on the basis of their research publications (cf. chapter 5). Indeed, "productivity" is almost synonymous with "publication." Out of 371 faculty respondents, Caplow and McGee reported that only fourteen (less than 4 percent) referred to teaching as being in any way "productive." As they put it,

> The academic man is judged almost exclusively by his performance in a kind of part-time voluntary job . . . . It is only a slight exaggeration to say that academic success is likely to come to the man who has learned to neglect his assigned duties . . . . The best teachers in educational institutions . . . often restrict themselves to a minimum of participation in the educational process (p. 221).

Encountering this same phenomenon in his own research, Berelson has added:

> It is important to recognize that the very people who have succeeded at the research game are running the show in the graduate schools, and it is hardly to be expected that they would give priority to . . . teaching (p. 40).

Having discerned these discrepancies, the student may also learn that few of his graduate courses will have direct relevance for his subsequent professional responsibilities. He will not be taught how to organize a course, initiate a research program, or give a job colloquium. He will not be tutored in grant writing skills or even in the construction of a vita. Instead of being taught *how* to think, he will be told *what* to think, and he may find that his professional survival skills are better taught by graduate peers rather than faculty.

For some students, these broader realizations may never occur. Hopefully, this is because their program is less guilty of the above abuses. Even when they are recognized, however, the student often succumbs to the system and—sooner or later—becomes still another product of its assembly line. As William James lamented in his 1912 essay "The Ph.D. Octupus," the student may muster even more resolve to attain those "three magic letters" which are assumed to be the union card of better employment. The corruption of scholarship has triumphed. Indeed, if he enters academia himself, the student may even have the opportunity to help perpetuate the system.

As he moves through the sequence of graduate hurdles, the student becomes more and more frantic to "get out." The light at the end of the tunnel may become all-engrossing. First-year anxieties take the form of second, third, and n-th year anxieties, which are often comprised of multiple factors. There is the perennial fear that the faculty will "find you out" for the moron you really are. Each academic term becomes an intrigue of calculated deception in which the student strives to prevent the discovery of his self-acknowledged incompetence. In addition to these are the anxieties stemming from the realization that the machinery of diploma production does not always run smoothly. There are vaguaries in requirements and an infinite array of things that *could* go wrong. Finally, there are the anxieties generated by one's uncertain future—will there be a job waiting? Will it allow some room for rest and recuperation from the graduate ordeal? Was this voluntary commitment to an ivory asylum a waste of time, effort, and money?

As these anxieties mount, the student may redouble his efforts to beat the system. Research publications begin to take on the form of professional redeemers and a vita starts to emerge. The behavior of successful faculty members is scrutinized and imitated from a distance. But two major obstacles remain between the aspirant and his goals—the comprehensive examination and the dissertation.

THE COMPREHENSIVE EXAMINATION

In addition to such prior hurdles as core courses, annual evaluations, and the master's thesis, most graduate programs require the student to survive what are called "comprehensive examinations" or "prelims." These usually consist of a set of written questions covering a wide range of topics in the given discipline. The student is allowed a certain number of hours (sometimes spanning several days) to respond in writing to these questions. This written exam is only half of the hurdle, however—the candidate must also survive several hours of unrehearsed interrogation by a faculty committee.

The alleged purposes of comprehensive examinations are to (a) test the breadth and adequacy of the student's knowledge, and (b) provide him with the professionally relevant experience of having surveyed his entire discipline. In a delightful satire on the orals portion of this examination, Mason contends that

> the basic purposes of the oral examination are: to make the examiner appear smarter and trickier than either the examinee or the other examiners, thereby preserving his self-esteem, and to crush the examinee, thereby avoiding the messy and time-wasting problem of post-examination judgment and decision (1956, p. 696).

Unfortunately, however, comprehensives are seldom a light or humorous element in graduate survival. Mason's satire is less of an exaggeration than one might desire. Depending on the student, committee, institution, and field, "comps" may range from a painful rite of passage to the most traumatizing event in the life of a young professional.

Perhaps more than any other graduate hurdle, comprehensives offer a lucid demonstration of "gamesmanship" on the part of both student and faculty. In the written portion, for example, the capable student has usually sized up the probability of various types of questions and the answers to which his captors will respond approvingly. Salient cues to these factors are usually apparent in prior interviews with faculty and in their lecture-imparted biases on what one should believe. Remembering that the word "diplomacy" has "diploma" as its root, the student usually writes with deft maneuvers which will allow him to cite the research or brilliant lectures of each of his committee members. Since comprehensive exam questions are usually submitted by each committee member, the discriminating student will also avoid the error of paying too much homage to one questioner at the slight of another.

The real drama of comps, however, usually occurs in the oral portion. This is an open-ended, no-holds-barred interrogation in which the student is asked to put his entire professional training on the line. With the pomp and appropriate decorum of an execution, the oral exam usually includes an "outside" (extra-departmental) member whose task it is to insure that the candidate is appropriately tortured prior to extermination. In the lingo of graduate handbooks, this is described as "fair and objective conduct of the examination."

In most oral comprehensives, committee members use a tag team strategy in which they rotate questioning and alternately rest themselves while they are wearing down the candidate. As suggested in the previously cited excerpt from Mason, one often gets the impression that the committee members are attempting to exhibit their erudition and impress their colleagues. They also seem to abide by some shared rules of interrogation:

> Make it clear to the examinee that his whole professional career may turn on his performance . . . . Throw out your hardest question first . . . . Do not permit him to ask you clarifying questions. Never repeat or clarify your own statement of the problem . . . . Every few minutes, ask him if he is nervous (p. 696).

Committee members are under a duress of their own, of course. The nature of the comprehensive exam may force them into the role of critic, even if they endorse the student's competency. These unwilling critics must therefore drill the candidate or risk appearing "soft" or non-discriminating to their colleagues. The student's adviser is often in this position and may ask broad, benign questions to satisfy the critic role without actually torturing the initiate. Unfortunately, these global queries often become the most difficult to answer and may lead to a faltering performance.

There are, on the other hand, committee members who seem to have accepted their academic mission as requiring the total humiliation of graduate students. For them, the oral exam is viewed as an intellectual beating which every student must receive, and they seem to relish in their power to administer it. Unless the candidate shows profuse sweating, voice tremors, and obvious humility, the examination has not been an optimal learning experience. Admissions of ignorance, involuntary urination, and apologies for inadequate preparation are considered much healthier signs.

This latter kind of committee member often draws upon impressive rhetorical skills in leading the student down a thorny path of self-contradiction and irrationality. Several of the most popular ploys in this endeavor are almost certain of success. In one, the student is asked to provide a clear and concise answer to some vague or universal question—often one which volumes of literature have failed to resolve. These problems generally take the form of "Define the universe and give two examples." This strategy is well illustrated in some of the sample questions suggested by Lipkin as preparation for a comprehensive examination in physics:

> List all elementary particles which have not yet been discovered, giving mass, charge, spin, isotopic spin, strangeness, and the reason why they have not yet been observed (1958, p. 12).

By well-timed lifts of the eyebrow and glances at the floor, the examiner communicates his disapproval as the student frantically jumps from one futile line of response to another. The second guerilla strategy might be called "expand your ignorance." Here, the committee member asks questions until he detects an area of weakness—and then he restricts his subsequent queries to this area. A third, but hardly the last tactic, is to force the student to take a stand opposite to that of another committee member. Veteran examiners can even wedge the student between *two* committee members who may disagree on some technical sub-issue. By cautiously avoiding sides, the student manages to alienate both.

When the debacle has ended, the student is asked to leave the room while a verdict is reached and his fate decided. It would, of course, be unthinkable that he should witness the deliberation. It has always intrigued me that anxiety researchers have failed to study the epitome of exhausted arousal—that lonely figure waiting in the corridor. Ever wondered what is going on in *his* mind at that moment? Does his life pass before him in sardonic commentary? Or is he simply numbed and drained to such an extent that the quiet solitude of a dark corridor is quite welcome?

If he still harbors any remaining illusions about the judicious conduct of academic affairs, it may be for the better that the student not witness his committee's deliberation. Academic etiquette usually encourages the student's adviser to defend him during this ordeal. If the student has wisely chosen an assertive or prestigious adviser, problems are less likely to arise. On the other hand, a timid and untenured defender may be the kiss of death. In that rare tragedy where the candidate has selected an adviser who is feuding with other committee members, his fate has probably been sketched (if not sealed) well before the oral exam.

When a student has performed well, the deliberation interval is brief. Faculty members congratulate one another for having produced such a fine specimen (although they will seldom be this generous in their direct feedback to the candidate). In marginal cases, the story is quite different. There is often a lengthy bemoaning of the deterioration of graduate education; good applicants are hard to find. Despite the fact that the aveage I.Q. of graduate students is relatively high, their intelligence is often berated by graduate faculty. As Berelson has put it, "in academic life, however good they are, they are never good enough" (p. 139). After maligning the student's aptitudes, motivation, and occasionally his race, the committee may decide to fail him on his oral performance. More frequently (I think), they adopt an air of patronizing charity (particularly in the case of minority students). "We've let him come this far . . . ." In those instances where the student fails to pass his oral exam, most departments are generous enough to allow the above torture to be experienced up to three times.

My evaluation of comprehensive exams may already be obvious. I consider them archaic, unnecessary, and inhumane rituals. This is, of course, a minority view, since Berelson reports that most graduate faculties favor the continuation or intensification of this practice. Some graduate students also favor it, although I suspect that many of its student supporters have already passed this hurdle in their own education.

The most common defenses of comps fall into three categories: (1) quality control, (2) professional preparation, and (3) justice and tradition. The quality control argument contends that comprehensive examinations offer one last chance to evaluate the breadth and adequacy of a candidate's knowledge. The implicit fear is that somewhere in one's graduate program there is a cunning moron who, up to now, has somehow managed to perform adequate coursework and research (presumably by some impressive legerdemain). Without comprehensives, this incompetent would enter the job market with a degree from *our department*, giving us a bad reputation and diminished prestige.

The second defense argues that comprehensives enhance the candidate's professional preparation by giving him the chance (as if it were an option) to round out his knowledge of the discipline. Having been forced to review broad areas in great detail, the student allegedly develops an integrated mastery of the field. Moreover, in arriving at this intellectual destination, the candidate is presumed to have improved his organizational and synthetic conceptual skills. A final sub-argument contends that the oral exam teaches the student that invaluable professional skill of quick thinking and critical dialogue.

The third argument simply contends that comps are a graduate school tradition which deserves preservation. The implicit (and sometimes explicit) corollary here is that "if I had to go through that hell . . . . "

In my opinion, none of the above arguments offer very strong reasons for the continued endorsement of comprehensive exams. For example, there is no evidence that these rituals are effective in their quality control efforts. It is somewhat puzzling that academicians presume that a single ordeal such as comps offers more accurate evaluation than three years of prior course work and tutelage. Given that these mythical morons have been adept enough to survive a barrage of prior courses and intermediate hurdles, what is the likelihood that they will be detected in one interrogatory marathon? How does one explain the apparently widespread concession that more than a few "incompetent" Ph.D.s have made it through comps (some of whom are now serving on comps committees)?

For the sake of argument, let us grant the assumption that comps *do* perform some sort of gross quality control function. Are they thereby justified? The answer, of course, depends on (a) how much one values "quality" in graduate education, (b) their magnitude of improvement relative to their costs (i.e., their "cost efficiency"), and (c) their relative effectiveness as compared to alternate quality control options. Regardless of whether it actually *exists* to any substantial degree, few would challenge the desirability of "quality" in graduate education. It is interesting to note that academicians are always eager to evaluate the quality of students' performance and are relatively defensive about having their own teaching performances evaluated. The premise here seems to reflect a double standard—"good" students are a product of a good graduate program; "bad" students are a product of inborn or irreversible personal (rather than teaching) deficits. At any rate, let us concede the necessity of some form of evaluation or quality control in graduate school. With this in mind, how "cost effective" is the system of comprehensive exams? Although I know of no research on the topic, it would be my guess that comps do very poorly—both in terms of improving quality (output), and in terms of the costs they require (input). Regarding the latter, I am not thinking here of faculty time or administrative hassles. I am not even questioning the value of a student having spent six months of preparatory studying. Rather, the costs which I find most disturbing are primarily emotional and psychological. Having seen students driven to anxious insomnia, desperate panic, and near-suicidal self-denigration, I feel that the benefits of comprehensives would have to be monumental to balance their debits. Can one really expect a science aspirant to develop confidence and professional self-assurance when placed in such a situation? What are the implications of such a practice for the student's self-image as a colleague or collaborator? Based on our knowledge of the relative effects of reward and punishment in learning, what are the consequences of making graduate school an avoidance marathon rather than an enrichment experience?

Another strong argument against the quality control defense is that there are alternate—and probably superior—methods of protecting program quality without incurring some of the extensive costs required by comps. Many of the more progressive—and I might add, top-ranked—graduate programs in the country have supplanted comprehensive exams with a more flexible curricular strategy which insures professional breadth while allowing the student to personalize his graduate training experiences. This alternative, which I shall call the personalized core, also avoids much of the perceived oppression and anxiety of the comps systems. A more detailed outline of the personalized core will be presented in my summary recommendations.

But we still have to face the argument that comprehensive exams offer an invaluable opportunity for "professional preparation." Let's look at how they might do this. Most students begin to make plans for their comprehensives nine to twelve months prior to their execution. For the final six months of preparation, the candidate often becomes a departmental ghost—attending and executing required functions, but spending all other available time pouring over an insurmountable literature. He rarely initiates any new research during this interval, and his social ties with faculty, peers, and sometimes family are seriously threatened. Knowing that he may be tested on minutiae, the student desperately pursues a "cramming marathon" in which he memorizes detailed specifics. As William James noted almost a century ago (and subsequent research in memory has borne him out), this style of learning is not only inefficient, but it may actually impede the more enduring and successful strategy of integrative learning and organizational memory.

In addition to the fact that much of a student's time and effort in preparing for comps is absorbed by rote memorization tasks, an additional inanity is the emphasis on *answers* in the exam itself. Rather than preparing him to ask *questions*—which is the basic task of the scientist—he is often forced to make sweeping conclusions and pronouncements. In at least some students, I think this may result in premature professional closure. The "world view" they were forced to construct for comprehensives becomes their permanent conceptual captor and they find it difficult to ever divest themselves of their first impressions.

Still another criticism of the longstanding emphasis on memorizing "facts" in graduate training is the realization that those "facts" are often very shortlived. This point was recently underlined by D.O. Hebb, who recommended that "in the present rapid growth of knowledge . . . the student should memorize as little as possible." Such a viewpoint is, of course, very compatible with the perspective I shall later endorse as a partial reform of graduate training—namely, that graduate education should be viewed as a flexible apprenticeship in learning and refining the *process* of inquiry.

When the date of the comprehensive exam finally arrives, the student is asked to perform a task which will never again be requested in his professional career—he is asked to sit in a room for two days and (often without books or notes) regurgitate everything he has ingested in the last six months. To stretch the metaphor, we need not doubt that the experience is nauseating. What I will question, however, is whether one can construe this as a "valuable professional preparation." Does it make sense to force a student into academic seclusion for half a year—to condone if not encourage admittedly inefficient study methods—and to force him to perform a professionally irrelevant and anxiously humiliating act? I think not.

But, again, let us concede the *possibility* that the above experience may have some redeeming features. For many students, it *does* force them to consult a literature which they might have otherwise ignored. For some students, it does help them to get some bearings on the breadth and depth of their field—forcing them to organize and communicate both their knowledge and their ignorance. These are, in my opinion, valuable experiences. However, I would again argue that these goals can be accomplished more efficiently with the alternative strategy of a personalized core. Until we start evaluating the cost-efficiency of our evaluation policies, however, adherents of both the comps and the core approach must confess to little substantiation in hard evidence.

I shall not even render a response to the "justice and tradition" argument. Its proponents have probably stopped reading this book long before now.

THE DISSERTATION

In his satirical taxonomy of *The Academic Bestiary*, Richard Armour describes the dissertation as *"magno iam conatu magnas nugas"* which means "to produce tremendous trifles with great effort" (1974, p. 51). Likewise, Berelson reminds us of Laski's definition of a dissertation as "an island of words in a sea of references." Judging from the fact that relatively circumscribed topics often receive over one thousand pages of discourse, both of these allusions to superfluity would seem to have ample defense. Its inflated size is perhaps a reflection of its assigned importance, for there can be little doubt that the dissertation is considered the magnum opus of graduate life—it is usually the last remaining requirement for the elusive Ph.D. degree. Theoretically, the dissertation is supposed to be "an original contribution to knowledge" which demonstrates the candidate's scholarship and research skills. There is often little consensus, however, as to what constitutes a "contribution" and even less regarding whether it is "original."

In many graduate programs, the master's thesis is viewed as a warm-up exercise for the dissertation. It is usually completed in the second year of a program and is often an essential prerequisite for subsequent "advancement to doctoral candidacy" (which, in turn, makes one eligible to take comprehensives and to form a dissertation committee). As Armour has put it, "The Thesis is born of Necessity. The other parent is unknown, wisely deciding to remain anonymous" (p. 147). Relative to the dissertation, the master's thesis is usually more circumscribed and less ambitious. Both its content and its purpose may vary widely from one institution and program to another. As the graduate dean at Harvard recently remarked, "The Master's degree is, at present, a bit like a streetwalker—all things to all men (and at different prices)" (Berelson, p. 185). Berelson notes that this intermediate graduate hurdle has declined in prestige over the last few decades, partly because prestigious universities and physical science departments have begun to eliminate it. Except for state universities, education departments, and institutions where it is the only graduate diploma, master's degrees appear to be declining in both popularity and function. However, they are unlikely to become extinct. In addition to serving quality control and apprenticeship functions, the master's services a huge body of intermediate level students (e.g., in education) who might otherwise further glut our already corpulent doctoral programs. Finally, the M.A., M.S., etc., (there are almost 100 kinds of master's degrees) may also assuage both faculty member and student in cases where an individual is dropped from further graduate studies. The master's becomes his consolation prize, so that he leaves the graduate jungle without empty hands and his faculty adviser feels fewer conscience pangs about his expulsion.

In Berelson's research with graduate faculties and recent Ph.D. recipients, he found an interesting ambivalence regarding the *purpose* of the doctoral dissertation. Both groups of respondents felt that it should be a dual-purpose endeavor, serving to expand our knowledge while it serves a research training function. Paradoxically, they felt that recent dissertations have been biased in favor of the latter function, and many favored an increased emphasis on contributions to public (rather than the student's) knowledge. In my opinion, this requirement imposes a number of counter-productive forces on both the student and his project.

First, it places an undue premium on "originality" at the expense of replication. In practice, if not in principle, controlled replication appears to be one of the lowest priorities in some contemporary sciences. I might add that in those fields where replication is least encouraged, scientific progress has been notably inferior. The bias against repetition has been reflected not only in the performance of studies, but also in their publication (chapter 5). For example, T.D. Sterling reviewed experimental articles in four psychological journals during one year. Out of 362 reported studies, not one was a replication. From an epistemological perspective, the costs of this originality bias have probably been substantial. In the social sciences particularly, investigators might do well to consider Harding's reminder that research might better be spelled with a hyphen (re-search).

In addition to the constraints imposed on originality, the "outcome" of the dissertation is often explicitly emphasized. It must yield "successful" or statistically significant results. Although this incidence is probably exaggerated, every doctoral candidate has heard the horror stories about previous students who were "shot down" because their dissertation failed to produce the desired results. Thus, he is encouraged to develop an implicit vested interest in the outcome of his study. As in many other research endeavors (chapter 6), this emotional involvement is most apparent when the data returns begin. The student shows unmistakable manic-depressive cycles as his data analyses reveal "positive" or "negative" results. Since many dissertations deal with sub-issues in the general research area of one's faculty adviser, the valence of the data are often critical. In my opinion, the practice of evaluating a dissertation on the basis of its outcome (rather than its relevance or methodology) is a travesty of science. It places undue restrictions on the type of research a student will propose. Rather than suggesting an innovative or unconventional question, he will stick to a more conservative issue. After all, he can hardly risk "failure" at this stage of his career. Having experienced four or five years of grueling professional preparation, the dissertation has become his sole reason for existence—it is the only remaining obstacle between him and his delusion of well-paid prestige. The student will therefore often choose a dissertation topic which incorporates minimal risk and maximal likelihood of a successful outcome. If he is particularly shrewd or fortunate, he will study a question for which *any* outcome would be interesting. It may turn out to be trivial in its relevance, but it will at least have been instrumental in the student's release.

Another side-effect of placing a valence on the data has to do with the "internal validity" of the study. As we shall see in chapter 8, experimenters often contaminate their results by a number of intentional and unintentional means. Although this may be more pronounced in experimentation with human subjects, it is certainly not restricted to this realm of science. In selecting their subjects, executing their procedure, and reporting or interpreting their results, researchers often demonstrate marked biases in favor of their experimental hypotheses. These prejudicial tactics are frequently subtle, and veteran researchers seem to be equally prone to (and probably more proficient in) their use. Needless to say, when the doctoral candidate's entire professional career may be riding on the outcome of his dissertation, there is ample room for bias. In discussing this problem with colleagues at a number of universities, I have been informed of half a dozen instances in which desperate doctoral candidates have performed glaring scientific sins to produce a "successful" dissertation—sins ranging from expedient data omissions to the epitome of empirical crime—data fabrication. These errant and intentional misdeeds are probably much rarer than those which are more readily rationalized as "legitimate" by the partisan researcher (chapter 8). Regardless of their form, however, the fact remains that the contemporary valuation of dissertation outcome exerts an influence on both the content and the conduct of doctoral research. In my opinion, that influence is not beneficial to either the student or to scientific progress.

Like many other graduate hurdles, the dissertation must be approved by a group of academic elders—the dissertation committee. This is usually accomplished by successive meetings during the proposal stage, followed by an austere "oral defense" of the dissertation. When the dissertation committee functions in the true spirit of graduate education—with generous encouragement, constructive suggestions, and substantial personal contact—the student may find himself in a uniquely stimulating and satisfying experience. Unfortunately, the conduct of such committees is rarely complimentary to academic ideals. Instead of being encouraged or advised, the candidate is often avoided or marginally tolerated. His ideas are seldom polished with constructive feedback; they are demolished with cryptic and authoritarian revision. Instead of being viewed as a feeling organism in a stressful dilemma, he is more often treated as a frustrating imposition upon a busy faculty schedule. The student's social skills are frequently taxed in this ordeal of subservience. He must not only tolerate and concede the often authoritarian changes requested, but he must also coordinate three or four difficult elders into a consensus of both scheduling and opinion.

Not every faculty member takes an avid interest in the dissertation he is supposed to be encouraging. Unless he is the committee chairman or the proposed study enters his private domain of expertise, it is a rare professor who invests much time or effort in reading or refining a dissertation proposal. This is repeatedly documented by anecdotes in the graduate student lounge, where candidates report that they inserted a five dollar bill or an obscene joke halfway through the pages of their proposal. The manuscript is frequently returned—pages unruffled and money intact—with vague mumbles of approval. Unfortunately, these disinterested sponsors are often the ones who raise objections *after* the study has been completed. They are reluctant to place their signature on an imperfect specimen of science.

I have omitted many other frustrations in completing a dissertation, such as:

1. the endless revisions in both the proposal and the final form;
2. the awkward contradictions requested when two committee members demand incompatible changes, or when the same committee

member suggests an addition which had been part of an earlier version but which *he* deleted;

3. the inane requirements of the Graduate Office, which often threaten rejection unless a perfectly typed manuscript is submitted on special weight paper prior to an impossible date and with no infractions of 84 incomprehensible "rules for preparation"; and

4. the pervasive (albeit unwarranted) fear that one's degree could be repossessed at any point in the next 40 years, should the Graduate Office discover a misplaced semicolon or a marginally legitimate data analysis.

Eventually, of course, the ordeal is ended. An approved research study has been milked for every conceivable implication and the long months of sleep deprivation and painful revision are over. The oral defense is passed, and each committee member participates in a ritualistic endorsement ceremony, symbolized by affixing their signature to the finished document. The rites of passage are past and, with awesome swiftness, the indigent peon has been ordained into the prestigious clergy of Truth Merchants.

It is perhaps, the rudest awakening of graduate life when the newly-crowned Ph.D. realizes that his travails have not here ended—they have just begun. Ahead of him lies a new role and different demands, many of which were totally ignored in his graduate education. He must survive the ordeal of job interviews, where Murphy's Law reigns supreme ("If anything can go wrong, it will"). Agnew and Pyke sum up the situation very well:

> Perhaps the most deceptive myth of all is that the Ph.D. represents the last hurdle in some kind of knowledge race. A student who has just cleared the jump should enjoy this illusion while it lasts. The science game now shifts to new ground with new rules. Your rating first depends on getting some articles out; then, once you've demonstrated that you can publish, your rating depends on whether you are publishing in respectable journals; then your rating depends on whether you have a good book out; and then .... (p. 146).

Before we move on to the rules of the science game, some reconstruction is in order. In this chapter I have been admittedly critical of contemporary graduate training practices. Although the model I have attacked is far from universal, I think that its elements are pervasive enough to make my portrait representative. If I am in error—and graduate programs are much more relevant and humane than I have portrayed—I shall delight in standing corrected. Meanwhile, I would like to share a partial list of recommendations for change.

IMPROVING GRADUATE APPRENTICESHIP: SOME RECOMMENDATIONS

The recommendations which follow will undoubtedly be met with mixed reactions. One of my reviewers has suggested that I have adopted the improvement of graduate life as my "mission," that I am trying to champion the apprentice. In a sense, this is true. But I disagree with the implied dichotomy—i.e., that one must either side with the faculty (and current practices) or defend the students (and demand reappraisal). The gap between these two groups is already much wider than I would prefer. Whatever can be done to improve graduate education will simultaneously enhance the lives of both. Moreover, as successive generations of scientists enjoy a more relevant and humane apprenticeship, we can expect to reap far-reaching benefits in our overall growth of knowledge.

Without examining and refining the crucial process of graduate training, we can hardly hope to *see*—let alone to see growth. Today's graduate students are the lifeblood of tomorrow's science; and more important, the tutors of generations to follow. If, after having reached the chairs of their own former mentors, they endorse traditional absurdities, then the inadequacies and inhumanities of the system may endlessly recycle. Evaluating these suggested changes may not be easy but, in my opinion, neither is enduring their absence.

Admissions Policies.   We have tenaciously clung to admissions criteria which have shown very poor relationship to individual performance either during or after graduate school. This suggests an embarrassing conclusion—that, as scientists, we prefer an incorrect hypothesis to none at all. Given that there are no competing predictors, why not continue to rely on our admittedly impotent (but pleasantly quantifiable) past criteria—grade point average, entrance exam scores, and so on? Besides its salient irrationality, this strategy probably encourages a post-admissions attitude of suspicion. Since we know that our selection criteria are poor, we try to keep up quality control aspects of our programs in a way which will allow *ad hoc* rejection of candidates.

It has always intrigued me that admissions committees tend to restrict their self-scrutiny to one of forward longitudinal logic. In their commendable efforts to refine selection criteria, they examine undergraduate variables and then correlate these with ratings of subsequent graduate and postgraduate performance. They seldom question these latter covariates—i.e., the reliability or validity of their "dependent" variables. Moreover, they rarely consider the reverse logic of interviewing "successful" students in an attempt to discover variables which may have been overlooked in their current regression equations.

In my opinion, the continued valuation of exceptionally high performance on intellectual tests is unwarranted in graduate admissions. Although some minimal criteria may be useful as flexible lower limits, we do not have much empirical justification for selecting one applicant over another on the basis of a few tenths of a point. Moreover, I would favor the development of standardized evaluation forms for sponsors of applicants. This might reduce some of the unfair advantage given to those prosaic letter writers who are most skilled at the use of convincing superlatives. Along these same lines, we might consider the establishment of a national clearinghouse for graduate applications. By centralizing this function, tremendous amounts of effort could be saved. Faculty sponsors would submit their recommendations only once (imagine the savings in secretarial time) and, at the student's request, graduate schools would receive files from this central source. For those who are enamored by factor analyses, consider the additional opportunities such a clearinghouse might afford for the refinement of admissions criteria. One could determine the *national* ranking of each student on any variable contained in the standard recommendation form. Moreover, by accumulating files, one could derive an index of each sponsor's conservatism in recommendations—i.e., whether he is generous or stingy with his superlatives. Each of these factors might offer invaluable opportunities for the refinement of our current policies.

Given the crudeness of present criteria, I would also favor research on alternatives to traditional admissions committees. For example, we need to better examine "apprentice selection systems" such as those explored by McGill and a few other universities. In this sytem, each member of a graduate faculty is given the chance to select his own student *on his own criteria*. This avoids the enforced prejudices of a committee which endorses traditional requirements. Moreover, by demanding that the faculty member take responsibility for selecting his own apprentices, we might expect to see an increment in their personal involvement and active participation in graduate training under such a system. The apprentice selection system could foster a tutelage relationship in which the student feels "wanted" by his sponsor who, in turn, feels a personal obligation to optimize and support the student's progress. As might well be expected, however, this alternative system is likely to have problems of its own. For example, how does one manage the funding of students? What if a student wants to change advisers or subspecialties? And perhaps most critically, would this kind of system hamper both faculty members and students by allowing them to exposure only to those who were already of similar interests and orientation? These potential problems are unavoidable risks in the exploration of alternative admission policies. However, as I have already indicated, they appear to be welcome risks when viewed against the inefficiency of our current traditions. Uncertainty and problems are part of the process called experimentation; but so also are growth and discovery.

Atmosphere. The ambiance of many graduate programs seems to be diametrically opposite to that recommended by educational researchers. There can be little doubt that it often fails to foster some of the presumably cardinal features of the scientist (such as independence and flexibility of thought). We should be little surprised if the science game is often colored by a fierce competitiveness and paranoid secrecy, for these are not uncommon components in our apprenticeship programs.

The unfortunate atmosphere of all too many graduate programs is one which encourages anxiety, confusion, and insecurity on the part of the student. He endures four to six years of indigent suffering, desperately striving toward a survival which is often marginal at best. Financially, socially, and psychologically, the graduate student is forced to sacrifice many of his "inalienable" rights. In some programs, he is hardly a second class citizen—particularly during the first two years. Until he has demonstrated some professional mettle, the student is often required to forfeit his opinions, his leisure time, and his self-esteem in return for the meager consolation of simply continuing his oppressed existence. In the more competitive programs, the tenuousness of his career is emphasized almost daily—with humiliating tasks, mechanically repetitive evaluations, and the occasional termination of a peer.

In my opinion, this atmosphere is not only a travesty of scientific apprenticeship, but also an affront to the dignity and sensitivity of the student. Even if it were extremely efficient in its product—which it certainly is not—one would be hard pressed to justify current policies as the optimal means. It is high time that we divorce ourselves from the austere model of graduate education, and strive toward developing a culture more conducive to professional training. If our goals are, in fact, the optimal preparation of young scientists, then we must begin generating an apprenticeship environment of respected collaboration and progressive independence. Our programs should emphasize personal freedom, conceptual flexibility, and the value of perpetual growth. In place of the frantic anxiety fostered by prevalent graduate policies, we should be encouraging the development of attributes which may be more compatible with scientific endeavors—self-assurance and personal valuation based on the pursuit of knowledge rather than its capture. One can hardly expect new paths to be blazed by those who have been immobilized by an enforced lack of confidence.

Quality Control. The foregoing comments do not imply the endorsement of a laissez faire policy of noncontingent progress through a graduate program. I do think that some degree of evaluation is beneficial for both the student and the profession. However, I think this evaluation needs to be modified substantially from prevalent policies. For example, it should emphasize broad and integrative conceptual knowledge rather than the humiliating and temporary rote memorization of technical minutiae. Likewise, the perspective of evaluation should be inverted. Instead of demonstrating their competence just to stay in school (i.e., the prevailing "avoidance model"), we should be *presuming* competence and integrity until, as rarely occurs, there is good reason to believe otherwise. Evaluation should also be reciprocal. There should be more emphasis placed on the assessment and improvement of graduate educators, and not just graduate students. Finally, graduate evaluation should be progressively removed (not intensified) as the student moves through a program. By the time he reaches his third year, he should feel (and be perceived as) an independent collaborator who can afford to pursue unconventional or counter-paradigm issues without fear of reprimand. In many contemporary programs, the "good" graduate student is one who can blurt out knowledgeable *answers* to a professor's questions. Very little recognition is given to the student who can formulate meaningful *questions*. I have sometimes wondered how graduate school would be affected by the rule that students must learn to "stump" each professor on their committee. Such a practice might be very healthy for both faculty and students alike.

Pursuant to the above guidelines, I would further recommend evaluation of the following possible changes in current quality control aspects of graduate training:

1. that the master's degree be made optional in those programs or instances where the Ph.D. is the ultimate pursuit; a less formal or ritualistic research project could serve as a substitute;
2. that comprehensive examinations (both written and oral) be made optional as a prerequisite for advancement; in their place, one might establish something like a personalized core of graduate courses in which the student demonstrates proficiency and breadth

by earning at least a "B" grade in n courses self-selected from among $n + x$ options; to insure breadth, the student may be required to take a specified number of courses in *each* of several broad disciplinary areas—e.g., 2 (out of 4) courses from Area I, 2 (out of 3) from Area II, and so on;

3. that the dissertation be defended and given *final* approval prior to the actual research—i.e., that the student defend his experimental design rather than his data;
4. that a student be able to exempt the formal dissertation requirement through prior demonstration of research proficiency; when a candidate has already shown adequate skills in independent research, he should be able to be certified by a committee and allowed to spend his final graduate year continuing his independent studies; and
5. that the evaluation of faculty by graduate students be made a standard and consequential policy; students should not only be given more voice in the determination of departmental policy, but their evaluations of individual faculty members should have direct bearing on the latter's salary and tenure.

There are, I think, ample arguments to defend each of the above recommendations, some of which have already demonstrated their promise at several of our more progressive institutions. In addition to improving the efficiency and atmosphere of graduate training, they may also offer considerable advantages to the faculty member. For example, several of the suggested changes actually reduce his work load, thereby allowing more time for alternate and more rewarding aspects of tutelage. They may likewise encourage a more active and conscientious participation by the faculty. When he realizes that his award of a "B" grade in a core course signifies his certification that the student has demonstrated proficiency therein, the instructor may revise his syllabus to present content breadth (rather than an autobiography of his own restricted research interests).

Content Relevance.   The marginal professional relevance of many graduate school experiences is a serious problem. All too much time seems to be spent evaluating and exploiting the student rather than preparing him for the responsibilities and assignments he is likely to encounter in his post-doctoral employment. The following suggestions offer some general guidelines for remedying our irrelevance:

1. students should be offered credit-bearing seminars or tutelage on appropriate topics of professional survival, such as course organiza-

tion and direct teaching experience (for prospective educators); helpful guidelines for the development of a program of research; grantsmanship and technical writing skills; how to construct a vita, write letters of recommendation, and give a job colloquium; the politics of an academic career; and so on;

2. students should be encouraged to develop a flexible breadth of competence which will provide them with a multilateral perspective as well as a valuable professional diversity; the *process* of learning should be emphasized as much as (if not more than) the *content* so that they will be well prepared to meet changing demands in job role or personal interest; and

3. the graduate program should emphasize the development of critical reasoning skills along with a cautious appreciation of the scientist's fallibilities; students should be taught *how* to think (rather than *what*) and emphasis should be placed on the value of such logical methods as "comprehensively critical rationalism" and disconfirmatory reasoning (chapter 7); experimental *replication* should be stressed as an indispensable element in scientific inquiry (and replicative research might be encouraged as a useful way of learning to conduct studies).

Pursuant to accomplishing the above mentioned goal of remedial relevancy, attempts should be made to collect appropriate feedback and suggestions from recent graduates.

Humane Modeling.   It is well documented in psychological research that a sizeable portion of complex human behavior—including values and attitudes—are acquired through vicarious means—i.e., the observation of someone else's performance. When the model is prestigious, his impact on an observer is enhanced. Needless to say, in graduate education faculty members are often selected as professional models by their young admiring students. This relationship can be conducive to either growth or deterioration, depending on the nature of their interaction and the types of behavior exhibited by the faculty model. His commentaries on professional matters will often color the perceptions and pursuits of his protegé. If he emphasizes personal rivalries, competitive secrecy, and political expedience, he can expect these performances to have some impact on the future conduct and perspective of his young admirer.

In addition to purely professional performances, the faculty member often imparts (albeit reluctantly) various characteristics of his personal life (e.g., the importance of family and friends), as well as his relative priorities within professional matters (e.g., teaching versus research) and between vocational and non-vocational endeavors (e.g., work versus family, the ability to extract himself from professional matters, and so on). As role models, I feel that faculty members have some obligation to share aspects of their personal lives with graduate students. The apprentice who never sees a professor except during frenzied snatches of office hours or in formal educational roles may easily develop misconceptions about his own future role. There is more to the scientist than usually meets the graduate eye. It is my bias that many of these unshared features may leave frustrating gaps in the professional self-image of the student. I can see little wrong with revealing our humanness.

REFERENCES

4, 7, 10, 21, 22, 50, 73, 78 ,81, 84, 86, 98, 101, 106, 115, 116, 122, 126, 171, 177, 179, 184, 190, 193, 195, 196, 205, 208, 210, 222, 228, 230, 231, 254, 255, 265, 266, 268, 275, 280, 281, 283, 287, 299, 330, 337, 347, 357, 360, 366, 373, 374, 375, 382, 383, 387, 389, 428, 438, 442, 446, 479, 482, 491.

Political influence may be acquired in exactly the same way as the gout . . . . sit tight and drink port wine.

F.M. Cornford

You have no notion of the intrigues that go on in this blessed world of science.

Thomas H. Huxley

The Principle of Limited Sloppiness: You should be sloppy enough so that the unexpected happens, but not so sloppy that you can't figure out what happened afterward.

Max Delbrück

The most impressive of all kinds of Professors is the Full Professor. It is not apparent at first glance precisely what it is full of, but there is an obvious fullness.

Richard Armour

No academic person is ever voted into the chair until he has reached an age at which he has forgotten the meaning of the word "irrelevant."

F.M. Cornford

In the beginning God made idiots—that was for practice. Then He began on the menagerie and labored along until finally He constructed the ass. Everyone could see He was then ready to create a professor, and He did.

Student X

Ivory towers are perhaps the easiest of all structures to build as an alternative to living.

Kitty Ben Herron

※ *Chapter 4*

Rules of the Game: Politics and Prizes

The travails of the science aspirant do not end with a graduate degree: in many ways, they have just begun. The young Ph.D. quickly learns that he has simply advanced to a larger pond and—reminiscent of his early graduate status—he is once again at the bottom of the pecking order. In *The Academic Marketplace*, Caplow and McGee convey some of the psychological aspects of early postgraduate employment:

> For those who survive (graduate training), the habit of insecurity and a certain mild paranoid resignation are standard psychological equipment. These characteristics are often strengthened by the discovery that the criteria which they must meet as faculty members are quite different from those . . . in graduate school (p. 223).

In some sciences, there used to be little concern over finding a job after graduate training. There were often more positions than there were qualified applicants. Things began to change in the 1960s and 70s, however, and the new Ph.D. soon found himself competing with hundreds of peers for a single (and often unattractive) opening. It was then, perhaps, that the tactics of job recruitment became the highest survival priority of the young scientist. In this chapter we shall explore some of the apparent game rules of academic science; with minor changes, I think they are also relevant for scientists in non-academic positions.

ACADEMIC POLITICS: FROM RECRUITMENT TO TENURE

In 1908, F.M. Cornford published a delightfully satirical pamphlet called *Microcosmographia Academica* in which he offers insightful guidelines for the "young academic politician."[a] The manuscript is basically a sardonic survival kit for the young and ambitious faculty member. Many of Cornford's observations remain relevant for today's educators.

Just as the mushrooming applications for graduate school have caused an abrupt escalation of (unreliable) admissions criteria, the Ph.D. "glut" has wreaked changes upon the recruitment scene. Two decades ago a young Ph.D. was often hired sight unseen, and he often presented a vita which was totally devoid of publications. Appointments were sometimes made by the chairman with little or no recourse to a "recruitment committee." In today's market, however, the job applicant is not only looked at but often extensively *tested* in a variety of surrealistic professional tasks. Moreover, his vita must often claim some minimum number of past or imminent publications and he must undergo personal interviews with a number of his prospective colleagues. Students coming from prestigious graduate institutions—with the endorsement of eminent sponsors—once again have a substantial advantage on the job market.

If the young Ph.D. is fortunate enough to attract the attention of a potential employer, he is invited to give a job colloquium. Formally, this is a brief oral presentation of his past or current research—often his dissertation. The colloquium allows the recruiting department to view the candidate under high stress conditions, and this single fifty minute performance is often considered an incontestable reflection of the candidate's teaching skills, intelligence and personality makeup. The colloquium, however, is only one small part of the overall evaluation which takes place during a recruitment visit. The job applicant can often expect to be faced with a large number of the following challenges, both intentional and unintentional:

1. the ability to pay your own way to and from the recruiting institution;
2. the ability to produce rational conversation with what often seem to be marginally psychotic hosts; this ability must be demonstrable upon request at any hour from 7 A.M. to 1 A.M., and regardless of personal health, sleep deprivation, or current blood alcohol content;

[a]I am indebted to Jack Hoey for bringing this work to my attention.

3. the ability to consume a critical amount of alcohol—sufficient to seem sociable but insufficient to produce either candor or coma;
4. the ability to be whirled through a day of blurred names and faces without forgetting your own;
5. the ability to suppress bladder and bowel responses for a minimum of six hours; and
6. the ability to withstand cynical comments and direct attacks upon your ideas or research without responding in counter-aggression.

If—*if* you can meet these kinds of challenges—then you may be deemed worthy of conditional (untenured) appointment as a *junior* faculty member. It has been my experience that most job recruitment decisions are based on four primary considerations: (a) the vita and its supporting letters, (b) personal interviews with faculty members, (c) social performance during the post-colloquium party, and (d) the adequacy of the colloquium presentation itself. When I was a graduate student, one of our faculty members gave us a long handout describing some "do's and don't's" of job colloquia. For example, we were told that the goal was to present oneself as a "self-assured smart ass"—competent and ambitious but not abrasive. I can still remember my revulsion at the thought that academic science was steeped in politics and impression management. I now smile at my naivete.

The intrigues and subtleties of job recruiting could consume a volume in themselves—as evidenced by the classic work of Caplow and McGee. Although somewhat dated, their research documents many of the inanities and inequities which continue to pervade academia—from the "publish or perish" rule to tenure and promotions. Their text might be an enlightening primer for the junior faculty member.

We shall soon turn our attention to the rewards which are often sought by *homo scientus*. However, since some of these involve intramural trophies within one's own institution and department, they deserve some treatment here. When the young Ph.D. is first hired, he is usually given a formal contract for one to three years as an "assistant professor" (some institutions require that one first serve as an "instructor" prior to receiving this rank). In this role, the individual is considered a "junior" faculty member—which usually means that he is untenured, ineligible for chairing doctoral committees, and most likely to receive the smallest office, worst teaching assignments, and farthest parking space. The life of an assistant professor is often harried and tenuous, particularly if he is a member of a competitive department. In order to survive (and receive contract renewals), the assistant professor must usually publish a certain number of professional articles per year. Interviews with faculty and administrators consistently reflect the pervasiveness of the "publish or perish" philosophy in appointments and promotions.[b] Despite the fact that he is paid for teaching, the fate of the academic scientist is primarily dependent upon his ability to get published. Unless he has a rare talent for administrative duties or committees which are onerous to his colleagues, the junior faculty member with sparse publications is usually doomed for termination. Teaching skills will not suffice—a fact which is reflected in the virtual absence of student input in faculty promotions.

Many universities have an "up or out" system; a junior faculty member must either be promoted or terminated. This decision is usually made in the sixth year of employment. Although they need not be related, promotion to "associate" professor is often paired with the granting of *tenure*. In place of his formerly tenuous year-to-year contracts, the faculty member is given a permanent contract and assurance of lifetime employment. Technically, this guarantee can only be negated by such extreme acts as prolonged negligence of duty or "moral terpitude" (both of which are either rare or common in academia—depending on one's value system). The purpose of tenure is to provide job security and thereby promote academic freedom. This is an admitted simplification, but I don't think it is misrepresentative. Without written assurance of job permanence, the faculty member might be reluctant to express or explore bold or innovative lines of thought. The tenured professor will supposedly venture on to conceptual and empirical planes which would be considered too chancy for his untenured junior colleagues.

I shall only briefly belabor my own views on the tenure system. Briefly, I think it is a counterproductive travesty of academic excellence. My reasons are as follows. First, it is a system which grants permanent noncontingent security on the primary basis of publications—a very dubious criterion. Although the institutional by-laws may state that *teaching excellence* is a prime consideration, the contrary evidence is almost staggering. Individuals who are blatantly incompetent as teachers are frequently granted tenure, and real teaching excellence is often met with termination due to sparse publications. The young faculty member quickly learns to compromise his ideals and invest his energies where they will be most expedient.

[b]Terry Wilson of Rutgers has suggested that this philosophy would be more aptly termed "publish *and* perish."

A second objection to the tenure system deals with its logical substratum. If its primary purpose is to provide a security blanket which will protect or encourage academic freedom, then why is this critical security postponed for seven years? Should not the younger faculty members receive this same assurance? If anything, historians of science tell us that bold and innovative ideas tend to come from the younger scientists. Isn't the system, then, reversed? Shouldn't guarantees be given early in one's career and gradually weakened with maturity? The answer, of course, is that the seven year wait is simply another evaluative hurdle in an endless marathon. The junior faculty member must "prove" his worthiness of noncontingent job security. How? By publishing, of course.

My third criticism also attacks the logic of the tenure system. If its primary purpose is to protect academic freedom, then—in my opinion —it has often performed that function very poorly. Although professional incompetence and negligence of one's educational duties are seldom grounds for the removal of tenure, political activism and unconventional beliefs about sex, religion, or morality are frequent correlates. In essence, tenure protects one's freedom to be a poor instructor, but it does not allow one much latitude in anything else.

Finally, I object to tenure on the grounds that it may encourage a counter-progressive pattern in research careers. The plethora of tenured cadavers in academia attests to the fact that this system often engenders stagnation. The "senior" professor has noncontingent security, and this is frequently reflected in the sharp decline of his post-tenure productivity. Actually, there are several different patterns in the productivity-tenure relationship:

	Pre-Tenure Productivity		Probable Post-Tenure Productivity	
	Quantity (QN)	Quality (QL)	Quantity (QN)	Quality (QL)
I	High	High	High or Medium QN,	High QL
II	High	Medium	Medium QN,	Medium QL
III	High	Low	Medium or Low QN,	Low QL
IV	Medium	High	Medium or Low QN,	High QL
V	Medium	Medium	Low QN,	Medium or Low QL
VI	Medium	Low	Low QN,	Low QL
VII	Low	Irrelevant	Tenure Not Granted	

These are, of course, subjective predictions and the matrix does not include all possible combinations. However, I think several of the more prevalent patterns are depicted. For example, in pattern I we see the researcher who is generally unaffected by tenure. His productivity remains quantitatively and qualitatively high even when his employment has been made noncontingent. In patterns III and VI, the prevalent post-tenure recession can be detected. Note that the theory behind these predictions seems to reflect at least two assumptions: (1) that the primary impact of tenure is to reduce the quantity, but not necessarily the quality, of publications, and (2) that individuals who do not sacrifice quality to secure pre-tenure quantity are often least affected by the granting of tenure. Whether the matrix is an accurate predictor is difficult to judge from the available literature. Likewise, if these patterns are valid, we must await further research for the identification of differentiating variables (e.g., preference of alternate incentives, "intrinsic" interest in research, etc.).

As an alternative to the tenure system, a series of renewable multi-year contracts would provide relative security without granting permanent noncontingency. In such a system, all faculty members would remain perpetually accountable for their work. The knowledge that he could be replaced by an energetic new Ph.D. might keep senior faculty members a bit more honest to their academic ideals; it might also help to distribute professional unemployment among the incompetent rather than just among the young. Hopefully, teaching skills and student input would be heavily emphasized. In the absence of drastic fiscal calamities, however, the tenure system is unlikely to be terminated in the next few generations. As long as the system is "up or out," even the dissenting junior professor must accept tenure or face unemployment. Moreover, as long as the jury is already tenured, the verdict will hardly be surprising.

Aside from special awards, the only remaining academic notch past the associate level is that of "full" professorship. This is the culmination of the academic ladder unless one aspires toward administrative posts. It usually carries additional political power and some intra-departmental fringe benefits, but is otherwise only an honorific promotion. Full professorship signifies one's "arrival" at a stage of recognized respect and academic rank. However, even the full professor may harbor feelings of insecurity and unrest. He has usually witnessed well over a decade of academic politics, and he knows that the only thing certain to occur is change. Cornford captures the recurrent cycle of academic life in his insightful condensation of professorial careers:

> While you are young you will be oppressed, and angry, and increasingly disagreeable. When you reach middle age, at five-and-thirty, you will be-

come complacent and, in your turn, an oppressor . . . . It will seem to you then that you grow wiser every day, as you learn more and more of the reasons why things should not be done . . . . If you persist to the threshold of an old age—your fiftieth year let us say—you will be a powerful person yourself . . . and far from below will mount the roar of a ruthless multitude of young men in a hurry. You may perhaps be aware what they are in a hurry to do. They are in a hurry to get you out of the way (pp. 9-10).

And the cycle continues. Cornford expresses pity for the young academician, but his sentiments toward senior politicians are not nearly as generous: "When you are old, if you will stand in the way, there will be no more pity for you than you deserve; and that will be none at all" (p. 10).

EXTRAMURAL TROPHIES

In addition to being appointed and promoted within an institution, the scientist usually strives for a variety of rewards from the larger scientific community. While these rewards may range widely in form, their basic ingredient is peer *recognition*. The scientist strives to be recognized and respected by his professional colleagues. As Ziman has noted, his research career and publication efforts are often dominated by the desire to win their approval and consensus. This energetic pursuit of recognition is a well documented aspect of scientific life which has led sociologist Warren O. Hagstrom to formulate the *recognition-exchange hypothesis*:

> In science, the acceptance by scientific journals of contributed manuscripts establishes the donor's status as a scientist—indeed, status as a scientist can be achieved *only* by such gift-giving—and it assures him of prestige within the scientific community.
> The organization of science consists of an exchange of social recognition for information. But, as in all gift-giving, the expectation of return gifts cannot be publicly acknowledged as the motive for making the gift (p. 13).

This latter point has also been noted by Merton in his discussion of ambivalences in the scientist role. Although many textbooks portray him as an unselfish devotee of truth—capable of unrewarded sacrifice and perpetual humility—the average scientist is faced with contrary data in his own very real aspirations for social recognition and professional respect. For many scientists, this contrast is probably a painful one. The storybook image tells him that he *should* be motivated only by "pure" incentives—the growth of knowledge and a communal sharing of effort. This idealistic portrait leaves no room for personal involvement; by its very nature science is a communistic (rather than capitalistic) endeavor. However, the conscience-ridden scientist may often be faced with his own human frailty—he finds himself hoping for or enjoying recognition and being upset or depressed when he is not awarded his due attention for an idea or discovery.

In my opinion, there is nothing demeaning about desiring the approval of one's peers. It is a necessary aspect of cultural conditioning and social survival. In technical and professional matters, concern for the opinions of respected experts or colleagues have obvious practical merit. Let us therefore repeal the unwritten norm of aloof humility and allow the scientist to openly acknowledge his desire for social recognition and respect; but let us also be wary of drawing illogical conclusions from such a repeal. It does not follow that the liberated scientist's life should now be transformed into a frenetic popularity contest. As in so many other areas of life, the question would appear to be one of *balance*. The wise scientist realizes that social recognition has its place in his career. It provides an important source of incentive at all levels of sophistication and eminence. In a sense, the social psychology of scientific communities offers an intriguing example of the power of peer approval in motivating effortful performance. Sociological studies have shown that scientists who receive recognition for their early work tend to be much more productive in their later careers and that the amount of recognition required is relatively nominal.

A second function of peer feedback (via recognition) is primarily epistemological rather than motivational. The stubborn skepticism of his colleagues is a critical factor in keeping *homo scientus* on his professional toes. He must double and triple check his instruments, his data, and particularly his logic. (Science is not the only profession in which some forms of paranoia and compulsiveness are adaptive.) Epistemologically, the researcher functions less efficiently when his peers are uncritically supportive. Effusive compliments and constant praise lead to a dangerous self-complacency. They may be emotionally satisfying, but their technical consequences are often tragic. The researcher begins to take his own veracity for granted. Prior caution and self-examination are replaced by an enthusiastic confidence which is repeatedly buttressed by incoming laurels. Rapid and cavernous leaps from "pilot" data to elaborate theories become a work style, and the scientist begins to show a laxness in his reasoning. In my opinion, this pattern is well documented in several contemporary paradigms. An eminent leader surrounds himself with enthusiastic disciples who voice energetic approval of his work. The leader becomes isolated from objective or contradictory feedback, and his ideas reflect a progression toward incredibility. The inadequacies of his theory become more and more obvious to outsiders but the isolated theorist remains buttressed by his loyal supporters (who now add oppression to their sources of unity).

Balance is a difficult thing to achieve. In my opinion, feedback from one's professional colleagues should be sufficiently important to motivate communal participation and perpetual self-scrutiny. They should not, however, be important enough to threaten personal integrity or primary reliance on one's self. It is often the stubborn isolate who makes dramatic discoveries. By refusing to allow expert opinion or consensus to overrule his ideas or his data, the renegade researcher frequently turns the tide of contemporary thought. Therefore, my recommendation regarding the emphasis placed on peer approval is intentionally cautious. It embodies a maxim which will find repeated use in the chapters to follow: *Never believe anything too much—including this maxim.*

Having forgiven the scientist his sin of coveting recognition, let us take a look at the different forms this recognition may take. Generally speaking, the scientist's rewards fall into two broad categories: (1) Administrative Invitations, and (2) Recognition of Contribution. In the first category we find such things as being asked to referee a journal manuscript or, more impressively, being invited to join the journal's editorial board. Also included in administrative honors are requests to serve on grant review panels or special professional committees. Each of these rewards involves an evaluative task and places its recipient in the role of a professional superior.

Most scientists are more apt to experience rewards from the second major category—recognition of contribution. This includes (a) having a manuscript published, (b) grant funding, (c) having one's work cited, (d) being invited to speak or write, (e) receiving invitations to move to another (preferably more prestigious) institution, (f) receipt of special awards of recognition (e.g., the Nobel prize), and (g) eponymity—having one's name used in the recognized title of an instrument, theory, or phenomenon (e.g., Darwinian theory, Euclidean geometry, Aristotelian logic). Each of the above conveys a recognition of the scientist's professional contributions. It should be noted, however, that the last six often presuppose the first. That is, getting published is frequently the major prerequisite for other forms of recognition. Because of its crucial role in the science game, an entire chapter will be devoted to publication.

Although very few scientists ever earn the most coveted awards of their profession, Glaser reports that most seem to be content with their allotment. Perhaps this is partly due to the fact that they are members of an elite fellowship which allows the majority of its constituency to share a communal pride and a sense of personal contribution. Although it is a small trophy, having an article published assures the author that his truth-seeking efforts are neither unnoticed nor unappreciated. As he logs each successive publication, the scientist senses a rise in his publicly recognized professional merit.

Like most societies, the scientific community is elaborately stratified. This characteristic seems to date back to the earliest professional societies, as documented in the works of Merton, Zuckerman, and Taylor. Interestingly, although it is a pervasively communal endeavor, science is also internally discriminatory. An "elitist" atmosphere can usually be found within any sub-group of scientists—especially when they are asked to compare themselves to some other sub-group. These comparisons are usually reflected in dichotomies which identify the individual as one of the "home team" or the opponents. Thus, he is either a scientist or a non-scientist, an experimentalist or a theoretician, a pure researcher or an impure (applied) researcher, and so on. The dichotomies extend from the broadest levels down into the sub-sub-specialties where individuals classify one another on the basis of complex technical and ideological preferences. At all stages, however, the elitism is very apparent. It is often reflected in formal membership criteria which require the applicant to be sponsored by current or past members of the elite fellowship.

The social processes and professional functions of the specialty fellowship are often most apparent during its first few years—i.e., when the specialty is a recent development or a minority group. Although the dissemination of information is an important function even at this stage, the primary purpose of the fellowship might be called "maintenance engineering." The participants band together for strength, mutual reassurance, and to promote organized growth. The essential characteristics of the elite fellowship are:

1. a small handful of revered leaders;
2. a spirit of optimism or enthusiasm regarding the group's potential or achievements; this is most apparent when (a) the fellowship is small and recent, and (b) the comparison in question contrasts the merits of this particular affiliation relative to alternate ones;
3. an enduring sense of paranoia regarding possible oppression, misunderstanding, or mistreatment (by more powerful fellowships, government granting agencies, the mass media, and so on); and
4. elaborate survival planning which usually includes formal encouragement of (a) proselytization (e.g., via teaching, publication,

etc.), (b) research, (c) group communication (e.g., via newsletters or technical journals), and (d) group cohesion (via conventions and special symposia); the cohesion function is also served by a guarded secrecy of internal troubles (both technical and personal)—empirical failure and personal rivalries are seldom acknowledged outside the group unless it has become securely established.

With stratification comes division of labor. The fellowship is usually divided into hierarchical rungs which provide rough groupings for the division of responsibilities. At the lowest ranks we find the *technicians*—research assistants, instrument specialists, apprentices, and so on. Their tasks range from menial to complex but they usually share the characteristic of being either nonimaginative or fundamental. In academic science the graduate student often occupies this role. He is usually denied formal membership in the professional society or is awarded a marginal (e.g., "associate" or "affiliate") status. Above the technicians we find a large population of *experimentalists*. Their primary function is to grind out data. In many ways they resemble the constituency of Kuhn's "normal science." Although he is usually granted more responsibility for initiating and conducting research, the differences between the experimentalist and the technician are often hard to detect.

In the next echelon we find a more heterogeneous group of semi-prestigious scientists who share the common characteristic of being *theoreticians*. This does not mean that they are exclusively theoretical and nonexperimental, but only that their relative emphasis is placed in conceptual realms. These workers are often upwardly mobile in the society's strata system and they are frequently the former students or associates of eminent leaders. Theoreticians perform the task of directing and interpreting experimental efforts. They share this responsibility with the top echelon of the hierarchy, the *luminaries*. For any given sub-discipline, there are seldom more than a handful of recognized authorities. Luminaries are usually somewhat older than their peers, and they are often well published. Most seem to show a progressive career pattern in which their contributions move away from original data and toward theoretical models. In other words, although they may have been early experimentalists, their claim to fame is usually based on their theorizing—a skill which they display with increasing passion as time passes.

Taken together, the top two echelons of the fellowship seem to serve a variety of communal functions:

1. navigation—they often suggest which issues are worthy of research by the experimentalist;

2. truth keeping—they often form the editorial review boards for journals and books;
3. fund allocation—as experts, their opinions are often sought in matters of granting;
4. propagation—they usually incur an implicit burden of proselytization via convention appearances, public relations, and so on; moreover, since their endorsements are usually powerful, the elite often fertilize the lower ranks with their preferred novitiates (graduate students and junior faculty);
5. historialization—since they are generally older, they are often given the task of protecting or reporting the history of their discipline; and
6. entertainment—as idols, their idiosyncrasies and private lives often form the culture's lore; their personal features are often touched upon in widespread gossip and the professional grapevine.

As a social system, the scientific community functions relatively smoothly. This is somewhat surprising in that its reward system is far from objective. For example, there is evidence to suggest that individual recognition is unduly influenced by institutional affiliation, and there are well known inequities in team research and financial support—not to mention some of the biases we will encounter in our upcoming discussion of publication. Perhaps the best known and generally accepted inequity of the scientist reward system is what Robert Merton has called the "Matthew Effect." This phenomenon was aptly described by a Nobel laureate whom Merton interviewed: "The world . . . tends to give credit to (already) famous people" (p. 37). It was more poetically stated in its biblical form:

> For unto every one that hath shall be given, and he shall have abundance: but from him that hath not shall be taken away even that which he hath.
> *Matthew 25:29*

According to Merton, the Matthew Effect is most apparent when a scientist of established prestige (a) co-authors an article with less prestigious colleagues, or (b) announces a discovery simultaneously with scientists of lesser eminence. In both of these situations, the scientific community is likely to award primary recognition to the person who may least need it—i.e., the already prestigious researcher. Even if he places his name last on a co-authored article, readers will assume that it was his idea or expertise that was important. Moreover, if he removes his name entirely so as to avoid this prejudicial recognition, he may often doom the article to nonpublication or obscurity. Without his name on it, it may never get read or printed. With his name on it, it will be credited to him—regardless of author orderings. The underlying principle in the Matthew Effect seems very apparent—whenever two or more researchers claim credit for a piece of work, give primary credit to the most eminent of the group. This strategy invokes the same self-fulfilling prophecy as accumulative advantage (chapter 3); recognition breeds further recognition.

Another prejudice in the distribution of rewards in science is what Merton has referred to as the Ratchet Effect. Briefly, this relates to the fact that—once a scientist has reached a certain degree of eminence—he never seems to lose ground. "Once a Nobel laureate, always a Nobel laureate" (p. 57). This should not be taken to imply that eminent researchers tend to rest on their laurels. While there is some evidence suggesting that one's scientific productivity may temporarily decline after receipt of a coveted award, there is general consensus that the most eminent scientists show little overall decline even in their later years. Although it is purely speculative at this point, one might predict that both the Matthew and Ratchet Effects are less pronounced in those sciences where there is higher consensus on research *quality* (e.g., the physical sciences) and more pronounced on the other end of the continuum (i.e., the social sciences). Some support for this speculation can be found in the excellent studies performed by Stephen and Jonathan Cole. Moreover, their work suggests that the biases due to author eminence, institutional affiliation and so on are greatest when the quality of research is low or mediocre. That is, a high quality contribution will tend to be identified and accepted regardless of these biases. When the reported work is more marginal, however, eminence and prestige will come into play.

There are, of course, many other sources of inequity in scientific recognition. For example, "original" contributions are given more weight than replications and quantity of output sometimes pre-empts quality in the distribution of professional trophies. All in all, however, the scientific community appears to tolerate the inefficiency of the system, and I shall here forego the temptation to speculate on the reasons for this complacency. Instead, let us move on to the *sine qua non* of scientific contribution and the essential prerequisite for almost all forms of recognition—publication.

REFERENCES

2, 7, 10, 25, 26, 34, 36, 43, 53, 65, 81, 98, 100, 101, 103, 107, 109, 110, 122, 124, 150, 151, 155, 156, 171, 177, 178, 187, 228, 236, 246, 256, 267, 268, 270, 278, 304, 306, 307, 316, 360, 361, 367, 401, 428, 429, 430, 435, 439, 465, 471, 491, 496, 497.

The (journal) referee is the lynchpin about which the whole business of science is pivoted.

John M. Ziman

Much hard-won truth is left to waste its sweetness on the desert air because it has not cleared the social hurdles on the path to publication.

D.L. Watson

There ought to be a law preventing the stealing of your ideas before you have them.

Joseph Zubin

There are three kinds of lies: lies, damned lies, and statistics.

Disraeli

Most of us still remain content to build our theoretical castles on the quicksand of merely rejecting the null hypothesis.

Marvin D. Dunnette

There never are any unsuccessful experiments.

Claude Bernard

There's this desert prison . . . with an old prisoner, resigned to his life, and a young one just arrived. The young one talks constantly of escape, and, after a few months, he makes a break. He's gone a week, and then he's brought back by the guards. He's half dead, crazy with hunger and thirst. He describes how awful it was to the old prisoner. The endless stretches of sand, no oasis, no signs of life anywhere. The old prisoner listens for a while, then says, "Yep. I know. I tried to escape myself, twenty years ago." The young prisoner says, "You did? Why didn't you tell me, all these months I was planning my escape? Why didn't you let me know it was impossible?" And the old prisoner shrugs, and says, "So who publishes negative results?"

Jeffrey Hudson

 *Chapter 5*

Publication: The Endless Quest

The primary day-to-day goal of the contemporary scientist is to have his work published—quickly, voluminously, and to a wide and respected audience. The storybook image of science would have us believe that this goal is based on the ideals of shared knowledge and communal cooperation. Research in the sociology of science has, however, left a very different impression. The conclusion to be drawn from that research suggests that most scientists strive for publication for more personal and expedient reasons. Getting published is a recognized and highly successful *means* for (a) enhancing personal recognition and prestige, (b) earning job security and advancement, (c) enhancing future chances of research funding and further publication, and (d) staking a publicly respected priority claim on some idea or discovery.

An observer of science can hardly doubt the central role of publication in the lives of contemporary researchers. There are over 40,000 current scientific journals and it has been estimated that articles for these journals are churned out at a rate of one every 35 seconds. Professional "productivity" is evaluated almost solely on the basis of published works, sometimes in the crudest of fashions (Andreski reports a department chairman who actually weighed each faculty member's publications on a scale!). Few scientists, however, have managed to be as prolific as the entomologist Theodore Cockerell, who authored 3,904 articles in his lifetime—about two per week during his peak.

A further indication that scientists publish primarily for personal reasons is the fact that relatively little of their published work will ever be read by their colleagues. According to Derek Price's figures, about half of the reading in contemporary science is done in less than one percent of the journals. Similarly, Merton has estimated that less than one percent of a scientist's hard-won publications are ever read by any sizeable audience. Parenthetically, he notes that what does get read is often determined by the author's prestige. In his work with British physicists Gaston also found that the motivation to publish is often much stronger than the motivation to read. His interviewees seldom read the journals in which they were so eager to publish.

One of the best analyses of scientific productivity and its correlates may be found in *Social Stratification in Science* by Jonathan and Stephen Cole. Their work has relied heavily on the *Science Citation Index*, a publication which serves as an implicit scorekeeper by listing the citations received by individual authors in over 2,000 journals. Cole and Cole have shown that frequency of citation is very strongly correlated with other measures of professional recognition and rated work quality. Earlier work by Hagstrom had suggested that the relationship between work *quantity* (number of articles published) and professional honors was moderately high ($r = 0.62$).[a] Using citation data, the Coles found that quantity was also related to *quality* ($r = 0.60$). They suggested that, at least in the physical sciences, the quality of one's research is a better predictor of professional success than is its quantity. The Cole's also offered a typology of scientific authors:

QUALITY

		High	Low
QUANTITY	High	Prolific	Mass Producers
	Low	Perfectionists	Silent

Interestingly, most of the physicists surveyed by them fell into either the prolific or the silent categories. This is congruent with a phenomenon previously explored by Derek Price. About half of all scientific papers are produced by fewer than 10 percent of the total scientist population; the vast majority of published research must

[a]It is noteworthy that Hagstrom also found a much weaker relationship between the number of students tutored by a scientist and his prestige ($r = 0.12$) or his prolificity ($r = 0.24$).

therefore be credited to a very small minority of researchers. This imbalanced distribution has been quantified in the form of Lotka's Law, or the Inverse Square Principle. Over a sufficient length of time (e.g., several years), the number of scientists producing n papers will be proportional to $1/n^2$. Thus, during a given decade, for every 100 people who published one article, there will be 25 who published two, 11 who published three, and so on. Price shows that Lotka's Law is apparently a very accurate predictor except at the extremes, and he suggests some refinements to remedy these slight discrepancies. The message of all this, however, is very clear. A very small proportion of scientists seem to produce the large majority of published work. Price has estimated that the number of average (nonprolific) scientists increases as the square of this minority. In a given interval, if the number of prolific contributors increases by 10, the number of nonprolific scientists increases by 100. The implications of this labor inequity are discussed at length by the Coles. They argue that a reduction in the total number of scientists would probably not retard progress. However, one should recall here the important function which Kuhn and others have ascribed to the work of the masses in normal science.

In an earlier chapter we discussed some possible patterns of career productivity as it might be influenced by the granting of tenure. The complexity of that relationship is increased by changing factors in the life of the publishing scientist. He may begin his career with a few painfully wrought articles, published primarily to protect job security or simply to demonstrate personal competence. After convincing himself and his peers that he can publish, the young author may then develop what Merton has called *"insanabile scribendi cacoethes"* (the itch to publish). His output begins to increase, and he may start aspiring to more prestigious journals. The scientist who is eventually prolific, however, may face an intriguing dilemma at this point in his career. Having mastered the strained art of getting published, he is now in a position where publication is easier. He has learned to write competitively and, at the same time, his previous articles have given him a visible precedent—journal editors may now be biased in his favor. On the other hand, the scientist begins to devalue "just getting published" and may start to aim for crystallized brilliance—a somewhat reduced frequency of higher quality productions. The dilemma, of course, stems from the temptation to publish in quantity. As he gains notoriety, the scientist can successfully publish papers which are progressively more mediocre. If he is seduced by this vicious cycle, he may end up communicating redundant trivia and spending more time in reminiscence than in research. Special invitations to contribute to books or other periodicals may tempt him to write the same article several different times, and the scientist may soon become more of a writer than an inquirer. This pattern can be observed in the careers of many eminent scientists. Although their output of words may increase with age and fame, there is a corresponding decline in their output of data.

The first scientific journals were established in the mid-1600s. In their first three centuries of existence, they published over six million articles, and current data suggest that each year brings an increment in the rate of article production. One might infer from all of this that (a) we know a lot, and (b) the rate of progress in knowledge is increasing. Both of these conclusions rest on the very tenuous assumption that our knowledge is accurately reflected in the size of our technical literatures. While one can hardly deny that we have made substantial progress in the last three centuries, I would argue that this progress is only crudely related to the mountains of paper produced by researchers. We have already seen that a very small percentage of technical articles are ever read or cited by the mass of scientists. The vast majority of research is apparently not essential for scientific progress. Moreover, with some qualifications, I would argue that the amount of precise knowledge in a discipline is often *inversely* related to the size of its literature. That is, those fields with greater paradigm consensus are likely to generate more condensed literatures in the sense that (a) their average article length will be smaller, and (b) the ratio of journals to scientists will be lower. In disciplines where there is greater consensus on critical issues and methodology, branch journals will more often be devoted to sub-topics (e.g., instrumentation) rather than to competing viewpoints. In less developed paradigms, there are multiple journals to service varied perspectives. These speculations are consistent with analyses of the lengths of dissertations in various fields. Lodahl and Gordon found greater consensus and paradigm development in the physical (versus non-physical) sciences. In Berelson's research on graduate education, Ph.D. dissertations were shortest in mathematics, physics, biology, and chemistry; they were substantially longer in the social sciences. Data on the verbiage-knowledge relationship are as yet meager. Hopefully, an interested (or incensed) reader may help to redress this situation.

The process of getting published is one which is very conducive to a game metaphor. Taking some polemical liberties, let us look at a hypothetical guide to the young scientist on how to play the publication game.

THE PUBLICATION GAME:
RULES FOR BEGINNERS

The goal of this game, of course, is to publish—and to publish volum-inously. The aspiring author should bear in mind, however, that in some quarters of science quality is weighed more heavily than quan-tity. Likewise, it should be remembered that publication is a *means* to other ends—personal recognition and professional advancement. It is therefore critical that the apprentice learn his skills well, and that he understand some of the standard and specialty plays which are likely to be received favorably by journal referees. With that goal in mind, a few basic guidelines are briefly noted.

1. **Watch authorship orderings.** If one of the co-authors is em-inent, he or she is most likely to be given primary credit for the work. However, his or her name on the article will also enhance its likeli-hood of being published and read. The young apprentice may have to accommodate this compromise early in his career. In general, the fewer the co-authors the better. The current trend, however, is for an increase in multiple authors. As the journals and job market be-come tighter, publications become a more precious commodity and the "gift" of co-authorship becomes all the more valuable. Younger colleagues and graduate students are rewarded for their work by such gifts. In some disciplines, the number of co-authors for even brief articles has sometimes exceeded two dozen. This phenomenon is probably most prevalent in team (versus individual) research. It has been half-facetiously suggested that these large conglomerates of scientists publish under a "team name," and some humorous possi-bilities have been offered. However, this concept of team authorship was recently adopted in at least one scientific article which credited only the institutions of the contributing writers. More illustrative, perhaps, is the well-known secret that the eminent mathematician Nicolas Bourbaki is actually a team of 10–20 French scientists. For almost four decades, this informal team has produced some of the most highly respected work in mathematics and, in partial whimsy, has continued to defend Bourbaki as a single (rather than poly-cephalic) author.

When co-authoring with equal-status colleagues, credit is gen-erally awarded to the first author (unless all authors are prestigious). Rules for determining order of authorship are often ambiguous. In most fields, each co-author is supposed to have been a contributor to the idea (hypothesis) or design, with "top billing" awarded to the primary originator. However, assertiveness, seniority, and grant ownership are probably additional determinants. Reflecting the differential valuation of theory over data in science, those individuals who actually' perform the experiment are given secondary authorship at best (and sometimes only acknowledgment in a footnote).

2. Push originality.   An article is more likely to be published if it shows creativity or originality. In some fields (particularly the social sciences), replicational research is almost impossible to publish. Moreover, even if it is accepted, it may be scored as a minimal achievement or even a negative reflection of the author's creativity or self-direction. "Scooping" a new idea or phenomenon is a professional plum. Being "first" here is critical. Put your ideas into print as quickly as possible—even if they are crude or totally devoid of data.

3. Use some fore-cite.   The bibliography of a technical article may significantly influence a referee's recommendation. In general, it is good to cite (a) a few classic works (this connotes erudition), (b) a few obscure papers (this connotes thorough knowledge), (c) at least one publication of each possible reviewer (if the likely referees are rivals, be careful not to take sides in the first draft), and (d) your own previously published work (regardless of relevance).[b] This latter practice of self-citation informs the reviewer that you are a productive researcher and, more important, it communicates an influential precedent if your prior papers appeared in a respected source (i.e., "other referees have liked my work . . . ."). Although they can be somewhat risky, personal communications and footnotes are additional sources of evaluation. If it is legitimate, footnote your gratitude to several eminent scientists. This communicates their implicit endorsement of your work, and the average reviewer will be duly impressed.

4. Stay in bounds.   Although your topic should be original, it must remain within the playing field of your discipline or paradigm.

---

[b]In a recent study by Alan Kazdin, Martin Kenigsberg, and myself, we sent identical manuscripts to journal referees. All manuscripts endorsed a relatively new application of some existing psychological principles, and buttressed these endorsements by reference to three fictitious studies which were alleged to be "in press" (accepted for journal publication, but not yet printed). For half of our referees, these "in press" references were listed as being written by the author of our experimental manuscript (i.e., they were self-references). For the other half, the "in press" articles were credited to someone else. Referee recommendations showed that self-referencing enhanced an author's chances of getting published.

Likewise, your experimental method and data analysis should not deviate from the respected norm. Do not challenge an accepted truth unless you have substantial backing (in the form of data or experts' opinions). With support, iconoclasm is professional paydirt; without it, you are simply inviting derision. Avoid polemics and personal rivalries (these are not to be put in print—only verbalized).

5. Set yourself up. With a properly worded introduction, virtually any research question can be portrayed as timely and relevant. Tie your research into the "big picture" and show how its findings will contribute to the extension or refinement of the paradigm.

6. Watch your language. The terminology of an article can be very important. Use the accepted terms of your paradigm as much as possible (regardless of their legitimacy). Whenever you have a choice between common language and technical argot, use the latter. The difference in products is well illustrated in an excerpt from O.L. Reiser's technical translation of a popular prayer (cited in Harding, 1931, p. 123):

> Give us this day our customary calories; forgive us our maladjustments as we overlook other loci their inadequate movements . . . . Though we walk through the valley of depressed metabolism, may we secrete no useless adrenalin.

Technical glossaries such as that offered by Graham may be very useful in translating personal opinions into acceptable form. For example, "I don't understand it" translates to "much additional work will be required."

Two remaining suggestions on language are frequently to quantify and qualify your remarks. Numbers are nice. Give the dimensions of everything (in the metric system, of course). *Quantophilia* is a widespread phenomenon in science. Likewise, regardless of your subjective certainty, be sure to couch all assertions in ample relativisms. This connotes a cautious suspension of judgment, and it often gives the author room for an honorable retreat if later data are contradictory. A very skillful author can camouflage his opinions sufficiently so that he can eventually claim to have been correct regardless of the ultimate evidence.

7. Groom your data. Present your results in a way which makes their implications obvious. Graphical illustrations are particularly powerful when the data can be drawn as a straight line. Huff and

Rudin have noted that this can be accomplished with almost any data if the author chooses the correct graph paper or applies an appropriate transformation to the data (e.g., square root, reciprocal, logarithm, etc.). Always highlight those data which confirm your hypotheses and ignore or explain those which do not. Unexpected results are unlikely to be published unless you offer an explanation for their deviance.

8. Anticipate your reviewers.   In discussing or interpreting your findings, acknowledge or defend any possible limitations or deficiencies in your research. This will force them to focus their criticisms on lesser flaws and it may enhance their estimation of your technical sophistication.

9. Always cite the need for further research.   This incantation is particularly appropriate at the close of an article. By acknowledging this need, you are keeping the scientific faith and voicing your endorsement of its epistemology. It is also an implicit confession and defense of the inadequacies in your isolated research efforts.

Many readers will have finished the above guidelines without knowing whether they were serious or satirical. After all, many of these strategies are widely practiced by contemporary scientists and their practical survival value is obvious. On the other hand, their expedience is often transparent. Was I offering an endorsement or an attack? In general, it was the latter. There are facets of the foregoing which are sometimes legitimate for reasons other than expedience (e.g., genuine citations or acknowledgments). Overall, however, I believe that our current publication practices are often political and dangerously inefficient. Gamesmanship ploys and inequities are much more prevalent than one might desire, and their epistemological consequences have yet to be fully appreciated. Let us take a brief look at the inadequacies of this core scientific activity.

APPRAISING THE GAME: THE PEER REVIEW SYSTEM

Most scientific journals employ the "peer review system" in evaluating manuscripts which have been submitted for publication. In this system, the journal editor or an associate editor sends the paper to one or more "referees," who may or may not be on the journal's editorial board. After an interval which may range from a few weeks to several months, the referees submit their recommendations regarding publication. These are weighed by the editor and are usually sent along (anonymously) to the author when he is informed of the editor's decision. Generally, that decision takes one of four forms: (a) accept as is, (b) accept with minor revisions, (c) accept with major revisions, and (d) reject.

Although the journal review system is a critical element in both personal and technical scientific progress, it has remained virtually unexamined until the last few years. Research by such investigators as Merton, Crane, and Zuckerman has recently begun to unravel some of the processes and parameters that seem to influence editorial decision. Their findings suggest that our neglect of this area has been a costly one—and one in dire need of immediate redress. As we shall see in a moment, the peer review system has often been shown to be relatively unreliable and quite prejudicial. Thus, for over a century scientists have subjected their ideas to painstaking experimental precision—only to allow their ultimate fate to be decided by a crude and often political social process which has survived unchanged by empirical default.

Before beginning our exploration of the journal review system, it should be noted that our comments will require qualification depending on specific disciplines and journals. For example, there is a vast difference in the rejection rates of journals in different fields. In their study of 83 professional journals, Zuckerman and Merton report that relatively few manuscripts are rejected in the physical sciences (approximately 24 percent in physics, 31 percent in chemistry, and 29 percent in biology). In psychology, political science, and sociology, however, about 80 percent of the papers submitted were rejected.[c] Although there are unquestionable differences among the various fields, it is noteworthy that journal acceptance rates seem to correlate strongly with degree of consensus and paradigm development. It is in those disciplines where there is less consensus—and where rejection rates are high—that we can expect to see more inequity and variability in the referee system.

For the sake of exposition, let us divide our attention among four different categories of variables which may interact in complex ways to influence the ultimate disposition of a paper. Viewing publication as a thoroughly social process, its constituents are (a) an author or authors, (b) a journal editor, (c) one or more referees, and (d) the manuscript itself.

Authorship. Who you are does make a difference. Moreover,

---

[c]In those fields where rejection is high, of course, one is more likely to observe a "perseverance to print"—i.e., the author will continue submitting the same manuscript to different journals until it is accepted.

where you are may influence your success at publication. Although the evidence is primarily correlational, it is clearcut—eminent authors and scientists at prestigious institutions have a much easier time getting published. One might argue that their work is also qualitatively superior, but this does not appear to account for their deferential treatment. As a matter of fact, the influence of prestige appears to be greatest when the manuscript is mediocre in quality. Zuckerman and Merton also report that eminent authors are more likely to receive quick reviews and are less likely to be asked for major revisions. There is a sad irony to the fact that eminence eases publication. Analogous to the Matthew Effect and accumulative advantage, eminence begets eminence. The more one publishes, the easier it is to publish. This inequity is most harmful to the young, unestablished scientist, and research has shown that he is most sensitive to the effects of manuscript rejection early in his career.

As noted by both Merton and Barber, journal editors have committed more than a few major blunders in rejecting classic works partly because their authors were not then prestigious. Waterston's work on molecular velocity was initially rejected as "nothing but nonsense" and classic papers by such scientists as Fourier, Mendel, and Krebs have often been initially turned down for publication. The influence of a prestigious name was humorously documented by R.J. Strutt, son of the eminent nineteenth century scientist, Lord Rayleigh. Rayleigh had submitted a paper on electricity to the British Association for the Advancement of Science. His name

> was either omitted or accidentally detached, and the committee "turned it down" as the work of one of those curious persons called paradoxers. However, when the authorship was discovered, the paper was found to have merits after all (p. 228).

Having recognized the potential bias introduced by authorship information, many contemporary journals have adopted a "blind review system" in which referees purportedly remain unaware of author and affiliation. This commendable effort is hampered by the fact that anonymity is often nearly impossible. If the referee does not have a good idea about who might have produced a certain piece of work, he can frequently satisfy his curiosity by looking at its bibliography—the most frequently cited author is a strong candidate.

Editor influence. It is my opinion that the most underrated figure in the science game is the journal editor. He controls the very lifelines of science, and in his hands may rest the fates of ideas as well as persons. In contemporary research, the unpublished thought is virtually impotent. Without communication to the professional community, it will seldom harvest either personal or technical advancement. It is the journal editor who ultimately decides *what* and *who* gets published. His potential influence is seldom appreciated (and hopefully seldom abused). The editor can subsidize or suppress emerging research trends—as well as aspiring scientists—by allocating journal space accordingly. Even when a blind review system is employed, the editor is aware of an article's authorship and can influence its evaluation by a judicious choice of reviewers. He knows the biases and preferences of his referees, and their assignment to manuscripts is far from random. Moreover, when the referees' comments are returned, the editor can still override their recommendations without their knowledge. In short, the fate of a manuscript may sometimes be sealed by a single person (the editor) irrespective of the peer review system.

In disciplines where there are multiple journals which service overlapping research topics, the power of a single editor may be diminished. However, until we appreciate and examine the behavior of this super-umpire, we have little room for complacency. It is hard to believe that we have so long entrusted the portals of Truth to such a small and unscrutinized segment of the scientific population.

The Referees. Most journal referees are selected on the basis of their expertise in an area of research relevant to the manuscript topic. They are drawn primarily from the middle and upper echelons of the field and are usually considered to be professionally "established." Although their recommendations are supposed to remain anonymous, many authors can determine the referee's identity through technical clues which may vary from his writing style to the watermark on the stationery. Perceived anonymity may occasionally tempt the referee to adopt a condescending or cynical stance in his remarks. Kay, for example, has commented on the abusive language of some reviewers in their lofty role of protecting precious journal space. Judging from the anecdotes of several dozen colleagues in psychology and responses to the survey conducted by Terry Kimper and myself (appendix), these abuses are not as rare as one might hope. The recommendation that referees publicly identify themselves may be a partial solution, but one which incurs problems of its own.

It may come as no shock to some of you that journal referees are often pathetically unreliable. As a matter of fact, it is this unreliability which helps to encourage perseverance to print. The rejected author knows that his manuscript may receive very different (and more favorable) reviews from other referees. I have yet to meet a social scientist who has not felt that the peer review system is frequently capricious and inequitable. In my travels to various institutions, colleagues have repeatedly volunteered anecdotes and illustrations of this problem. Comments by referees are sometimes so divergent that one wonders whether they were actually reading the same manuscript. Those who have experienced referee idiosyncrasies may need no further evidence—a few salient personal episodes may have already convinced you of the system's inefficiency. However, the data on referee incongruence is more than just anecdotal.

In their excellent discussion of the peer review system, Zuckerman and Merton report reliability rates for referees from various journals. It should be noted that reliability per se is not as defensible as a *sufficient* index of referee competence. Reviewers may agree with one another regarding the final disposition of a paper without serving the "best interests" of their field. For example, in the physical sciences (where acceptance rates are very high), a referee can adopt the strategy of "when in doubt, accept." The opposite strategy seems to be employed in the social sciences. In both instances, the reviewer is assured of superficial consensus with other referees by the simple fact that *most* papers suffer identical fates. Similarly, since unconventional methods or anomalous data are seldom condoned in many fields, our hypothetical referees can be highly inter-reliable in rejecting critically significant manuscripts. Shared prejudices produce high reliabilities.

So far, the evidence on referee agreement suggests wide variability across disciplines, journals, and—of course—referees. Here again we are confronted with an apparent difference between fields where there is greater paradigm consensus (primarily the physical sciences) and those where there is not. In the former, referee reliability appears to be higher. This might be due to their emphasis on clearcut and quantifiable criteria in reviewer evaluations. When we look at referee agreement in the social sciences, however, the picture is quite different. For example, Bowen and his colleagues found inter-referee agreement to be 0.11 on eight papers reviewed in consumer psychology. Similarly, Scott reported a reliability of 0.26 for 328 manuscripts submitted to the *Journal of Personality and Social Psychology*. In another study with psychologists (which will be described in a moment), I found that rater agreement was meager. In this particular study, referees were also asked to estimate their degree of reliability on each of the factors they had been asked to evaluate. Their average self-predictions contrasted sharply with the obtained values:

Factor	Self-Predicted Reliability	Actual Reliability
Topic Relevance	0.74	−0.07
Methodology	0.69	0.03
Adequate Data Presentation	0.72	0.30
Interpretation (Discussion) of Results	0.72	−0.01
Scientific Contribution	0.72	0.30
Summary Recommendation	0.72	0.30

Although the evidence is still sparse, there is some indication that rater unreliability is sometimes exacerbated by personal biases and professional rivalries. Since the referee is usually an expert on the manuscript topic, he may hold strong opinions or even claim theoretical monopoly on his area. When he is asked to review papers submitted by rival theorists or containing offensive data, his objectivity can easily be strained. The opposite, of course, is also true—he may be tempted to approve manuscripts which pay homage to his theory or lend it further support. The role of personal factors in the competition for journal space and recognition has been repeatedly cited by scientists themselves. It is documented not only in contemporary interviews, but also in the historical biographies of eminent researchers. Thus, in a letter to a friend, the young Thomas Henry Huxley wrote:

> You have no idea of the intrigues that go on in this blessed world of science. Science is, I fear, no purer than any other region of human activity; though it should be. Merit alone is very little good; it must be backed by tact and knowledge of the world to do very much.
> For example, I know that the paper I have just sent in (to the Royal Society) is very original and of some importance, and I am equally sure that if it is referred to the judgment of my "particular friend" _____ That it will not be published. He won't be able to say a word against it, but he will pooh-pooh it to a dead certainty .... For the last twenty years _____ has been regarded as the great authority on these matters, and has had no one to tread on his heels, until at last, I think, he has come to look upon the Natural World as his special preserve, and "no poachers allowed." So I must maneuver a little to get my poor memoir kept out of his hands (p. 97).

As Mitroff has succinctly summarized, the history of scientific progress may be more aptly portrayed as a competition among persons rather than among ideas.

The Manuscript. As was implied in my earlier satire on guidelines for the young author, the content and style of a manuscript may dramatically influence its final disposition. One thing the author can be sure of is that his referees will suggest *some* changes. They have been cast in the role of critics, and they see it as their duty to find inadequacies. They may have to settle for such trivia as spelling errors, but they *will* find fault. To do otherwise would seem non-discriminating.

In the social sciences—where replication is barely tolerated—one's topic or approach must be sufficiently original to merit a distinction between "new" and prior research. Replications are generally disfavored unless (a) they extend or refine a previous idea, or (b) they challenge it by obtaining opposite or different results.

In all sciences, of course, the paper topic must be within the proper playing field—bizarre or unconventional excursions are tolerated only when accompanied by strong data or author eminence. Topics or terms which are currently in vogue may also influence editorial decisions. This is often seen when authors adopt a recently popularized label to describe what might have previously been given a more mundane description. One's technical language and methodology are important, too. *Quantophilia*—the passion for irrelevant numerical descriptors—is common in scientific journals. There are obviously some epistemological reasons for valuing quantification in science. The problem here, however, is the reliance on excessive, exclusive, or irrelevant quantification to legitimate a manuscript. Technical terms convey an aura of rigor and sophistication which may have been entirely absent in the reported research.

Abraham Maslow has used the term "methodolatry" to describe scientists' passion for agreed-upon procedures of inquiry. Technical instruments and conventional research methods exert a tremendous influence on the kinds of questions asked by scientists. This has been extensively documented by Kuhn. It is the rare scientist who will deviate from conventional methods of research (and survive to tell about it).

Each of the above components may contribute to a manuscript's chances of publication. However, it is my hunch that the strongest determinants lie in the Results and Discussion sections of a paper. That is, the disposition of an article may be influenced more by its data or their interpretation than by its topic, language, or method. Ideally, of course, one might hope that manuscripts would be published solely on the basis of some objective assessment of their relevance and methodological adequacy. Given a significant research question and adequate experimental procedures, *any* obtained data should be considered meaningful and contributory. To evaluate whether this ideal is practiced, I sent out 75 manuscripts to guest reviewers from a well-known psychological journal. All manuscripts were anonymously authored and contained identical introductions, method sections, and bibliographies. However, one-fifth of the referees received a results section which reported data congruent with their presumed theoretical viewpoint. In another group, the manuscript results contradicted that viewpoint. Two additional groups read a results section which reported data of mixed outcome—but the paper's discussion section drew conclusions which were either favorable or unfavorable to the referees' paradigm. In a final group, reviewers were asked to evaluate the manuscript without seeing any results or discussion. The five groups, then, were:

	Introduction	*Method*	*Results*	*Discussion*
I	Standard	Standard	Positive	None
II	Standard	Standard	Negative	None
III	Standard	Standard	Mixed	Positive
IV	Standard	Standard	Mixed	Negative
V	Standard	Standard	None	None

Referee evaluations were dramatically affected by the direction of the data. Manuscripts which were identical in topic and procedure were recommended for publication when their results were positive; they were consistently rejected when the data were negative. Moreover, reviewers rated the same experimental procedures as significantly more adequate when they had allegedly yielded the preferred data. A measure of critical reading showed that reviewers of negative results manuscripts were much more scrutinizing than those who read supportive articles; the latter seldom detected a relatively obvious mistake in the method section. Contrary to my hunch, the discussion section did not exert much influence on reviewer's judgments. Mixed results were consistently met with rejection regardless of their interpretation; ambiguity was not tolerated.

The foregoing study was intended to redress some of our continuing ignorance of the factors involved in journal review practices. Interestingly, the unsuspecting reviewers were generally supportive when they learned of their participation. Many felt that this kind of research was long overdue and they often expressed appreciation of my interests and efforts. A small minority felt that the project was unethical in that it had deceived its participants. Even though there is a good reason to believe that preinformed referees would have given very different (and less meaningful) responses, a few of the reviewers felt strongly enough to submit formal protests of unethical conduct to the American Psychological Association. Although I share their general reluctance to condone experimental deception, I also feel that its alternative was no less imbued with ethical issues. To have abandoned this research—or to have conducted it in a way which would have seriously jeopardized its validity—would, in my opinion, have been much more unethical. Having now been indicted by some of my own colleagues for conducting research which is critical to the refinement of our shared profession, however, I can better understand the longstanding neglect of *homo scientus*. There are at least some members of the species who seem to be very strongly opposed to their own scrutiny.

The fate of the manuscript describing the aforementioned study is an ironic illustration of inequities and possible prejudice in the journal review process. Many behavioral scientists believe that the journal *Science*, which is highly respected as a medium of exchange, is biased against manuscripts emanating from such fields as psychology. In my own case, this prejudice had already been suggested by the fact that an earlier manuscript on the critical reasoning skills of scientists (to be described in chapter 8) was forthright rejected, apparently without any peer review (there were no accompanying remarks to explain the manuscript's unsuitability). After consulting with half a dozen colleagues, I learned that this was not an unusual occurrence with this journal. Nevertheless, after completing the study on the peer review system, I submitted it to *Science*. After several months, I received copies of the comments of three referees. One was extremely positive, opening his review with the statement that the "paper is certainly publishable in its present form." The other two referees were also positive—describing it as "bold, imaginative, and interesting"—but requesting some minor revisions in the presentation and interpretation of the data. Notwithstanding these three positive reviews, *Science* editor Philip H. Abelson decided to reject the manuscript! Making the minor changes mentioned by the reviewers, I resubmitted the article along with a letter to Abelson noting the positive tone of the reviews and expressing puzzlement at his decision to reject. Abelson returned a three sentence letter saying (a) the manuscript "is obviously suitable for publication in a specialized journal," (b) if "it were shortened it might be published as a Research Report" (in *Science*), and (c) that I should qualify my conclusions regarding "the area of research and publications which are covered." It is not clear whether this latter remark was intended to imply that the peer review system in the physical sciences is not as flawed as that in the social sciences. In any case, I shortened the article, emphasized the study's limitations, and noted the researchable possibility that different results might have been obtained with a different sample of referees or in a different discipline. My efforts were rewarded several months later when Assistant Editor John E. Ringle returned the manuscript with a five sentence rejection letter, recommending that I *lengthen* the article and submit it to a psychology journal. Once again, I received no referee comments to defend this apparently arbitrary editorial decision.

ENFORCED IGNORANCE: THE COSTS
OF PREJUDICIAL KNOWLEDGE

In addition to the foregoing inadequacies of the peer review system, contemporary science is also hampered by several epistemological conventions which affect publication policies. These prejudices sometimes vary from one field to the next and they overlap with several of our earlier topics. Their summary here may therefore seem partially redundant, but I think the topic is important enough to merit reiteration. Moreover, the comments which follow may help to integrate some of the earlier themes of this chapter and to clarify their practical implications.

In its barest essence, science is a search for order; it is an attempt to describe relationships among events. When description precedes the events in question, it is called *prediction*; when it follows them or substitutes alternate terms, it is often said to be an *explanation*. In either case, the power of scientific knowledge lies in its application. Accurate and valid functional laws facilitate the development of *control*, although this is seldom a simple task. For example, one of the pioneering discoveries in surgery was the relationship between germs and postoperative infections. This knowledge suggested the possibility of controlling the latter by reducing germ exposure during surgery. However, this innovation was dependent on still other relationships (that between germ concentration and various components of the operation itself—i.e., the surgeon's hands, sanitized linens, sterile instruments, and so on). Finally, the improvement of these variables necessitated an understanding of some of the ways to influence the behavior of surgeons and other hospital staff.

The methods of scientific research are designed to explore and refine these complex matrices of functional relationship. From an ideological philosophy of science perspective, the nature of one's methods and the content of any observed relationships are basically irrelevant. So long as a reliable and publicly replicable phenomenon is reported, it is supposed to be warmly welcomed into the family of scientific knowledge. As we have begun to see, however, science is seldom practiced according to these ideological guidelines. The prejudices of contemporary science are often most apparent in technical publication policies. There are procedures which are favored or forbidden, topics which are licit or illicit, and findings which will be sanctified or suppressed. These prejudices are often less prevalent in fields of high paradigm development, but they are never totally absent. Let us briefly review their major categories.

Topic and Language.   The scientist who aspires to publication (and therefore survival) is seldom granted much liberty in his choice of research problems. They must lie within the popular playing field, and they must be described in an argot which conveys their relevance to today's game. The renegade researcher can, of course, venture off into forbidden regions, but he usually does so at some personal risk. If he is already eminent, these excursions are usually tolerated as the idiosyncrasies of a genius or—if he is over fifty—the beginnings of senility. Should he hit paydirt on one of these illicit journeys, the established scientist will fare much better than his obscure peer in having his discovery acknowledged or accepted. Even so, however, the rules are much more stringent when one is dabbling with prohibited topics. For example, the phenomenon of extrasensory perception (ESP) is generally rejected by psychologists. Hence, it has been extremely difficult for renegade researchers to publish their work on the topic (especially if it is supportive). ESP investigators have been forced to employ procedures which are considerably more rigorous than those found in conventional psychological research. Their results have also been viewed with less leniency than more legitimate data. Thus, although it is easy (and common) for psychologists to publish relatively crude experiments on personality prediction (where less than 10 percent of variance in the dependent variable can be accounted for), this will hardly be tolerated in an ESP article. Even if the renegade has performed an exquisitely controlled study with impressively powerful results, his chances of getting published have been very slim.[d] I suspect that this same pattern could be documented in many disciplines (e.g., with UFO's in space science, astrology in astronomy, and so on).

Experimental Procedure.   One must not only restrict the content

---

[d]This state of affairs has been partially ameliorated by the development of technical publications focused upon parapsychology. As often happens in science, the renegade can publish (and survive) only if he establishes his own channels of publication. These, in their turn, will discriminate against the next generation of explorers.

of one's questions; their form must also be conventional. Standard plays involve standard equipment—instruments and methods which are well recognized and respected. The technological myopia thereby fostered is seldom appreciated by the researcher. The behaviorist tradition in psychology had laid out a playing field and a methodology which amply illustrate this consequence. Cognitive processes such as thoughts and images were *defined* out of psychological relevance and the core of acceptable experimental procedures did not permit any contra-doctrine questions. It was only after several generations of "mindlessness" that psychologists began to deviate procedurally—and to find that the forbidden cognitive variables could substantially increase their predictive accuracy.

Although I may have already belabored the point, the devaluation of replication warrants reiteration here. With some exceptions in the physical sciences, journal editors are reluctant to publish purely repetitious experiments. The consequence, in my opinion, can be likened to the fate of a mountain climber who seldom rechecks the stability of his rigging. Unfortunately, however, in the thin atmosphere of theory, unreplicated findings never fall—so that the whole ambitious climb is often built upon an ephemeral void. The eager researcher continues to scramble onward, impervious to the instability of his footing, and unaware that "onward" and "upward" can be two very different directions.

The average physical scientist would probably shudder at the number of social science "facts" which rest on unreplicated research. The antireplication rule has harvested a culture of strained improvisation in research. The social scientist knows that an exact replication cannot get published. On the other hand, truly innovative ideas are rare and, besides, he may want to stay in the settlement rather than push back the frontier. The result? A hybrid called "partial replication and extension." In this strategy the basic components of a previous idea are replicated, but with minor changes (to satisfy the editor's and culture's passion for originality). In and of itself, this strategy is epistemologically justified. However, because of the originality prejudice, researchers have often gone to great depths of trivia to muster some claim to originality. In many cases, exact replication would have been much more meaningful. This is because of the inferential logic which is expediently applied in "partial replications." Let us say that a previous study found event A to be correlated with event B. The scientist now modifies the former to A′ in order to meet the originality requirement. If A′ also correlates with B, he claims a replication and extension of the phenomenon. If it does not, however, he seldom questions the original finding. Instead of challenging the original A-B study, he simply concludes that the A-B relationship is restricted to some values of A. This reasoning, of course, protects the earlier finding and its hypothesis from ready falsification.

Acceptable Data.   Contrary to the storybook image, scientists are not totally open to *any* data. This was readily illustrated in the referee study discussed earlier. In general, one's data are unlikely to be acknowledged or communicated unless they are presented in the proper form. Re-enter quantophilia. It is apparent that many scientists do not believe that nominal scale categorization is a legitimate form of quantifying some data. Unless they can claim an ordinal or equal-interval scale, the data have little hope of acknowledgement.

More important than their form, perhaps, is their direction. Again with some notable exceptions, most scientific specialties are very intolerant of data which contradict conventional "laws" or their derivative hypotheses. These *negative results* are generally characterized by the fact that they fail to support an accepted or expected relationship. There are psychological differences, of course, in the threat posed by different kinds of nonsupportive data. Imagine, if you will, a continuum which ranges from "weak" and slightly negative data to very blatant counter-theoretical findings. I shall refer to the latter as *anomalies*. They are often considered most threatening to a paradigm due to (a) their acknowledged deviation from expectancy (in terms of raw data deviance, extensive replication, or endorsement from an authority), (b) their relevance to central (rather than peripheral) tenets of the paradigm, and (c) their accompaniment by direct acknowledgement of crisis or even an invitation to revolution. In contrast, data toward the weaker "negative results" end of the continuum tend to be (a) marginally deviant and equivocal (e.g., their validity is often challenged), (b) less threatening to the paradigm (either because they bear on peripheral tenets or because they are strongly outnumbered by prior positive results), and (c) often presented with an apologetic explanation which is offered as an account for their deviance.

With sufficient replication and endorsement, of course, a particular phenomenon may move toward the anomalous end of the continuum. When this occurs, there is an interesting shift in its "publishability." Generally speaking, the first reports of a contratheoretical phenomenon are very difficult to get published. The researcher may himself discount them as having been due to measurement error or the inadequacy of his experiment. Unless the scientist is an authority or can strongly document his unexpected findings, their most likely fate is seldom pleasant. As we shall see in chapter 8, they are sometimes suppressed by the investigator—not in a malicious cover-up, but in the honest belief that they were invalid. Occasionally, they will be communicated verbally and they often end up being bantered about at conventions. At this stage, their only hope for publication is in a journal which is marginal or antagonistic to the challenged paradigm (and here they may be warmly welcomed). This may be followed by letters to the editor by defenders of the paradigm, and a rash of salvage experiments may ensue. These are usually intended to show the phenomenon as having been spurious. If the negative results are encountered by these stalwart defenders, the phenomenon quickly becomes anomalous and a vogue topic. Where it had been previously impossible to get published, it is now very easy—the editor's criteria shift toward relative leniency.

With replications of the increasingly popular anomaly, there develops a frenzied race for its *explanation*. Theories are offered to "account for" the phenomenon, ranging from patched-up revisions of a prior model to relatively comprehensive alternate views. The motivation behind this frantic race is not hard to decipher—science is generous in its treatment of theorists. It will be the truth spinner who will often receive the most recognition for the phenomenon—not the experimentalist who reported it. This may be part of the reason that researchers often suppress an anomaly until they have had time to formulate their own theoretical account of it. I find it intriguing that the requirement of *sensibility* is so pervasive in scientific publication, and yet it is seldom acknowledged. The data must "make sense" and, until they do, they are unlikely to be accepted as valid. The researcher must be able to show how they fit into some broad conceptual model, and we again face the significance of Kuhn's analysis. Without an encompassing paradigm, anomalous data are poorly tolerated. When they are rendered "reasonable" by a new conceptual model, their reception is more hospitable. The philosophical implications of this pattern are profound. We demand that reality make sense. When it does not, we overlook or deny its transgressions until we are forced to compromise the rules. It is obvious that we are not non-discriminatory in our acceptance of evidence. We do not welcome data which contradict our sensibility. As Thoreau pointed out, "We shall see but little if we require to understand what we see." The problem is that our perceptions are often dependent upon our conceptions.

It is noteworthy that the bias against negative results and anomalies is most prevalent in the "less advanced" sciences. This prejudice has undoubtedly contributed to their slow and erratic progress. As documented by Kuhn and others, anomalous data play a critical role in paradigm refinement and scientific revolution. When these data are effectively suppressed by inequitable publication policies, the consequences are epistemologically expensive. The social sciences—which are usually eager to imitate their physical science cousins—might do well to emulate this particular aspect. While their acknowledgement is sometimes grudging, anomalies are far more likely to be communicated and explored in the physical sciences. As long as we continue to hide our theoretical failures, we shall be deceived and misguided by our successes.

Data Analysis. The publication of "raw" data is rare in most sciences. Experimental results are more frequently expressed in transformations, graphic illustrations, or summary measures which use descriptive statistics. Even when the original data are reported, however, many fields require certain conventional methods of data analysis. Once again, the scientist's interest lies less in the data themselves and more in their conceptual implications. To get published, he must not only report his results; he must also interpret them via condoned methods of inference.

Most controversies in contemporary science focus upon preferred methods of data collection and analysis. In psychology, for example, we see the phenomena of *statophilia* and *statophobia*. Statophiles are scientists who refuse to acknowledge any relationship which fails to claim statistical justification. They tend to criticize or ignore the research of the statophobic, who views statistical analysis as rarely legitimate and frequently misleading. The statophobic can, of course, muster ample support for at least some of his avoidance behavior from such sources as Huff's classic *How to Lie with Statistics*, and the statophile will often defend the merits of statisticulation. In addition to these two extreme positions, there is a broad array of interim controversies over the appropriate statistics (or non-statistical analyses) for various problems.

It is not my intention to here resolve these controversies, nor to place myself in the camp of either extreme. However, in terms of journal publication policies, one can hardly ignore the significance of statistical considerations. This is due to the fact that the dichotomization of data into positive/negative categories is more prevalent in disciplines which employ inferential statistics in their data analyses. Under these circumstances, experimental results are deemed "successful" only if accepted statistical tests support their probable validity.

In the social sciences the dominating statistical strategy is known as *null hypothesis testing* (which I shall hereafter abbreviate as NHT).

Its procedural sequence is as follows. The experimenter specifies a "null hypothesis" and its alternative, the experimental hypothesis. The null hypothesis is the one which the researcher considers false, and he sets out to reject it with his data. For example, let us imagine that a scientist has developed a drug which could have potential relevance for human obesity. His experimental hypothesis is that recipients of the drug will either lose more or less weight than non-recipients. However, the focus of his research will be on the null hypothesis—i.e., that no difference will be found. It should be noted that the null hypothesis is usually *exact*—it specifies a discrete value for one or more population parameters. In the above example, the null hypothesis stated that weight loss among drug recipients will be (exactly) equal to that among non-recipients. In contrast, the experimental hypothesis covers a wide range of potential parameter values.

After specifying his hypotheses, the researcher selects and applies a statistical test to his data. The purpose of this test is to determine the probability that the obtained results could have been due to "chance" (sampling error) given that the null hypothesis was true. The statistics here offer a decision rule to help the experimenter avoid two types of errors—incorrectly rejecting the null hypothesis (Type I error) or failing to reject it when it is, in fact, false (Type II error). The maximum risk allowed here is called the "critical significance level"; it specifies the criterion of improbability. For example, five percent is a popular significance level in the social sciences. The obtained data must be attributable to chance factors no more than five percent of the time. If their calculated probability is less than this, the null hypothesis is rejected (and the experiment is considered to have yielded "positive" results). Results which are not statistically significant do not allow the experimenter to do anything other than retain the null hypothesis.

In a study of over 300 manuscripts published in four psychological journals, Reginald Smart found that less than ten percent reported "negative" results. The influence of statistical significance is apparent. A researcher's hopes for publication may rest precariously on the passive judgment of conventional statistical tests. This might not seem so disastrous if one has sufficient faith in the tests. I, for one, do not. This is not to say that I would discourage the use of descriptive statistics; I think their utility is frequently very apparent. However, inferential statistics are much more limited than some researchers seem willing to admit. For example, many studies in the social sciences have failed to satisfy some of the critical prerequisites for meaningful statistical analyses. These can, of course, be sidestepped via a judicious choice of sample size. However, there are scientific questions for which NHT is logically inadequate. In the conventional use of NHT, *only differences are significant*. There are many situations, however, where a non-difference would be more interesting or heuristic. In a study which I shall describe later, the reasoning skills of scientists and non-scientists were compared. From a strict NHT perspective, that study would be publishable only if the two groups were different. This suggests that their comparative equivalence in reasoning would *not* be a significant or contributory finding. Finally, as Greenwald, Rozeboom, and others have pointed out, the logical foundations of NHT are far from unequivocal. It will be shown in chapter 7 that, in addition to their practical problems, all forms of contemporary inferential statistics are irrationally based.

The practical consequences of data partiality merit serious consideration. If we continue to deferentially publish "positive" results, then we may expect each of the following to continue or accelerate:

1. *probability pyramiding.* Researchers will write up only their "successful" studies and, through selective publication, the technical literature will reflect a degree of reliability or consensus which is misleading.
2. *research myopia.* Investigators will tend to pursue only those questions which can be easily evaluated by null hypothesis testing, and they will favor those which are most likely to yield results which are statistically significant (versus epistemologically relevant). This may encourage what Mitroff and Featheringham call "the fallacy of misplaced precision" or Type III error—having solved the wrong problem.
3. *data hounding.* There are so many different statistical tests and manoeuvres that one can, with perseverance, usually find one which will yield a significant result. With publication hanging in the balance, the researcher will transform his data (e.g., to reciprocals, logarithms, etc.) in an endless pursuit of statistical success. He will scrounge for subcategories of results which show a significant trend and then highlight them. His primary concern becomes the outcome of his statistical tests rather than their appropriateness.
4. *distortion.* If pressed far enough, the investigator may misrepresent either his procedure or his results in order to satisfy publication requirements. This may be done by an expedient elimination of troublesome data points or by rewriting his method or hypotheses to fit his results. This practice is seldom considered illicit by the investigator—there are well known strategies for "winsorizing" one's data or eliminating "outlying" data points. Unfortunately,

the scientist's own biases can readily influence which data are ejected.

In addition to the foregoing, investigators will continue to equate statistical significance with acceptable knowledge. A finding which is significant at the five percent level is published; one at the seven percent level is not. Such arbitrary criteria stand in the way of more legitimate standards, such as a *relative* increase in the precision obtained. Consider the possible consequences if social science research were published—not because it had passed some static and arbitrary significance level—but because it increased the prevalent level of precision for the phenomenon in question.

In an insightful analysis of theory evaluation in physics and psychology, Paul E. Meehl has noted an apparent paradox:

> In the physical sciences, the usual result of an improvement in experimental design, instrumentation, or numerical mass of data, is to increase the difficulty of the "observational hurdle" which the physical theory of interest must successfully surmount; whereas in psychology and some of the allied behavior sciences, the usual effect of such improvement in experimental precision is to provide an easier hurdle for the theory to surmount (p. 103).

This paradox stems from the fact that the physical sciences tend to adopt progressively more stringent criteria as their precision increases. In NHT, however, the criterion is a fixed level of improbability. The null hypothesis usually specifies an exact parameter value. It is, of course, unlikely that the obtained value will be *exactly* equal to that predicted by the null hypothesis. Since increased precision enhances one's chances of detecting some difference (no matter how small), the null hypothesis can often be rejected with progressive ease. As Meehl points out, this means that in NHT, theory corroboration becomes weaker as precision increases!

CHANGING THE GAME RULES

This chapter has argued that publication is a critically important element in the life of the modern scientist. In their present form, however, many journal publication policies seem to work against optimal knowledge growth. In some fields, progress has often been achieved despite (rather than because of) the journal medium. I have argued that aspects of contemporary journal policies:

1. show an inequitable preference for eminent authors and prestigious affiliations;
2. are often unreliable;
3. encourage forms of research which are unduly restrictive; and
4. often produce a dangerously misrepresentative image of the quality and quantity of current knowledge.

Out of consideration for the individual scientist as well as the adequacy of our knowledge-seeking endeavors, I believe that journal publication practices are in dire need of reform. Since an entire volume could (and perhaps should) be devoted to this topic, the comments which follow are necessarily selective. Likewise, each suggestion should be read as a question, not an answer. Without empirically scrutinizing the impact of each reform, we have no way of knowing whether they have wrought improvement.

First I suggest that we drastically alter the peer review system, and particularly the role of referees. Judging from the available evidence, journal referees invest a tremendous amount of time in rendering verdicts which are dismally unreliable. Zuckerman and Merton point out that reviewers may often serve the function of professional decoys in protecting the editor from the ire of rejected authors. It is apparent that referees may contribute precious little to the objectivity of editorial decision. Although I know of no study on the topic, I would predict that an editor could perform his responsibilities without referees and suffer little or no loss in reliability. If anything, the review process would be much quicker and—assuming that the editor were at least self-consistent in his biases—less capricious. Given the current inefficiency of peer review, two alternate reforms present themselves: (1) eliminate peer review and allow editors to personally evaluate manuscripts, and (2) develop alternate referee sources. Both options have problems of their own, of course, but I think they are less acute than those encountered in current practices. I doubt that editorial fiat would be more biased than peer review. However, to effect this option one would probably have to divide responsibilities among several editors in order to provide sufficient breadth of knowledge and competency. A single editor is rarely an expert in all the topics of his discipline.

Since our current referees have shown very poor agreement with one another, we might also look to alternate reviewer sources. Graduate students, for example, might be ideally suited to this task; they are frequently at a career point in which technical knowledge is impressive and critical skills are sharpest. Moreover, since they are less entrenched in paradigms or their own pet theories, they might well be more objective than "established" referees. The experience of reviewing contemporary research could be an exciting and stimulating addition to graduate training. Unfortunately, this option presumes the same fallacy as the current referee system—namely, that some subclass of scientists is naturally reliable. If we want to increase referee agreement, then it will be necessary to resort to the same strategies which are required for the development of other forms of interpersonal agreement. Investigators who employ human observers in their research do not presume reliability—they produce it through training. The same is true of referees. If we want reliability, then we must train our raters. This, of course, raises the issue of criteria; what shall we train them to evaluate? Do we have consensus on what constitutes an adequate design in social science research? If we can't agree on the basic criteria for acceptable inquiry, how can we expect to agree on the merits of a study? The answers are not simple. However, it is my belief that dramatic progress could be made by this kind of empirical soul-searching. By isolating our disagreements we may illuminate our biases. To neglect these biases is to concede their supremacy.

It is noteworthy that some sciences cannot agree on acceptable methods of research until after the research is completed. In the referee study reported earlier, the same experimental procedures were given diametrically opposite ratings depending on the data they allegedly produced. The message here is clear. We can't agree on the adequacy of the question until we see the answer. Its corollary is as subtle as it is malignant. Instead of refining our inquiry *process*, we invest our faith in *outcome*. If the results of a study are "positive" or "significant," then its procedures are vindicated. This capricious style of inquiry is hardly a monument either to reason or to cost-efficiency. While it may sporadically uncover regularities in phenomena, its "hit rate" is usually low. It is time that we place our trust in good questions rather than cheap answers.

The foregoing excursion leads me to my second major recommendation for reform: *manuscripts should be evaluated solely on the basis of their relevance and their methodology.* Given that they ask an important question in an experimentally meaningful way, they should be published—regardless of their results. In the peer review system, papers sent to referees would contain only an introduction and a procedure section (perhaps supplemented with a brief description of how the data would be presented or analyzed). After the reviewers had rendered their opinions, the results would be appended. An even better option would be to have *contracted publication*. In this system, the researcher submits his idea and experimental procedures to the editor *prior* to their execution. If the editor (with or without re-viewers) approves, the researcher is guaranteed subsequent publica-tion of the work. This strategy would avoid mountains of unre-warded (and uncommunicated) inquiry and it could provide the researcher with invaluable assistance in the early design of his exper-iment.[e] It also places evaluative emphasis on the question rather than on the answer. Upon hearing this suggested reform, several col-leagues remarked that it would flood the journals. I disagree. In fact, if we were to publish only adequately conducted research, it might reduce journal backlogs and reduce the time to publication. Our varying opinions on the matter are readily open to empirical eval-uation.

In terms of the manuscript itself, there are many potential reforms which merit consideration and scrutiny. For example, the discussion section at the end of an article warrants examination. It supposedly summarizes and interprets the study's findings. In my own reviewing experience, however, I have often encountered discussions which bore little or no relationship to the data reported. What would happen if someone other than the author were asked to write an article's summary? I would not be surprised if authors and independent readers were to write very different interpretations of the same study. This would offer an interesting exercise in the exploration of personal biases.

I am obviously in favor of blind reviewing, notwithstanding its limitations. I would also support a policy of *multiple submission* in which authors can simultaneously submit the same manuscript to several different journals. This is currently prohibited, so that the author must submit and wait for a reply—which often takes any-where from two to eight months. If his manuscript is accepted, there is another delay of six to 24 months before it actually appears in the journal. If it is rejected, he can re-submit to another journal—and be-gin the waiting all over again. Editors claim that it would be a waste of reviewer time if multiple submission were possible. I fail to see how it makes a difference whether the redundant reviewing is simul-taneous or sequential. Perhaps editors would hasten their evaluations if they knew that a manuscript might be "scooped" by a rival period-

---

[e]Not surprisingly, this strategy could also create problems. For example, it is not unusual for a research project to deviate from its proposed methodology simply because of unforeseen problems. Likewise, a researcher could submit a study as if it were a proposal when, in fact, it had already been conducted. This would be a risky and unnecessary locution, however, if the reviewers requested changes and if their evaluations of an already completed study would have hinged on exactly the same document (i.e., a relevant question addressed via an adequate methodology).

ical. Incidentally, some editors have also suggested that multiple submission would present copyright problems. This is incorrect. The copyright on a paper is not established until it is in print.

There are an infinite number of other researchable issues in the refinement of journal reviewing. For example, should journals be required to publish their reliability rates?[f] What would be the consequences of publishing the identity of reviewers (along with the manuscript) or of listing all submitted manuscripts prior to their review? Should there be any attempts to institute reforms in the review and publication of books (versus articles)? If, as my friend and colleague Ted Rosenthal has noted, scientists are a community of consumers, to what extent are journals liable to antitrust (monopoly) laws and the like? The list could go on and on, and I haven't even talked about other facets of the publication game. For example, I harbor little hope that we will soon see a decline in the importance of publication quantity. Chairmen and recruiting committees will continue to weigh verbiage over value and the surviving scientist will sometimes have to accommodate. Even if journals were to adopt a lenient "publish everything" policy, it would not alleviate this malady—it would only inflate its arithmetic. Nor would it mean that emphasis would shift to work quality. While there is little consensus on the latter, quantity is an easily understood description. It is perhaps one of the sadder moments in the young scientist's life when he realizes that his contribution to the music of science will be judged less on its calibre than on its volume.

REFERENCES

7, 20, 25, 26, 36, 43, 48, 59, 60, 81, 88, 90, 92, 98, 99, 100, 107, 108, 111, 124, 142, 150, 162, 163, 164, 167, 171, 173, 177, 178, 194, 197, 200, 203, 217, 220, 246, 268, 270, 271, 273, 274, 276, 278, 282, 292, 293, 298, 304, 307, 316, 317, 320, 325, 332, 358, 360, 367, 368, 390, 393, 394, 402, 421, 422, 428, 434, 452, 465, 471, 483, 484, 491, 494, 495, 496, 498.

[f]We should not, incidentally, presume that reliability is a sacrosanct criterion in our refinement of the journal review process. Referees can be perfectly reliable by simply sharing the same counter-progressive prejudices.

The state of mind which enables a man to do work of this kind is akin to that of the religious worshipper or lover. The daily effort comes . . . straight from the heart.

Albert Einstein

Satisfaction of one's curiosity is one of the greatest sources of happiness in life.

Linus Pauling

Science is a willingness to accept facts even when they are opposed to wishes.

B.F. Skinner

We think very few people sensible, except those who are of our opinion.

Rochefoucauld

Science advances as much through the opposition of men of differing persuasions as it does through the opposition of different ideas.

Ian I. Mitroff

Of all crimes the worst is the theft of glory.

Robert Frost

The task of the scientific theorist who wishes to be recognized in his lifetime is as much a matter of weighing the likes, dislikes, prejudices, and intellectual honesty of office holders as it is of questioning phenomena.

D.L. Watson

There is no more envious race of men than scientific discoverers.

Jules Verne

Man is the only animal that blushes—or has reason to.

Mark Twain

❋ *Chapter 6*

Passions of the Scientist

I was tempted to call this chapter "The Sensuous Scientist," but decided that such a title might place too much emphasis on the wrong organs.

You will recall from chapter 1 that one of the cardinal features of the storybook image of the scientist deals with his stubborn objectivity. Displaying skills that transcend the frailties of most mortals, the mythical scientist is said to be capable of dispassionate judgment and unbiased inquiry. He can set his personal views aside and force his rational skills to reign supreme over his emotions.

As we shall see in the present chapter, this long-standing image could well be considered one of the most delusional ideas in contemporary science. The scientist is not only subjective in the execution of his professional role—he is often downright passionate. Until a few years ago, the existence of emotions in the scientist *qua* scientist was seldom acknowledged. Despite the fact that such men as Michael Polanyi, Karl Popper, E.G. Boring, and Albert Einstein were underlining the role of emotion in scientific inquiry, the autonomic nervous system of *homo scientus* remained a taboo topic. This was clearly illustrated by the lively (and ironically emotional) responses to James D. Watson's *The Double Helix*. In this autobiographical account of the research which led to the Nobel Prize for discovering the molecular structure of DNA, Watson described many of the personal and subjective aspects of scientific research. He was sharply ostracized by his peers, some of whom condemned his candid exposé as an exercise in sensationalism and muckraking. The intensity of these reactions was an ironic illustration of some of Watson's very contentions—e.g., that *homo scientus* is often an emotional creature. Commenting on the impact of Watson's book, Robert Merton points out that the message of *The Double Helix* was hardly a surprise to those familiar with the history of science. In a captivating survey of great scientists, Merton goes on to document the pervasiveness of emotionality in both the conduct and communication of research.

It is perhaps a sign of progress that Ian Mitroff's group of geoscientists were unanimously in agreement that the "notion of the objective, emotionally disinterested scientist" was naive. The degree and pervasiveness of their emotional behavior was noted by Mitroff, who remarked that his 261 hours of interviews with prominent scientists "document . . . the intense emotions which permeate the doing of science." Interestingly, however, many of Mitroff's subjects seemed to be most convinced of emotionality in their colleagues rather than in themselves. This personal "psychology of exception" is one which may have important implications for you, the reader, as well as me, the author. In this critical analysis of *homo scientus*, it is easy to slip into the role of an immune spectator—rather than an active contributor—to the fallibilities of science. By exempting ourselves from the portrait, we may smile (or scream) at the inanities of our colleagues, and plod on in self-righteous ignorance of our own needs for refinement and self-appraisal.

The scientist may be *more* passionately involved in his vocation than almost any other professional. His is not simply a nine to five occupation which brings in a paycheck. Relative to other professions, it offers little financial incentive and questionable job security. And yet, in terms of prestige and respect, it is surpassed by few vocations.

If psychology has taught us anything in its first century of research (and there are more than a few who would question this conditional), it has been that the human organism is primarily hedonistic. That is, we will work to produce or prolong certain classes of events and to avoid or reduce others. This superficially trite summarization is complicated by the fact that these classes of events (crudely dichotomized as "pleasures" and "pains") are:

1. distributed along a continuum of valence,
2. often idiosyncratic to specific individuals,
3. not restricted to simplistic "biological drives,"
4. tremendously influenced by the person's "conceptual world" (value and belief systems), and
5. subject to change with time or situation.

This rhetorical tangent is by way of explaining an opinion—namely, that it may behoove the scientist to be more emotionally involved in his work than other professionals. Were the pursuit of a career in science dependent upon its financial lucrativeness, we would have damn few scientists. If it is generally true that humans will not long pursue any effortful endeavor unless they *perceive* it as being worthwhile or "need-satisfying," then it may be adaptive that *homo scientus* sees his vocation as full of "worth." This is not to imply that all other professionals are therefore inspired only by the dollar or that they see no other values in their work. However, again invoking the concept of a continuum, I think the scientist may well have a stronger personal (psychological) investment in the non-financial aspects of his career.

Recall that the fundamental task of the scientist is to increase and refine our knowledge. Given that he may be satisfying a variety of personal needs in pursuing that goal, it seems reasonable to suggest two tentative speculations:

1. that the scientist will respond emotionally to events which are perceived as enhancing or challenging our current state of knowledge (e.g., new discoveries or paradigms), and
2. that the scientist will respond emotionally to events which are perceived as reflecting his personal competence or contribution to the task (e.g., the success or failure of his experiments, the receipt of acknowledgment or recognition for his work, etc.).

In what follows I shall attempt to elaborate on these two broad categories of emotion—those dealing primarily with the *paradigm* and those which are more *personal* in nature. While it is admittedly arbitrary, this manufactured distinction may help to structure our exploration of the subjective sides of science. Likewise, I have no delusions about the relative crudeness of the portrait which follows. The pervasiveness of emotionality in science is very clear, but its nuances have yet to be reliably examined. Finally, it should be noted that the present chapter focuses upon sources and types of emotions in science. The possible influence of those emotions on other behavior—e.g., the conduct of research—will be addressed in chapter 8.

PARADIGM PASSIONS

Many of the scientist's emotions are associated with his perception of the adequacy of the paradigm(s) to which he ascribes. If the paradigm is solving problems and making ostensive progress, then his emotions may range from complacency to strong enthusiasm. On the other hand, if the paradigm is encountering difficulties, the scientist may respond with frustration, anxiety, or depression. Finally, depending on his current degree of satisfaction and the nature of the paradigm's problems, the scientist may eagerly welcome or energetically fight the emergence of competing perspectives.

The scientist's emotional reactions to the paradigm are thus variable and complex. An analysis and description of their complexity is complicated by the multiplicity of apparently influential variables. For example, a cursory survey suggests that each of the following may affect how the scientist feels about events bearing on the paradigm:

1. the recency (age) of the paradigm,
2. whether the scientist is a recent recruit or convert,
3. whether it is a majority or minority perspective,
4. whether its deficiencies appear to be methodological rather than theoretical,
5. the extent, history, and credibility of its empirical failures,
6. whether its deficiencies deal with central rather than peripheral issues (e.g., negative results versus anomalies),
7. whether the inadequacies of the paradigm are being publicly cited or acknowledged,
8. whether the paradigm is being attacked internally (by respected peers or authorities) versus externally,
9. whether there are competing alternative paradigms which are claiming or demonstrating superiority, and
10. whether the scientist is publicly recognized (or self-perceived) as a primary contributor (founder) of either the old or the competing paradigm.

Needless to say, it would be foolish to offer universal aphorisms on such a complex phenomenon. Given the multiplicity of factors involved and the current lack of controlled research, it might also be naively ambitious to even offer tentative and global impressions of scientist emotions. However, I believe that such a portrait might help to stimulate more refined explorations of the phenomenon. A crude sketch usually elicits more of a reaction than a blank canvas, and it is this premise which motivates me to climb out on some descriptive limbs here.

Perhaps it would be best to begin with another fallible distinction between what I shall call *atmospheric* versus *event-related* emotions. Atmospheric emotions refer to general day-to-day feelings which form the affective background for the scientist's work. While they are more stable than their event-related counterparts, these emotions may reflect trends in the individual's satisfaction with the paradigm. Event-related emotions are usually more intense and momentary feelings which are cued by specific incidents. These events eventually have their impact on affective atmosphere, but their distinguishing feature is their acuteness. Emotion-eliciting events may range from theoretical insights and empirical discoveries to ambiguous, perplexing, or "negative" experimental outcomes. The nature of the event here merits consideration. Notice that they are neither restricted to physically "external" incidents nor to experimental outcomes. They may take the form of an idea, a colleague's remarks, a technical article, and so on. The identification of an emotion-eliciting event is determined phenomenologically (from the internal perspective of the scientist). It does not rest inherently within the event.[a]

Examples of emotional responses to specific events are readily available in science. As Merton indicated in his article on "The Behavior Patterns of Scientists," for example, the *Eureka syndrome* is well documented in both early and contemporary science. Thus, we see Kepler exclaiming joy "beyond his fondest hopes" at his discovery of the third planetary law and William James "all aflame" with the idea of pragmatism. The recurrence of this intense emotional response is likewise illustrated in the book *Moments of Discovery* and in many contemporary accounts of research. In his personal account of discovering the double helix structure of the DNA molecule, James Watson describes his racing pulse as he "happily lay awake with pairs of adenine residues whirling in front of my closed eyes." The fact that he was openly racing for a Nobel Prize and saw this discovery as a means of personal recognition also reflects the inseparability of personal and paradigm passions.

Few experiments yield earth-shaking discoveries, however, and most scientists are probably more familiar with what might be called the *blahshit syndrome*. Here, the reaction is one of disappointment, frustration, or depression. When the emotion-eliciting event has to do

[a]One must be careful here not to fall into the beckoning tautology that identification of an "event-related emotion" somehow demonstrates the emotion-eliciting capabilities of the event. We are talking about a crude taxonomy of emotions, not a causal explanation. Thus, if a discovery is correlated with some intense emotional response on the part of a scientist, we can—according to the present definition—describe the *emotion* as "event-related." We cannot, however, use that definition to defend the contention that the *event* elicited the emotion. The latter would require demonstration that the event-emotion correlation meets conventional criteria for the attribution of cause (e.g., elimination of competing causal candidates, replicability, etc.). These criteria, of course, have their own share of problems (chapter 7).

with someone else "scooping" an idea, anger and aggression are not uncommon. These latter reactions will be discussed in a moment. For now, it is worth noting that over half of the scientists who participated in our survey (appendix A) reported that they experienced disappointment when their research yielded negative results. Judging from the fact that about one-third of their experimental outcomes were reported to be "negative," it would appear that this emotion is not a stranger to many scientists.

The emotions that are elicited by a particular event are influenced by factors other than the event itself. Negative results and anomalies, for example, may generate either frustration or elation depending on the circumstances which surround them. If they relate to one's personal hypotheses, they may be met with negative affect. However, if they bear perceived implications for a discovery or breakthrough, they may be joyously welcomed. Recently, in the unexpected discovery of two new elementary physical particles, the researchers first reacted to their serendipitous results with frustration and doubt. They "sat on their data" for several months fearing that they were invalid and not wanting to risk a public report. When word leaked out that another laboratory had independently observed (and suppressed) the same phenomena, these "anomalies" immediately turned into "the thrill of a lifetime."

Some emotional patterns in the scientist seem to correlate roughly with various stages of paradigm growth and revolution. Thus, new paradigms often engender an atmosphere of energetic enthusiasm. When the scientist is a new recruit or a "convert" to the paradigm, his excitement may approach missionary zeal. This phase might then be called the "ecstacy of truth" (or "isn't it great to be right?"). It is probably more common for adherents of a young and "healthy" paradigm to feel complacently confident. While there may be some frustration stemming from unsolved problems, the "true believer" assumes that these will be dealt with in time. During this phase, of course, perplexities and failures reflect on the inadequacies of the scientist or his instruments, so that the negative emotions they engender are more likely to be directed toward the person than the paradigm. Thus, in his delightful account of the early research linking rapid eye movements (REMs) with dreaming, William Dement describes his agonizing feelings of personal doubt when an artifactual error caused him to question the validity of his own work.

A scientist's emotional commitment to a paradigm is probably most apprent when it is under attack. While his daily affect may have previously been one of quiet contentment, this complacency is seldom maintained in the face of attack. Here again, however, the scientist's reaction may range from defensive rebuttals and persecution of the challengers to patronizing pity for the misguided skeptics. It is interesting to note that the *source* of the attack may influence the reaction it receives. Threats which are posed externally by competing paradigms often induce increased solidarity and commitment. Depending on the nature and strength of the attack, a counter-offensive may be launched, and it is not uncommon to see recurring skirmishes. As Kuhn has pointed out, these exchanges are often futile in the sense that proponents of the competing perspectives presuppose the validity of their own argumentative premises. When this occurs, a "cold war" may evolve in which the competitors spend less and less time in skirmishes and each learns to tolerate or disregard the "absurdities" of the other.

Internal threats to the paradigm are often much more upsetting to the scientist. This may be due to such factors as the use of a shared language and conceptual model, increased "credibility" of the source, and so on. If the challenge is either weak or outrageously revolutionary, the malcontents may be ignored or chastised. Should they start to attract a sizeable following, their nuisance value increases and there may be a drawing of clear and public faction lines. This fragmentation may be particularly clear when the challenge has been posed or endorsed by one or more recognized authorities in the field.

Although there is some historical evidence to suggest that newcomers to a paradigm are more likely to make breakthrough discoveries and stimulate revolutions, we do not yet know how to accurately predict which scientists will *convert* to the new view. As noted by Planck and others, age seems to be the best predictor, but it is far from perfect. There are many exceptions to the rule that younger scientists are conceptually more pliable than older ones, and I suspect that at least some of these exceptions may be attributed to "open versus closed" thinking styles (chapters 7-9). Other factors might include the characteristics of the new paradigm, the scientist's personal contribution to the previous or challenging perspective, and so on. From the available analyses of scientific revolutions, however, the following seem clear:

1. Paradigm crises and revolutions are usually accompanied by intense emotional reactions on the part of the individual scientist;
2. The rejection of a paradigm is rare in the absence of an alternative paradigm; that is, "agnosticism" in science is infrequent;
3. Conversion to a new paradigm is often slow and sometimes rare; many new paradigms enlarge their constituency primarily by

proselytizing to the uncommitted (students) rather than convert-
ing their rivals;
4. Data often seem to play a substantially less important role in conversion than personal and psychological factors; and
5. Threats to a paradigm are often met with disregard and intolerance
—occasionally with persecution.

This last points bears elaboration in that it denotes some of the behavioral correlates of the scientists' emotions. Contrary to his mythical image, the scientist is often energetically intolerant of new ideas
and contra-theoretical claims. This pattern is well illustrated in
Bernard Barber's classic paper on "Resistance by Scientists to Scientific discovery." Here we are told that the great astronomer Tycho
Brahe "remained a life-long opponent of Copernicanism" and helped
to postpone acceptance of the new doctrine. Likewise, despite their
superiority over previous views, the theories of each of the following were vigorously resisted: Helmholtz, Lister, Harvey, Planck,
Young, Galton, Roentgen, Rutherford, Mendel, Newton, Pasteur,
Darwin, Magendie, and Einstein. The list could easily be multiplied.
Many of these scientists have remarked on the intensity of their
opposition and the personal anguish of being scorned and sometimes persecuted. Thus, for his absurd claim that unsanitary surgical procedures might be responsible for the high incidence of post-
surgical infection, Ignaz Semmelweis was scorned and ridiculed.
After he had collected evidence to support his hypothesis, he was
fired from his job—eventually dying in an insane asylum.

The more recent uproar over Immanuel Velikovsky is another case
in point. If you have any doubts about the ability or willingness of
scientists to engage in the violent and bigoted persecution of their
colleagues, I recommend perusal of the September 1963 issue of the
American Behavioral Scientist. There Alfred de Grazia and his colleagues document some of the incredible atrocities committed against
Velikovsky. In his controversial theory, he had outlined several
radically different ideas about the earth's history and the development of other planets in our solar system. His hypotheses included
such claims as interplanetary collisions and violent changes in the
earth's surface. These events were alleged to have occurred prior to
our solar system settling down to its current patterns of planetary
orbit. Velikovsky described the derivation of his theory as well as
specifying several potential tests of its accuracy. Despite his repeated
attempts to stimulate research, Velikovsky was snubbed by hundreds
of scientists—some of whom refused to even *read* his theory. The
popular press picked up some of the sensational aspects of the theory,

and diatribes against Velikovsky were soon offered by scores of his colleagues. He was not allowed to publish rebuttals, even when some of his astronomical claims had been unexpectedly verified by his detractors. After rejections from many other publishers, the Macmillan company agreed to publish a book version of Velikovsky's ideas, titled *Worlds in Collision.* When word got out that a contract had been offered, the Macmillan company began to receive threats from the scientific community. After some hesitation, Macmillan went ahead with publication—and immediately felt the wrath of organized science. Their other books were boycotted and their sales representatives were refused appointments at several major universities. Letters demanding cessation of publication were received. In response to this book, the American Association for the Advancement of Science proposed that future publications of new scientific hypotheses be restricted to authors who could claim sponsorship from "a proper professional body." Individuals who voiced tolerance or support for Velikovsky's views—such as the Chairman of the Astronomy Department at the American Museum of Natural History —were threatened with being fired if they did not withdraw their support. The pressure finally became so great that the Macmillan company capitulated. They ceased publication and sold their rights to the manuscript. Several years later, Velikovsky documented the verification of several of his "preposterous" claims (such as the extremely high surface temperature of the planet Venus and the emission of radio waves by the planet Jupiter). His letter was apparently returned unread by *Science* editor Philip Abelson. The incidents go on and on; and the issue, of course, is not whether Velikovsky was correct. The fact that he was so energetically persecuted and denied access to means for rebutting his critics is a sad chapter in the history of science.

Equally sad, perhaps, but less publicized is the tragedy surrounding research on Darwinian versus Lamarckian theory, earlier in this century. Biologist Paul Kammerer was a lonely defender of the latter perspective at a time when it was violently resisted by the more populous Darwinians. In his account of Kammerer's personal struggles, Arthur Koestler (*The Case of the Midwife Toad*) paints a vivid portrait of oppression. In addition to several other bits of evidence, Kammerer had produced a biological specimen which offered strong support for Lamarckian theory. When his antagonists questioned the existence and authenticity of such a specimen (which had taken several years to produce and was the sole survivor of his prewar laboratory), Kammerer agreed to submit it to public inspection. Surprisingly, however, his primary opponent (William Bateson) refused to inspect the specimen when it was brought to him at Cambridge. Several other biologists examined it at that time and found it to be authentic. Kammerer returned to his Vienna laboratory and was soon visited by another of his detractors who insisted on seeing the deteriorating specimen. Kammerer agreed, and his young antagonist subjected the specimen to a thorough examination. His conclusion was quickly printed in *Nature*: that the specimen had been artificially altered by the injection of India ink. An independent chemical test was performed by one of Kammerer's friends and it verified that the specimen had been altered. Despite the earlier public inspections, Kammerer was "accused of the worst crime a scientist can commit"—i.e., fabricating his data. Although he was convinced that someone had intentionally contaminated his specimen, Kammerer felt little hope in protesting his innocence. He had already been persecuted and ridiculed for well over a decade. Six weeks after the "scandal" was publicized, he climbed a mountain path in Austria and put a bullet through his head. In his suicide note, he gave his body to science and remarked, "Perhaps my worthy academic colleagues will discover in my brain a trace of the qualities they found absent from the manifestations of my mental activities while I was alive."

PERSONAL RECOGNITION:
THE PRIORITY RACE

Our discussion has thus far focused on emotions primarily associated with changes in the paradigm—discoveries, anomalies, attacks, and so on. As we have seen, it is impossible to separate the personal component from these situations. To the extent that he is committed to and influenced by a paradigm, the scientist will react emotionally to changes in its status. When he is personally responsible for some of these changes, he is even more likely to greet them with fluctuations in his autonomic (as well as central) nervous system. This may be partly due to his taking pride in having made a personal contribution to communal knowledge. While this "altruistic" motive is unquestionably an important one, it is probably misrepresentative to say that scientists derive their primary satisfaction from the growth of knowledge. As defined by science, "knowledge" is a public—and therefore *social*—phenomenon. An idea or discovery is not "contributory" until it is acknowledged and accepted by the scientific community. Thus, in his book *Public Knowledge*, John Ziman argues that the primary goal of the scientist is consensus—the persuasion of his peers. He is, in essence, a truth merchant. But the market in which he trades is an unsteady one in that the quality (validity) of his wares is complexly dependent on whether or not they are purchased. There is an interesting paradox here which will be further examined in chapter 7—namely, that the ultimate criterion of truth does not lie in experimental outcomes. While the data—which are themselves very fallible—may play a role in the process, the ultimate standard of knowledge is psychosocial. A "fact" is not a fact until it has received peer approval, and herein lies at least one reason for scientists' quest for recognition. If they want their work to be contributory, they must strive to get it publicly "recognized"—i.e., acknowledged, replicated, expanded, and so on.

But there is another meaning to the term "recognition" and another kind of motivation surrounding it. Up until now, I have referred to it as a fundamental prerequisite in knowledge—an epistemological nuisance which must be tolerated by the researcher. In its psychological sense, however, "recognition" refers to a form of personal evaluation—commendation, respect, peer approval. We have already discussed Hagstrom's "recognition-exchange hypothesis" (chapter 4) regarding the reciprocity between knowledge-sharing and personal recognition. As I have pointed out, I do not see this quest for recognition as a corrupt or counter-progressive element in science. From both epistemological and psychological perspectives, it appears to be an essential ingredient in rational inquiry. Unfortunately, while it may be an essential ingredient, it is also a problematic one in that some of science's darkest hours have been spawned by the quest for recognition. Since I believe that an awareness of these problems is a prerequisite to their reduction, we shall take some time here to explore them.

For most scientists, their work—and particularly recognition of their work—is far from a dispassionate endeavor. The scientist wants not only to expand our knowledge, but also to be given *credit* for this accomplishment. The importance of that credit is well documented by the intensity of emotions surrounding it. First, we find a long list of violent disputes over the rightful "ownership" of ideas and discoveries. Surveying some of the more infamous battles, Merton concludes that:

> The fact is that almost all of those firmly placed in the pantheon of science—Newton, Descartes, Leibniz, Pascal, or Huygens, Lister, Faraday, Laplace, or Davy—were caught up in passionate efforts to achieve priority and to have it publicly registered (1969, p. 7).

In two vitriolic volumes, Galileo defended his theoretical claims against the "calumnies" of other claimants, and levied harsh attacks at those who "attempted to rob me of that glory which was mine." Newton, who is often depicted as a paragon among scientists, was described by astronomer John Flamsteed as "insidious, ambitious, and excessively covetous of praise." He fought with Robert Hooke over several issues in optics and celestial mechanics. When Leibniz and Newton independently discovered the calculus, the two became embroiled in a long and bitter struggle over rightful paternity. The animosities exchanged were violent and scurrilous. Shortly before Leibniz's death Newton exercised his power as president of the Royal Society and hand picked a committee to decide the rightful claimant.

The pattern repeats itself again and again, touching some of the most eminent scientists of the time. Hobbes, Cavendish, Watt, Lavoisier, Bernoulli, Comte, Nobel—and these are only the spectacular battles. There were, of course, exceptions—scientists who declined to participate in priority disputes (e.g., Franklin, Darwin)—but their pacifism is clearly overshadowed by the fierce territoriality of their colleagues.

Based on some research he conducted with Elinor Barber, Merton has concluded that intense priority fights have declined in recent times. This may be due in part to a greater appreciation of the fact that independent "multiple discoveries" seem to be a common and inevitable phenomenon. Working from very different perspectives, scientists have often hit upon the same discovery or idea independently. The annals of science are filled with hundreds of incidents in which researchers—sometimes separated by continents—have made the same breakthrough almost simultaneously. In some instances, their discoveries were literally separated only by hours!

The awareness of this simultaneity is indicated in interviews with scientists. Hagstrom reports that over half of his sample expressed concern about being "scooped" and an even greater percentage said that they had already experienced this phenomenon. It is interesting to note that the prospect of *theft* also weighs heavily on the minds of some scientists. History has recorded only a few verified instances of outright stealing (Laplace, for example, was noted for it), but a sizeable minority of scientists seem very concerned about its ever-present threat. This was expressed by several of Mitroff's subjects and, in Gaston's study of high energy physicists, over one-sixth believed that some of their work had been stolen. In our own survey (appendix A), physicists, biologists, sociologists, and psychologists estimated that an average of fourteen percent of their colleagues had plagiarized other's ideas. The seriousness of these beliefs is reflected in such events as the Piccioni lawsuit regarding a "stolen" Nobel Prize, but it is even more apparent in the secretiveness of scientists.

Whether it is due to appreciation of simultaneity or fear of theft, there can be little doubt that *homo scientus* is an energetically secretive creature. He is cautious in divulging unfinished work and very discreet in concealing his unsubstantiated hunches or hypotheses. The contemporary scientist is no innovator in this paranoid secrecy, however. According to Arthur Koestler (*The Watershed*), Galileo was in the habit of using anagrams (scrambled letters which contained a hidden message) in order to protect his priority claims. Thus, when he saw the moons of Jupiter in 1610, he disguised his find by sending this note to an ambassador in Prague: "SMAISMRMILMEPOETALEUMIBUNENUGTTAURIAS" ("I have observed the highest planet (Saturn) in triplet form.") The use of anagrams to disguise tentative hunches and unpolished hypotheses was not uncommon in early science.[b] Judging from interviews with contemporary scientists, their secretive functions have been usurped by more discreet methods of protection.

There is a certain paradox in the unofficial norm of secrecy in science. The researcher begins by covetously protecting his ideas. However, once he is confident of their validity and significance, he transforms from a reclusive tortoise into an ambitious hare. Where he had previously spoken in whispers, he now shouts his discovery and rushes into print quickly so as to stake his claim. Publication in some form is, of course, the title to one's conceptual property. These frenzied efforts in the race to print are reflected in harried letters to the editor, the "preprint" ritual, and "accidental" leaks to the popular press. The sense of urgency is pervasive. Fertile ideas are a prize, and the competing scientist is caught up in a landrush on an infinite frontier. He must, in Faraday's words, "work, finish, publish," for the race is a close one and there is an infinite gap between first and second place.

In addition to the urgency and paranoid secrecy, there are themes of personal rivalry and even animosity in science. Thus, we see James Watson and Francis Crick celebrating an error made by their rival Linus Pauling in the race for the structure of DNA. Even more striking are the interview transcripts reported by Mitroff when he inquired of scientists' feelings about one another. They were marked by a "sheer

[b]According to Hart, Leonardo Da Vinci had a particularly unique code for his personal notes—he wrote them backwards, in mirror image.

intensity of emotion, vituperation, and overall vindictiveness." One of the more eminent scientists summarized his feelings with a rather sweeping evaluation of his peers: "Look, *they're* all fucking ass-holes!"

The saga of subjectivity in the scientist and the quest for recognition could go on and on. We see the race not only for priority but also for visibility. The scientist must not only publish fast, but also furiously. Number of articles, order of authorship, prestige of journal —they are all measures of his socially (and self-) defined worth. We see reactions of indignation when his work is not cited and vituperative attacks at convention "rumor mills." There are political factions, personal animosities, and even glimpses of espionage. But perhaps my point is already made. The scientist is not dispassionate.

REFLECTIONS ON EMOTIONALITY IN SCIENCE: A QUESTION OF BALANCE

In marked contrast to his storybook image, we have seen that the scientist is often very emotionally involved in his work. He is not objectively flexible, welcoming contrary opinions and respecting the integrity of their proponents. Instead of an open "communal" sharing of knowledge, he is often secretive and, in contrast to his mythical humility, he is often fiercely protective of his fame—resorting to personal attacks and acrimonious disputes over recognition.

Where does this leave us? The scientist, as practitioner, does not fit his "ideal" mold. We therefore have three options—accept (tolerate) the discrepancy, reform the scientist, or reform the mold. It is my opinion that we will probably need to do a little of each, but with particular emphasis on reforming our "ideal image" of the scientist. The concept of dispassionate inquiry is epistemologically absurd. While we can strive to minimize the subjective elements in knowledge, they can never be totally eliminated. But it is not just the *content* of knowledge which is inherently subjective—so also is its *process*. Inquiry requires incentive, whether it be Polanyi's "heuristic passions" or a less esoteric variety. This relationship has been noted by many. Max Weber talks about the "strange intoxication" which is required in research and David Watson asks, "Would we *have* any science if truth did not inspire passionate devotion in the searcher?" Abraham Maslow talks of the need for love, devotion, and fascination in the scientist; and even Karl Popper states that he is quite ready to admit that "nothing will ever be achieved without a modicum of passion." In defending the role of feelings in science, Mitroff argues that:

strong emotions—the often hostile feelings between various types of individuals, the intense commitment to particular preferred positions—are not by themselves necessarily detrimental to the ideal of scientific objectivity.... Some scientists are keen observers precisely because of their commitments, not in spite of them ... to eliminate strong emotions and intense commitments may be to eliminate some of science's most vital sustaining forces (pp. 247–48).

With the exception of Mitroff, these defenses of the scientist's feelings are primarily focused upon *intellectual* rather than *psychosocial* incentives. The researcher's feelings are applauded so long as they stem from curiousity and a thirst for knowledge. While I concur in the value of these cerebral motives, I am concerned about our neglect of their apparently less virtuous siblings. Is the quest for personal recognition an unacceptable source of motivation? As we have seen in this chapter, it is often the "priority race" which seems to stimulate some of the least admirable behaviors in *homo scientus*. In brief review, it looks as though competition for recognition is often associated with such phenomena as:

1. secretiveness,
2. personal rivalries and credit disputes,
3. hasty research and publication,
4. voluminous research and publication,
5. experimental and conceptual risk taking,
6. perseverance,
7. endorsement of the practice of "idea ownership," and
8. differential valuation of innovation (over replication) and theories (over data).

While it may be clear that some of these patterns probably facilitate scientific progress, it should also be apparent that some may not. Would a "cooperative" rather than a "competitive" approach be more productive? The effectiveness of "communistic" research programs in China and Russia may shed some light on this issue, but I suspect that we will find an ever-present need for personal gratification of the scientist. Indeed, although I have criticized the *accuracy* of the storybook image, I wonder whether it may not serve some psychological *functions* in the scientist. To the extent that both he and the public believe it, a comfortable percept is created—*homo scientus* can view himself as dedicated, honest, self-sacrificing, and so on. Unfortunately, the image contrasts sharply with daily experience, and the scientist is faced with some unresolvable conflicts (e.g., cooperate *but* compete, strive for recognition *but* deny its personal importance, etc.). As noted by Merton and others, these conflicts between the "ideal" and actual norms of science frequently stimulate intense feelings of ambivalence and perplexity.

My conclusion is necessarily tentative. Were I asked to translate this chapter into practical implications for further action, I would offer the following: First, I think that the scientist should be made more aware of the subjectivity of his enterprise and the possible role of emotions in both the process and the product of his research. It is time that he be liberated from the perplexity of dual norms and manufactured self-deception. Second, we need to explore (both logically and experimentally) the various forms of motivation to do research. What are our options in refining the incentive system such that it is optimally tuned for the growth of knowledge and the personal satisfaction of the scientist? Finally, as an interim strategy, we should probably encourage the scientist to strive for a balance in his emotions. Rather than deny or disguise their existence, he can consciously monitor their contribution to (as well as conflict with) the execution of his research. Inquiry may require incentive, but it need not be unrestrained. In the "love affair" metaphor of Agnew and Pyke, the scientist can be encouraged to allow himself the pleasures of a romance or marriage to his ideas and peer group—but he should always remain open to the option of divorce.

REFERENCES

4, 6, 25, 36, 39, 46, 49, 70, 96, 117, 118, 120, 122, 124, 127, 135, 143, 145 149, 153, 156, 162, 170, 171, 180, 183, 215, 216, 224, 228, 233, 235, 251, 259, 269, 275, 295, 297, 302, 303, 306, 307, 309, 315, 316, 321, 322, 329, 334, 341, 350, 356, 367, 387, 389, 399, 400, 412, 427, 437, 443, 444, 449, 450, 451, 462, 463, 464, 493.

Not to be absolutely certain is, I think, one of the essential things of rationality.

Bertrand Russell

The number of rational hypotheses that can explain any given phenomenon is infinite.

Robert M. Pirsig

Human thought, before it is squeezed into its Sunday best, for purposes of publication, is a nebulous and intuitive affair: in place of logic there brews a stew of hunch and partial insight, half submerged.

Liam Hudson

A . . . persistent sour note in the symphony of modern science comes from the scientist's expiring faith in logic as a dependable ally. . . . On closer examination, however, "logical rigor" has proved to be but a changing fashion. . . . Logic, like science itself, is open to distortion by human frailty, and is no sure guide either in discovery or criticism.

D.L. Watson

It is always a bit ironical when a house which professes to virtue topples under censure by its own precept. This is to some extent the history of empiricism. . . . Empiricism itself is culpable, yet we have found no reliable substitute for a knowledge supported by the fact of its public communicability.

Merle B. Turner

All scientific knowing is indirect, presumptive, obliquely and incompletely corroborated at best. The language of science is subjective, provincial, approximative, and metaphoric, never the language of reality itself. . . . The best we can hope for are well-edited approximations.

Donald T. Campbell

Philosophy may provide a reconstruction of scientific knowledge once it is achieved, but it falls to psychology and sociology to explain the nature and acquisition of human knowledge, and, hence, the nature and growth of science.

Walter B. Weimer

✳ *Chapter 7*

The Rationality of Science

Up until now, the scientist appears to be a flawed but not incompetent purveyor of knowledge. Some might even argue that the evidence thus far presented is irrelevant to the issue of whether he performs his job well. What if he *is* ritualistic, competitive, emotional, and so on—as long as he is efficient in producing knowledge, we should be able to tolerate his shortcomings. If the scientist is paid to churn out "truth," then perhaps our concern should be only with the products (rather than process) of his efforts.

While the process/product dichotomy may be an alluring one, it is also misrepresentative. This and the next chapter will attempt to show that the scientist is often an inefficient Truth Spinner, and that this is at least partly attributable to his processes of inquiry. This obviously does not mean that the scientist is always (or even usually) wrong in his claims to knowledge, but that his efficiency is clearly hampered by the ways he goes about his work. Three primary sources of inefficiency will be explored: (1) the traditional systems of inquiry in which most scientists are steeped (Chapter 7), (2) the fallibilities of the scientist as a critical thinker, and (3) the fallibilities of the scientist as an objective collector of data (Chapter 8). These three are, I think, inter-related and those of you who survive these two chapters will hopefully discern some of their interactions.

In the process of their professional acculturation, scientists are usually indoctrinated in a theory of knowledge which can be roughly termed *empiricism*. This indoctrination is often implicit in that the scientist is seldom tutored in *epistemology*—theories of knowledge

Rather, he is exposed primarily to empirical approaches to knowledge, and sometimes to only one subset of those approaches.

For a variety of reasons, many scientists seem to have an aversion to the discipline of philosophy—and particularly to its encroachments on their *modus operandi*. With a few notable exceptions, scientists tend to view philosophers as experts in pedantic irrelevance. It should be noted that this perception is not infrequently reinforced by philosophers, some of whom seem to relish in their esoteric absurdities. The unfortunate consequence of this is that some scientists tend to prejudicially reject *all* philosophy as worthless. This assertion may elicit in you (the reader) dire apprehensions about what lies in store in the next few pages. Let me here offer some brief assurances. First, while acknowledging the inconsistency of their track record, I think that certain aspects of philosophy (particularly epistemology) have critical daily relevance for the scientist. This assertion will (I hope) be borne out by the material to follow. Second, I don't think that philosophy has to be esoteric. It is unfortunate that their obstruse discourse has led to the assumption that many philosophers believe "incomprehensibility reflects genius"—that is, that if no one understands what you have said, you are on the road to eminence. I disagree with that maxim and hope to risk the costs of being comprehensible.

In the pages which follow I shall offer a brief and superficial survey of metatheory (theory of theories) and epistemology, concluding with some remarks on its importance for the practice of science. In condensing broad and variegated perspectives into manageable size, you should recognize that I will occasionally resort to some distortions and oversimplifications. I have defended these (to myself at least) as acceptable misdemeanors, particularly if they enable me to better communicate the relevance of these disciplines for *homo scientus*. For those of you who would like a more detailed and comprehensive discussion of the topics which follow, I would recommend perusal of Walter Weimer's two volumes.

SELECTED PROBLEMS IN THE CONVENTIONAL VIEW OF SCIENCE

In chapter 1 we discussed the storybook image of the individual *scientist*, but we have yet to come to grips with popular views of *science* as a collective enterprise. What is it that distinguishes scientific from non-scientific approaches to knowledge? What are the processes of discovery and knowledge growth? How are theories evaluated? These are just a few of the issues which have stimulated controversy among analysts of science. One of the more recent and dramatic developments has been the emergence of a consensus that traditional views of science are sorely inadequate. Prevalent theories about the nature of science have been virtually destroyed by recent thinkers, and the long popular image of science as a fact-finding, truth-yielding enterprise appears to be fading into the history books as a newly recognized myth. It is important to note that these recent insights do not threaten the *value* or *conduct* of science—they simply challenge our *understanding* of the processes of scientific inquiry. Let us take a moment here to explicate traditional views of scientific process, after which I shall offer a brief synopsis of their inadequacy.

In its barest essence, science is viewed as a search for (a) structure and (b) order. It is an attempt to describe the nature of reality both in terms of things in themselves and in terms of relationships among things. These two broad interest areas are termed *ontology* (theories about the essence or structure of reality) and *cosmology* (theories of causal influence). In its endless quest for more adequate descriptions of reality, science endorses an *epistemology* (theory of knowledge) which is called empiricism. This epistemology is allegedly distinguished from several others (e.g., rationalism, mysticism, etc.) by the fact that it makes sense experience the ultimate source of knowledge. For the empiricist, all genuine knowledge must derive from or ultimately relate to sense data.

According to the folklore of elementary textbooks, the scientist goes about his business in a rather straightforward, common sensical manner. First, he collects data. This is accomplished via sophisticated observational skills which allow the scientist to detect and record the most minute detail. As the data begin to accumulate, the scientist looks for orderly patterns—correlated events. These are the keys to functional laws. At some point in time, an hypothesis (or theory) begins to form and the scientist makes the leap from his data to a speculative assertion about reality. The assertion then becomes the focus of intense and critical scrutiny via crucial experiments. The results of these experiments determine the fate of the scientist's hypothesis. If the data support the hypothesis, it is said to be confirmed or proven. If they contradict it, the hypothesis is considered refuted or disproven.

While there have been several variations to the above caricature, it is undoubtedly one which is very widely preached to science students. Observe, hypothesize, experiment: this is the catechism of science.

Students have been led to believe that this is how science has always been done and, indeed, how it *should* be done. Thus, as argued by Weimer, the average contemporary scientist probably believes that:

1. scientific knowledge is grounded in empirical facts which are known for certain;
2. theories are derived from (and therefore secondary to) these facts;
3. science progresses via the gradual accumulation of facts;
4. since facts form the foundation of our knowledge, they are independent of theory and fixed in their meaning;
5. theories (or hypotheses) are logically derived via the rational process of induction; and
6. theories (or hypotheses) are retained or rejected solely on the basis of their ability to survive experimental tests.

According to contemporary philosophers of science, *each of the above assertions can be shown to be false!* Demonstrations of their inadequacy have centered around several key features of the conventional view. What I shall present here are the more fundamental issues, and I again defer to the writings of Weimer for a more extensive explication.

    1. The Demarcation Problem. What is it that distinguishes science from non-science? This may seem like a disarmingly simple question, but its answer has remained perplexingly elusive. Attempts to set science apart from other approaches to knowledge have been numerous . . . and unanimously unsuccessful. Two of the most recent and popular efforts have taken the forms of *logical positivism* and *falsificationism*. Both of these perspectives used a definitional criterion to demarcate scientific from nonscientific problems. The logical positivists adopted the criterion of "meaningfulness" and argued that a statement was scientifically meaningful if (and only if) it were potentially verifiable. Verifiability thereby became the touchstone of meaningfulness. Truly scientific problems (or hypotheses) were those for which one could specify the data by which they could be proven true. This obviously implies that the core activity of science should be the verification of hypotheses.

    The principle of verifiability had hardly been pronounced before its inadequacies were recognized. It is to their credit that many of the positivists were themselves the first to recognize these problems. Briefly, it is easy to show that many ostensibly "meaningful" scientific statements are not technically verifiable. For example, consider universal propositions of the form "All Xs are Ys." Since it would be impossible to ever exhaust an infinite set of observations, these propositions are unverifiable. Thus, to assert that "all plants contain carbon" is hypothetically meaningless since one could never test *all* plants (past, present, and future). The same is true for historical hypotheses and what philosophers call "counterfactual conditional assertions" (e.g., "if the earth were square, it would rotate slower"). In both of these instances one cannot feasibly hope to bring the hypothesis to an unequivocal test. Another problem lay in the fact that logical positivism was—by its own criterion—meaningless. That is, it could not defend (verify) its claim that verification should be paramount.

Recognizing these inadequacies, Karl Popper proposed the alternative of "testability" to demarcate science from pseudo-scientific endeavors. For Popper, the essence of testability is the potential for falsification. He proposed that a statement is scientific to the extent that it is testable, and an hypothesis is testable if it is capable of being falsified (at least in principle). This involves a considerable shift from positivism. The principle of verifiability was intended to separate sense from non-sense (it was a theory of meaningfulness for statements), and the positivists simply *assumed* that science was meaningful and that its alternatives were not. Popper's falsificationist approach to testability, however, did not equate science with sense and non-science with non-sense. Testability (or falsifiability) is the essence of being scientific, but not a prerequisite for being meaningful. For Popper, a statement could not be considered scientific unless one could specify the data which could refute it. Consider the assertion, "There is a god." What are the potential events that would disprove this statement? According to falsificationism, untestable assertions were (by definition) unscientific, and it was the scientist's task to guard against them.

The logic of falsification is very different from that of verification and Popper was quick to point out that his proposal remedied the problem of universal assertions. While the principle of verifiability could not deal with such statements, the principle of falsifiability could: it takes only one disconfirming observation to refute a universal statement. Popper's endorsement of falsification was based on a number of other considerations, however, and we shall explore these in a moment. For the time being, suffice it that falsificationism succeeded in overthrowing the logic of verification, but it too failed to provide an adequate solution to the demarcation problem. As we shall see, the logic of refutation (or disconfirmation) has become acknowledged as the most powerful strategy available to the scientist. However, falsifiability does *not* distinguish science from non-science. Many ostensibly scientific statements are not falsifiable. For example, non-universal hypotheses such as "some Xs are Ys" cannot be refuted. Popper felt that these kinds of hypotheses are less central to science than are universal laws and that the latter are readily addressed by falsificationism. Philosophers of religion were quick to point out, however, that there were other hypotheses which were immune to falsification. "There is a life after death." This statement is termed *eschatological* (meaning "in the end") and is potentially verifiable but completely unfalsifiable. Other problems arose when philosophers and historians showed that many scientific theories come replete with qualifiers and implicit assumptions which effectively prevent any truly critical tests. We shall expand this point in a later section.

Perhaps the most critical flaw of falsificationism, however, was its inconsistency—it was not defensible on its own criterion. Popper's assertion that meaningful scientific hypotheses must be potentially falsifiable was, itself, unfalsifiable.

Thus, attempts to erect a single criterion for demarcation have failed miserably—even to the point of public concession by their originators. Nevertheless, the contemporary scientist goes on waving the banners of positivism and logical empiricism as if they were the undisputed champions of scientific process. Were he to take a moment to look behind him, the scientist would see that he has been long since abandoned by his philosophical comrades; they are off fighting other battles. If the scientist thinks that the beat of epistemological drums has become faint because he has moved so far ahead of philosophers, he should listen more closely . . . he may find that he has been marching to a hollow echo.

2. The Nature of Data.   A second major thorn in the side of conventional views of science has to do with the purity of its empirical data base. According to the canons of empiricism, scientific knowledge is anchored in sensory experience. The "facts" of experience are the *source* of theoretical conjectures and the ultimate *judge* of theoretical adequacy. They are the firm foundation of truth and it is their accumulation which marks "progress". Thus, the data are of crucial importance to the conduct of science. Our theories may be wrong, but "the data never lie."

This notion of data supremacy is probably as prevalent as it is naive. Since several writers have already laid this myth to rest, I shall only briefly exhume it. Perhaps our autopsy should begin with Weimer's exercise on the conceptual nature of facts: "Observe carefully and write down every fact you see." This assignment presents insurmountable problems. How does one distinguish a "fact" from a "non-fact?" If the two are indistinguishable, then the term becomes meaningless. Despite some early attempts at salvaging the purity of "raw data," even the most staunch defenders have now conceded *factual relativity*—i.e., that facts acquire their meaning only in conceptual perspective. This verdict was grudgingly accepted on the basis of several strong arguments:

1. *the untenability of naive realism* (or what Friedrich Nietzsche called the doctrine of immaculate perception); we can get no closer to reality than our own sense experience and we have no sure way of evaluating its correspondence with the real world;
2. *the demonstration of structural biases in our perceptual systems;* we are biologically wired in a manner which constrains how and what we see in the world;
3. *the demonstration of conceptual biases in perception;* the same experiential events may be seen very differently depending on one's assumptions, conjectures, and expectancies; and
4. *the admission of factual impermanence;* the allegedly immutable facts of yesteryear are often rejected and replaced by newer data.

Actually, the arguments extend far beyond these four. Recent philosophers have gone so far as to claim that scientific data always presuppose some form of conceptualization. The essence of this idea was, of course, proposed by Immanuel Kant almost two centuries ago, but it has been substantially elaborated by subsequent thinkers. In a sense, theories may be said to *generate* (rather than reflect) data. This does not imply that there are no external referents for data or that science is no more than an elaborate delusional system. It simply means that "data" require (a) a perceiver, (b) an explicit or implicit rule for what constitutes a datum, and (presumably) (c) some causal event linking the datum to the perceiver.

Even though the most ardent defenders of data supremacy have come to admit the conceptual nature of facts, few have realized the gravity of this concession. If data are relative and changeable, then one cannot reasonably claim that the empirical foundations of science are firm. The admission of factual mutability destroys the notion that science progresses by data accumulation. Data are not the firm building blocks of knowledge. In at least one sense, they are the products of theory—not its parents. In place of a firm foundation of known facts, we find that science rests upon a shifting substructure. As mentioned above, this does not mean that data are totally ephemeral constructions. We must (pragmatically) assume some crude correspondence between "the world as it really is" and our selectively constructed data. However, we are also compelled to reject the naive assumption that our scientific knowledge is securely grounded in facts. We must confess that our constructions of reality are more like the clay models of a sculptor than the steel girders of an architect.

3. **Inductive Inference and Discovery.** Recall that conventional views of science emphasize its dependence on the process of induction. The scientist is thought to be a rational processor of information whose theories and hypotheses are guided by the logic of inductive inference. Systematic observations lead to a clean and cumulative implication, and it is the task of *homo scientus* to make those observations and discover their implication.

Before exploring the problems of this viewpoint, it might be well to review the most familiar forms of inference. In Western thought, induction and deduction are considered the two primary categories of inference. Induction involves a conceptual (or conjectural) leap to a conclusion whose content exceeds the information contained in its premises. A typical inductive leap takes the familiar form of moving from specific instances to a generalization:

1. X_1 is a Y, X_2 is a Y, X_3 is a Y, . . . X_n is a Y
2. Therefore, *all* Xs are Ys.

Deduction, on the other hand, refers to inferences whose conclusions do *not* lay claim to more information than is contained in their premises. Deductive inferences merely draw out the (logical) consequences of that information. Aristotle's syllogistic reasoning (elementary class logic) is prototypic:

1. All Xs are Ys
2. All Ys are Zs
3. Therefore, all Xs are Zs

Here it is obvious that the conclusion merely restates information that is already available in the premises.

The difference between induction and deduction is solely a matter of warrant for the conclusion. In deduction the conclusion "follows from" or is a derivation from the premises. The concept of (logical) *proof* is an explication of what is involved in such derivation, and it is correct to refer to the conclusion of a valid derivation as "proven". In induction, however, the conclusion leaps beyond the premises, and is not a derivation or "proof" at all: one can never prove an inductive inference to be true. From the standpoint of logic, inductive inferences are always risky for—no matter how many instances support an inference—it can never be certified "true" in the manner of deductive inferences. This is why there is a problem in justifying induction as a valid source of knowledge, and this problem has plagued philosophers from Hume's day to the present.

Parenthetically, one should note that the familiar definitions of induction as "going from the particular to the general" and deduction as "going from the general to the particular" are not entirely accurate. Both forms of inference occasionally fit *both* of these patterns. The technical distinction between induction and deduction is not the direction of inference, but rather the warrant for the conclusion. In conventional views of science, these two forms of reasoning are thought to be coordinated. Thus, the scientist is said to employ "hypotheticodeductive" methods in which hypotheses are inductively inferred (from observations) and then deductively cultivated for testable predictions.

Now then, the problems of inductive inference have to do mainly with two related issues: (a) whether it is, in fact, the primary source of scientific hypotheses, and (b) whether it is logical. With regard to the former, most contemporary writers agree that the scientist does, indeed, operate in an inductive fashion. However, there has been recent debate about the explicitness of his reasoning. N.R. Hanson, Michael Polanyi, and Arthur Koestler have been among those who have argued that the processes of hypothesis formation are much less polished than science historians have claimed. Polanyi's concept of *tacit knowledge* has been particularly well received, and such writers as Kuhn and Weimer now grant substantial importance to pre-awareness (or unconscious) forms of thought in scientific discovery. Their speculations are consistent with many phenomenological accounts of scientific thought, and have also borne up well in recent research in cognitive psychology.

The second issue deals with the logical status of inductive inference. Despite the fact that David Hume recognized the impossibility of an "inductive logic" almost two centuries ago, many philosophers of science have continued unsuccessful salvage attempts. As we saw earlier, "logic" refers to a set of (derivation) rules which govern the legitimacy of conclusions. They allow one to judge the truth value of a proposition which has been derived from other propositions. Thus, a true premise necessitates a true conclusion and a false conclusion necessarily implies a false premise. Propositional logic is simply a calculus which dictates how and when the truth or falsity of a premise bears on the truth or falsity of a conclusion, and vice versa.

The history of attacks on induction has been long and somewhat bloody—scientists have been reluctant to part with their faith in its rationality. For the sake of brevity, I shall here offer the three most popular affronts:

1. Hume correctly argued that the process of induction makes an assumption which is clearly indefensible by logic alone (i.e., that the future will resemble the past);
2. according to Popper, Fries (in 1828) showed that logical relations apply only to propositions and that propositions can only be derived from other propositions, not from facts. Data can never *necessitate* an assertion or generalization, and without this necessary inter-relationship there can be no logical inference; and
3. to be logical, inductive inference would require (a) facts which are known to be certain and immutable, and (b) derivation rules which would dictate a necessary relationship between given facts and a specific conclusion. However, it has been shown that facts are relative and unstable, that the same set of data are frequently invoked to defend contradictory conclusions, and that necessary derivations apply only to deductive inferences.

These and other arguments have forced leading philosophers to concede the logical indefensibility of induction, but the practicing scientist has remained steadfast—sometimes invoking faith (rather than reason) as his defense. The implicit fear seems to be that if one concedes the non-logical nature of inductive inference, then one has rendered science its death blow. This, of course, is still more illogic. The fact that scientific discoveries and theoretical conjectures may be arrived at illogically (or alogically) does not (logically) entail that science is either wholly irrational or unwarranted. Unfortunately, many scientists find it frustrating (or embarrassing) to confess that we don't know how scientists generate hypotheses or that the process is not demonstrably logical. These embarrassments, however, are unnecessary and counter-productive. Research in cognitive psychology has recently begun to untangle some of the processes in hypothesis formation and, as we will see in a moment, the rationality of science can perhaps be salvaged at a later stage of the inquiry process.

There are a few less devastating problems which arise at the level of deductive predictions in science. For example, many theories (particularly in the social sciences) are so loose that their derivations could claim more paternity in psycho-logic than in formal logic. This, however, is a practical rather than inherent impediment. More critical, perhaps, is the demonstration by Kurt Gödel that no formal theoretical system can be simultaneously consistent *and* complete. Put another way, Gödel showed that any internally consistent axiomatic system must necessarily invite propositions which it can neither prove nor disprove. This complicated exercise in logic has been considered one of the greatest intellectual achievements of recent times, but its ramifications for science bear primarily on the impossibility of completeness. Given our contemporary distance from that goal, I doubt that too many scientists have lost sleep over Gödel's proof. Let us therefore move on to a more fertile source of insomnia.

4. Theory Evaluation. In the lore of how-to-do science, one reads that hypothesis testing lies at the very heart of empiricism. The scientist formulates his hypothesis, performs elaborately controlled experiments which are critical to its evaluation, and then abides by the verdict of his data. Evidence which is consistent with the hypothesis is considered supportive or confirmatory; it increases the scientist's confidence in his position. Non-supportive results weaken that confidence.

This all sounds straightforward and reasonable, but theory evaluation is perhaps the most misunderstood aspect of scientific practice. It is also the site of widespread irrationality. To demonstrate this, I must insert a brief (but hopefully painless) digression on the logic of valid inference. For those with more than a casual interest in propositional logic, I have summarized some of the basic ingredients in table 7-1.

From the rules of propositional logic, there are two valid forms of implication. These are diagrammed below. For any "if/then" proposition:

Proposition	Information	Valid Conclusion
1. If the premise (p) is true, then the conclusion (q) is true	p is true	q is true
Example: If Rex is a dog, then Rex is a mammal	Rex is a dog	Rex is a mammal
2. If the premise (p) is true, then the conclusion (q) is true	q is false	p is false
Example: If Rex is a dog, then Rex is a mammal	Rex is *not* a mammal	Rex is *not* a dog

Table 7-1. Definitions and Assumptions in Propositional Logic

1. *Definition:* A proposition is an assertion of relationship expressed in symbolic form.
2. *Law of the Excluded Middle:* A proposition is either true or false, but not both.
3. *Conjunction:* The conjunction of propositions is expressed "and"; it is true if and only if all of its constituent propositions are true.
4. *Disjunction:* The disjunction of propositions is expressed "or"; it is true if *any* of its constituent propositions are true.
5. *Negation:* The negation or denial of a proposition always has a truth value opposite to that of the proposition; in cases of double negation, the original truth value is maintained.
6. *Equivalence Relations:* An element of a proposition is said to be equivalent to itself (the *identity* relationship); a proposition is said to be *symmetrical* when its truth value is unchanged by reversing the order of its elements (i.e., p relate q = q relate p, such as in p + q = q + p); equivalent terms may be *substituted* in a proposition without changing its truth value (i.e., if r = p, then r relate q = p relate q).
7. *Implication:* A compound proposition which asserts that an antecedent condition entails (requires or necessarily implies) a consequent condition is called an implication (symbolized as $p \to q$, or "if p, then q").
8. *Truth Status of Implications:* An implication is false only if the antecedent is true and the consequent is false (i.e., $p \to$ not-q); otherwise it is true. From this, it follows that:
   (a) a true antecedent occurs *only* with a true consequent;
   (b) a false consequent *always* indicates a false antecedent;
   (c) a false antecedent has no necessary bearing on the truth value of the consequent; and
   (d) a true consequent has no necessary bearing on the truth value of the antecedent.
9. *Contradiction:* The conjunction or implication of any proposition with its own negation is false (sometimes termed *reductio ad absurdum*).
10. *Transitivity:* If the consequent of a true implication is itself the antecedent of another true implication, then it is true that the antecedent of the first necessarily entails the consequent of the second (i.e., if $p \to q$ and $q \to r$, then $p \to r$).

The first form of implication is known as *modus ponens*, or confirmatory reasoning, and second is called *modus tollens*, or disconfirmatory reasoning. According to the rules of logic (table 7-1), these are the *only* valid forms of conclusive inference. Note that they embody the crux of formal logic: a true premise must yield a true conclusion, and a false conclusion necessarily implies a false premise. Unfortunately, humans—and, as we shall soon see, scientists—are not inherently logical creatures. Their two most common errors are *affirming the consequent* (invalidly reasoning that a true consequent implies a true premise) and *denying the antecedent* (inferring that a false premise must imply a false consequent). Now then, let us look at the most typical strategy of theory evaluation in science. The scientist arrives at a theory or hypothesis (p) which predicts some

Proposition	Information	Invalid *Conclusion*
1. If the premise (p) is true, then the conclusion (q) is true	q is true	p is true
Example: If Rex is a dog, then Rex is a mammal	Rex is a mammal	Rex is a dog
2. If the premise (p) is true, then the conclusion (q) is true	p is false	q is false
Example: If Rex is a dog, then Rex is a mammal	Rex is *not* a dog	Rex is *not* a mammal

experimental or observational phenomenon (q). He (implicitly or explicitly) reasons that "if my hypothesis is true, then I will observe such-and-such." When he subsequently makes these observations, he illogically concludes that they "verify" his hypothesis. That is, *the reasoning used in theory evaluation is often the illicit form of affirming the consequent!*

Popper pointed out that valid confirmatory reasoning is of little use to the scientist, since the information therein required is the question at issue (i.e., the truth value of one's hypothesis). In order to comply with the logical rules for confirmation (*modus ponens*), the scientist would have to follow this sequence:

Proposition: "If my hypothesis is true, I will observe X."
Information: "My hypothesis is true."
Conclusion: "Therefore, I will observe X."

This is obviously a blatant case of question-begging, since the scientist cannot know that his hypothesis is true. Popper went on to recommend the use of disconfirmatory logic (*modus tollens*) as the most viable approach to scientific knowledge. In a strictly technical sense, disconfirmation is the *only* form of valid conclusive inference currently available to the scientist. This is because *successful predictions, no matter how numerous, have no necessary logical bearing on the truth status of the theory or hypothesis from which they were derived*. They may spawn *subjective* confidence in the sense that the hypothesis has repeatedly escaped disconfirmation, but—until we develop other forms of valid scientific inference—*it is only unsuccessful predictions which have conclusive logical implications*.

The logical supremacy of disconfirmation is generally conceded by contemporary philosophers of science. However, as was previewed in our earlier discussion of the demarcation problem, falsificationism has not succeeded as an adequate model of scientific practice. It is certainly not descriptive of how science is currently conducted. This is readily apparent in two well replicated phenomena:

1. virtually all scientific theories are discrepant with some set of data even at their inception so that, in a technical sense, they are born refuted; and
2. there are no truly "critical" (or crucial) tests of any theory.

This second assertion is known as *the Duhem-Quine thesis*, and it is well illustrated in the annals of science. *Any theory can be permanently saved from refutation by internal revisions and adjustments.* As will be seen in chapter 8, the Duhem-Quine thesis is not just a potential insulator against disconfirmation; it is actively practiced. Thus, it is not just the case that theories are malleable in their predictions, but also that scientists are more inclined to salvage than to reject. Both the theory and the theorist are imperfect.

We are thus left with three clear implications regarding theory evaluation: (1) it is often approached with demonstrably illogical reasoning, (2) disconfirmation appears to be our only viable means for valid scientific inference, and (3) disconfirmation is limited in its scope and fails to depict actual patterns of scientific conduct.

COMPREHENSIVELY CRITICAL RATIONALISM

As if the above considerations were not enough to destroy any lingering complacency about the rationality of science, a recent treatise has effected what appears to be a convincing demolition of the most fundamental substructure of scientific rationality. In a still neglected book titled *The Retreat to Commitment*, William Warren Bartley III took a long and revealing look at the logical defensibility of all rationalistic (reason-embracing) approaches to knowledge. Using what he calls the *"tu quoque* argument" (i.e., "how do you know?"), Bartley shows that all traditional approaches to knowledge are inherently irrational! The *tu quoque* argument may be introduced by considering the authoritarian structure of traditional epistemology. Our conventional approaches to knowledge have always invoked some form of ultimate epistemological authority—sense data, logic, revelation, or whatever. However, the authority of *this* authority is always taken on faith. That is, as one pushes the proponents of one or another rational authority into a corner with successive requests for proof, each must ultimately "make a dogmatic irrational commitment" to their *faith* in the authority. They cannot invoke the authority in its own defense without begging the question at issue.

This inevitable leap of faith (or "retreat to commitment") is an element in all forms of what Bartley calls *justificational* philosophies, theories of knowledge which claim or presume justification or certification of their legitimacy. Although these philosophies include the major religious perspectives, we shall restrict our attention ·here to *rationalism*, the form endorsed by conventional science. In its most comprehensive form, rationalism (a) accepts any proposition which can be defended (justified) by appeal to logic, data, or related rational criteria, and (b) it accepts *only* those propositions which can be so justified. Bartley points out, however, that these two criteria are contradictory. That is, if we concur with the second—that one should only accept rationally justified assertions—then we must reject both, because the authority of rational criteria cannot be justified. Indeed, any attempts to make rationality rational are instances of question-begging (and therefore irrational): "A man cannot, without arguing in a circle, justify the rationality of his standard by appealing to that standard."

The *tu quoque* argument begins by acknowledging the failure of comprehensive rationalism. It may be summarized in these three propositions:

1. because of the logic of the situation (i.e., the infinite regress of standards requiring justification), rationality is limited; everyone must sooner or later make a dogmatic commitment;
2. therefore one may make any commitment one desires;
3. therefore no one can criticize anyone else's commitment, nor can anyone be criticized for making a commitment.

Within the confines of authoritarian epistemology, which identifies knowledge with proof and authority, one can never know that a claim is genuine knowledge. Traditional approaches to rationality (everywhere, not just in science) are thus bankrupt. Even the more recent attempts to salvage a reduced form of rationalism (via "relative truth" and "probabilified knowledge") have been unsuccessful because of the *tu quoque* argument. With a straightforward simplicity that is rare in philosophers, Bartley appears to have slain the Goliath of traditional rationalism in all its myriad forms.

Does this mean that we are necessarily doomed to irrationalism? Not according to Bartley. He argues that the inherent irrationality of traditional rationalism stems from its pretense to justifiability, and that one can resolve the above problems by basing one's rationality on criticism rather than justification. This perspective, which he calls *comprehensively critical rationalism*, is an elegantly presented non-justificational approach. Instead of presuming or attempting to justify its own rationality, comprehensively critical rationalism (let's call it CCR) always doubts it. Thus, from the CCR perspective, a truly rational rationalist is one:

> who holds *all* his beliefs, including his most fundamental standards and his basic philosophical position itself, open to criticism; one who never cuts off an argument by resorting to faith or irrational commitment to justify some belief that has been under severe critical fire (p. 146).

What Bartley proposes is, of course, a staggering paradigm shift which bears far-reaching implications for scientific postures. In fact, you (the reader) may now be doing a conceptual double-take—rereading the above paragraphs and experiencing a mixture of confusion, skepticism, and curiosity at the perspective Bartley has offered. Let us explore it a bit further.

While Bartley credits Popper with having first waved the non-justificational banner of criticism as the best foundation for rationality, CCR goes well beyond Popperian falsificationism in several respects. Since these differences would require more elaboration than is warranted here, I shall forego their enumeration. Suffice it to say that CCR encompasses testability (or at least its essence of criticism) and then addresses itself to issues much broader than the criteria for meaningfulness and the nature of hypothesis testing.[a]

In an admirable exercise of self-scrutiny, Bartley applied the criteria of CCR to itself. Is the contention that "all one's beliefs should be open to criticism" itself open to criticism? The answer, surprisingly, is affirmative. Bartley has apparently proposed the first epistemological perspective which is truly rational in the sense of not being contradicted by its own contentions! He goes on to show that the comprehensively critical rationalist—since he is not "committed" to any authority (including the authority of criticism)—should (theoretically) argue himself (or be argued) out of CCR. This observation, which is logically consistent with the model, is an intriguing (or as one colleague has said, "mind-fucking") corollary. Recalling the *tu quoque* ("how do you know") argument, Bartley shows that it is inappropriate to the CCR position. To ask for proof or justification

---

[a]In his more recent writings Popper has recognized some of the problems in his earlier philosophies. He has proposed two non-justificational alternatives—*critical fallibilism* and *neutral epistemology*—which are summarized and critiqued by Weimer.

as a "defense" of CCR is to presuppose a justificational perspective—which is, of course, the fallen competitor here. Indeed, Bartley argues that the *tu quoque* is what makes justificational approaches irrational. By claiming absolute defensibility, these perspectives automatically invite their own destruction. They must—by their own criteria—address the *tu quoque* and since they cannot defeat it, each is forced to ultimately retreat to an irrational commitment. CCR, on the other hand, does not claim to be indubitably rational and thereby avoids the *tu quoque* entirely. If someone asks, "How do you *know* that CCR is rational?", Bartley's answer is "I don't know for certain—but then I never claimed that it could be proven." The *tu quoque* presupposes justificationism, but for the comprehensively critical rationalist, the perpetual openness to criticisms of his rationality "is explicitly *part* of his rationalism." For Bartley, "The rationality of a belief will be relative to its success in weathering criticism." Thus, the goal of CCR is not to *defend* beliefs in the sense of proving them true (as in justificationism), but to *offend* (attack) them, retaining (at least tentatively) only those which survive the onslaught. The strategy is not to produce guaranteed truths, but to reduce errors.[b]

Bartley goes on to catalog four methods of reducing error via criticism—(1) logic, (2) sense observations, (3) conflict with well-tested scientific hypotheses and (4) problem-solving adequacy. Each critical method is, of course, open to criticism on its legitimacy, and none is infallible. On the issue of logic, however, Bartley points out that the potential for "revisability" is limited. One can suggest alternative rules of logic only so long as they comply with *modus ponens* and *modus tollens* (i.e., that true premises always yield true conclusions and that false conclusions always indicate false premises). This is not because CCR is "committed" to these logical forms (which it is not), but because these forms are *presupposed* in critical argument. Thus, although logic is not immune to criticism, its rejection brings argumentative suicide:

> The point is that the practice of critical argument and logic are bound together. We can reject logic, but to do so is to reject the practice of argument (p. 171).

[b]Bartley aptly notes that, in the past, the concept of "criticism" has been illegitimately fused with that of justification. Thus, many philosophers have endorsed the use of *tu quoque* as if it were critical. Asking for "proof" is not, according to Bartley, true or "comprehensive" criticism since it presupposes a justificational approach. Likewise, one cannot escape the rationalism dilemma by confessing to a first leap of irrational commitment and then saying, "But after that leap, the system makes sense." A leap of faith is a leap of faith; once it is executed, the "leaper" has no logical grounds to criticize anyone else's leaps and the door is opened for unlimited irrationality.

Like falsificationism, CCR recognizes the logical power of disconfirmation. Indeed, one could crudely assert that Bartley has taken Popper's criterion of criticism and comprehensively applied it to itself. It is, I think, ironic that in my several public presentations of these issues, critics of CCR have been unable to divest themselves from their justificational heritage. They have often been aggravated by the glaring simplicity of Bartley's argument, and they quickly demand "reasons" that *prove* the superiority of CCR. In so doing, of course, they are invoking the *tu quoque* and this is exactly the question at issue. A criterion of knowledge (or source of authority) cannot be invoked in its own defense without begging the question. The dilemma is analogous to one in which one patently accepts the verbal testimony of a person who has been accused of dishonesty. CCR avoids the dilemma by making no claim to absolute (proven or demonstrable) rationality. Indeed, the revised form of rationality toward which CCR aspires is intentionally tenuous—it invites its own criticism. By saying that no theory of knowledge (including the present) is unequivocally "good" (true, defensible, perfect), CCR emerges as a refreshing epistemological alternative. While denying the attainability of indubitable truths, it simultaneously retains its own internal consistency.

Despite its unique epistemological strengths and salient implications for the conduct of science, CCR has remained a relatively obscure viewpoint. This is doubly unfortunate in that scientists have been unable to explore its practical value and, at the same time, CCR has been denied the critical scrutiny which it welcomes. Until CCR has been translated into "programs of action" for the practicing scientist, we will not be able to evaluate its ramifications for research.[c] Likewise, until it is subjected to more critical philosophical analysis, its epistemological status must be tentatively regarded as singularly adequate—by far the leading contender.

PSYCHOLOGICAL FALLIBILISM

In a comprehensive survey of metatheories and epistemology, Walter B. Weimer presents a much more detailed discussion of the problems of

[c]It should be noted that Bartley does not view CCR as prohibitive of practical action. It does not force the scientist into complete skeptical immobility. Rather, one can *rationally* adopt and act upon hypotheses, theories, and paradigms. These beliefs and actions only become irrational when the scientist becomes "committed" to them in the sense of conceptual closure and behavior patterns which are geared toward justifying (confirming) rather than criticizing (disconfirming) his beliefs.

justificationism—as well as their recognition and apparent resolution via the non-justificational theories of Popper and Bartley. As I indicated in the foreword, I am personally indebted to Weimer and Norman J. Lesswing for calling my attention to some of these issues and developments. In addition to his valuable review and evaluation of varying philosophical perspectives, Weimer integrates several of his own ideas with those of Thomas Kuhn regarding the processes of scientific revolutions. For example, he reiterates the untenability of the popular belief that science grows by "accretion"—the sequential accumulation of more and more "facts." This, as we saw earlier, is challenged by the phenomenon of *factual relativism* (i.e., that facts change with paradigms; they are not immutable pieces of truth). Similarly, Weimer concurs with Kuhn that "theories are not evaluated in isolation against neutral facts," but rather are evaluated against competing theories. Science grows not by confirmation or refutation via data, but by the successive confrontations of competing viewpoints. While endorsing the promise of the comprehensively critical approach (CCR) in our search for truth, Weimer rejects Popper's assertion that we can either assume or evaluate science's successive approximations to that goal. He claims, on the contrary, that we will (and can) never know if we are "getting close." Finally, extending some of the views of Thomas Kuhn, Weimer offers the doctrine of *psychological fallibilism* which contends that "psychology is indispensable for epistemology." In contrast to Popper and others who view scientific revolutions as totally explicable by philosophical analyses, Weimer claims that "the growth of science is ultimately a matter for the psychological sciences to explain." The acceptance and rejection of various theories and paradigms are, according to this perspective, problems which are best understood in terms of socio-psychological processes. This point is elaborated by Lesswing, who cogently argues that the method of "conversion" in science is primarily one of rhetoric, not logic. Formal criteria for theory evaluation are said to function more as camouflage for the underlying sources of scientific revolution—namely, argumentation. Thus, we again encounter the notion that science grows via ulterior processes— the personal competition among scientists (Mitroff) and the quest for consensus via persuasive communication (Ziman). While data may be an element in the arguments, it is the arguments themselves which are the instruments of conversion. Scientists face arguments (in print or in person) much more often than they face data. The critical issue then becomes one of psychological demeanor—what are the parameters of scientific "believing?"

SUMMARY AND CONJECTURES

Since I have condensed a large amount of material which may be new to the reader, it might be worthwhile to outline the contrast between conventional (justificational) views of science and some of the more recent (non-justificational) perspectives. Depending on the philosopher and viewpoint in question, there are points where this demarcation is less clearcut, but it may be generally simplified as follows.

Topic	Conventional View	Recent Revision
1. Nature of Knowledge	true (provable) assertion	warranted (fallible) conjecture
a. ultimate authority	logic (reason) and sense experience (data)	no *ultimate* authority
b. nature of data	certain, immutable facts	factual relativism
c. role of theory	secondary to data	prerequisite for data
2. Nature of Progress	accumulation of facts	reconstruction of "facts"
a. discovery	logical (by induction)	psychological (by induction)
b. theory evaluation	instant rational assessment of one theory at a time (via reason and data)	simultaneous competition among theories (via data, rhetoric, conceptual elegance, politics, etc.)
3. Science Practice	monolithic enactment of a logical script; totally explicable by philosophy	poorly understood complex of conjecture, tacit knowledge, and personal belief; only explicable if psychosocial influences are acknowledged

Some of the practical implications of these recent revisions merit at least brief mention. For example, it should now be obvious that popular publication practices and the reverent use of inferential statistics need to be reappraised from a logical perspective. Weimer has cogently argued that *all* contemporary inferential statistics are inherently justificational (and therefore irrational) in the sense that they are employed to defend a knowledge claim (by assigning either a dichotomous or a probabilistic truth status to an hypothesis). If they are to be used rationally, statistics may be descriptive but they may not assume the role of ultimate authorities for decision-making purposes. There is a double irony in the current popularity of Fisherian null hypothesis testing in that the insult of its irrationality is added to the injury of its prejudicial endorsement of confirmatory publications. The costs of that practice are, unfortunately, all too apparent in the social sciences.[d]

After reading this chapter, you may well be wondering how it is that science has made *any* progress what with the pervasive irrationality of its inductive research programs. I would argue that the indisputable progress made by science is attributable *not* to the justificational illogic of its practitioners, but rather to the fact that nature has forced the scientist to face anomalies (disconfirmations). One wonders how much more rapid our progress would have been had the scientist been consciously looking for (rather than avoiding) these events. Likewise, it is important to bear in mind that most of the problems addressed in this chapter deal with our inadequate *understanding* of how science works, not *whether* it works.

A second implication of this chapter bears on the revolutionary tenets of CCR. As I have already noted, its practical implications have yet to be outlined by its adherents. Essentially, the gist of CCR would appear to be that our "best bet" (albeit not a *sure* one) for a "rational" epistemology is one which grounds itself in criticism rather than justificationism. Such an epistemology is, at least, self-consistent. In this respect CCR picks up where falsificationism fell down. When it was first proposed, falsificationism was a justificational model in that it claimed its own rationality. Bartley's message is clear: (1) we cannot claim to be *certain* of our rationality without being self-contradictory, and (2) we can salvage a tentative form of ratiionality only if we base it in criticism.

On first reading, some of you may have interpreted Bartley's comments as being fatally destructive of science; that he leaves us with nothing but ruins and the embarrassed realization that we have perpetrated unreason for several centuries. But CCR is not simply destructive; it does offer an alternative (and one which is unique in its self-consistency). The scientist who adopts a CCR perspective need not abandon all of his beliefs, terminate his research, and reject any

---

[d]Some of you may be pondering whether null hypothesis testing does not fulfill the criteria for disconfirmation. After all, the null hypothesis supposedly predicts observations which are contrary to those expected by the experimental hypothesis. Although Fisher did found NHT on disconfirmatory logic, he made the mistake of defining the null hypothesis by denying the antecedent. That is, he illogically reasoned that—if the experimental hypothesis predicts a difference —then the null hypothesis should predict no difference. As outlined in our earlier discussion of logic, not-p does not logically imply not-q. This same logical error is made in other assumptions in NHT. For example, the law of equally probable events (based on the "principle of insufficient reason") can be shown to be an instance of denying the antecedent. These illogical elements are exacerbated by the fact that NHT is a justificational procedure.

references to authority. According to Bartley, the critically rational scientist can (and—if he aspires to conduct inquiry—*must*) accept theories, test hypotheses and hold convictions. The crux of his "new" stance, however, is a tentativity and skepticism which pervade all of these undertakings. He must never retreat to a leap of faith in order to end an argument (or to calm his own doubts). In a sense, the CCR adherent must force himself to perform "unnatural" acts—to perpetually scrutinize his hypotheses, his theories and even his epistemology (CCR). He must fight the complacency of conceptual slumber by intentionally reawakening himself with whispers of skepticism. In his most fundamental assumptions, he must walk a tightrope of conviction—granting them enough credibility to enable him to act upon (and thereby assess) them without making that leap of faith which would immunize them to subsequent criticism.

CCR is not an immobilizing philosophy. It does not sterilize scientific inquiry, nor does it invite a sedentary nihilism. Skepticism need not be passive. Indeed, after sweeping away the ruins of justificationist rationality, it may be seen that CCR has left us with many proscriptions which are certainly not foreign to previous illusions of science. Skepticism, tentativity and organized programs of criticism—are these such "radical" endorsements? The merits of CCR lie not only in its provision of a self-consistent epistemology, but also in the possibility that it may actually encourage the *practice* (rather than simply the *preaching*) of these pursuits.

Related to this promise is the final implication raised by this chapter—that changes in the practice of science presume an understanding of both the scientist and his institutions. As Kuhn and Weimer have argued, the processes of scientific "knowing" are the processes of human knowing. Up until now, we have left the analysis of scientists to philosophers and historians. Recognizing the essential role of cultural influences in science, sociologists have now begun to devote their technical skills to the problem of scientific knowledge. Need I reiterate that the psychologist is long overdue in following suit? Since this point is at the core of my appeal for a "psychology of science," I shall briefly sketch its emergence from the themes of this chapter.

Among other things, science may be said to be a search for order—an attempt to condense the flux of our sense experience into symbolic rules. The enterprise is a complicated one in that it strives to develop a détente between two very foreign realms—one of perpetual experience and the other of semantic propositions. Like a harried ambassador, the scientist is continually negotiating between the two—recognizing that each has its own idiosyncrasies, its own "language" and its own demands. There are unquestionable problems of translation and inevitable points of difficulty. The semantic (theoretical) realm sets up its artificial rules of self-consistency, logical inference, and so on, while its perceptual neighbor imposes its own non-semantical demands. To add to the dilemma, the scientist is not only caught between the two realms but is also a partial prisoner of each. One of the implications of CCR and psychological fallibilism is that the détente will always be a tenuous one, and that we can never know how "good" our theory-reality relationship is.

In his search for order, the scientist resorts to two general strategies: (1) naturalistic observation, and (2) experimentation. For both of these strategies he must *categorize* (divide) his perceptual experiences so that he can then look for correlations among the categories ("factors," "variables," etc.). Naturalistic observation is used most extensively in those sciences which have fewer options in terms of manipulating (systematically altering) the status of one of the variables. In astronomy, for example, the researcher has little hope of being able to alter planetary orbits so that he must settle for summary descriptions of "naturally" occurring correlations. Experimentation is a more ambitious undertaking in the sense that the scientist actively intrudes upon nature by making systematic changes in one variable and looking at correlated changes in other variables. The manipulated factor is usually viewed as the "cause" (or "independent variable") and those factors which show consistent covariations are deemed "effects" (or "dependent variables"). The essential strategy of experimentation, then, is to look for changes in one variable which consistently follow changes in the other. Unfortunately (for the scientist, at least), *all* variables seem to display an inherent variability (which may be due to unexamined influences, measurement errors or intrinsic degrees of indeterminism). Thus, nature is noisy, and the scientist's task is to decide whether changes in one variable produce (are followed by) changes in the other which are greater than those it normally displays. This, of course, was the impetus for the birth of inferential statistics—a branch of mathematics which would aid the scientist in deciding whether or not observed variations ("changes") were greater than those which might be normally expected. And it is here—in the realm of "significant differences"—that the scientist must answer to psychological (rather than logical) directives. The dilemma can be paraphrased as follows:

1. scientific theories generally make assertions about specific aspects of structure or order in reality;

2. because of logical considerations, the truth status of a scientific theory can only be addressed via disconfirmatory reasoning;
3. therefore, the crux of theory (or hypothesis) evaluation lies in the criteria for *declaring* an observation as "disconfirmatory."

The dilemma here is a very simple one: *There can NEVER be any purely logical criteria for making that decision!* All decision-making criteria invoke some form of authority and, as Bartley has shown, such appeals to an ultimate authority are demonstrably irrational.

This does not mean that we can never make any evaluative decisions in science, or that we cannot pragmatically invoke some (admittedly arbitrary) criterion to judge whether our experimental results were disconfirmatory or not. However, I am saying that the "meaning" or disconfirmatory status of any set of data can never be arbitrated by logic. *Theory evaluation (and knowledge growth) are psychological (not logical) phenomena and, moreover, they must remain so.* This conclusion is an obviously staggering one, particularly when it follows on the heels of our earlier discussion. The practicing scientist must (a) reject the popular practice of quasi-confirmatory theory evaluation, (b) accept the sole supremacy of disconfirmatory logic in those few areas where it is applicable, (c) entertain the unsettling perpetual paranoia demanded by CCR, and—now—(d) accept the inescapability that his data evaluations can never be made on truly logical grounds.

While it may be discomforting, I do not think that the inevitable subjectivity of science need have a paralyzing effect. While we cannot hope to salvage its rationality by discovering some elusive logical decision rule, we can at least aspire to a better understanding of the "psycho-logic" on which it rests. What are the subjective criteria for a "significant difference?" How do these vary with such factors as the current state of the paradigm (normal science versus crisis), the content of the hypothesis, and the individual psychological make-up of the scientist? What factors account for the different beliefs of scientists who are confronted with the same data and, more important, the same arguments?

My brief survey has not even touched on some of the better known philosophical embarrassments of science (e.g., the assumptions of determinism and causality or the ideologies of operationism and parsimony). But perhaps I have said enough already. Hopefully, it is now more apparent that epistemology *does* have something very relevant to say to the practicing scientist. The fact that most contemporary researchers are inductive justificationists should, at this point, stimulate some perplexity in those of you who survived this chapter. Out of tradition, complacency, ignorance, momentum or whatever—the vast majority of scientists today accept, practice, and preach an approach to knowledge which is demonstrably irrational. As Paul Meehl has put it,

> Meanwhile our eager-beaver researcher, undismayed by logic of science considerations . . . has produced a long publication list and been promoted to full professorship. In terms of his contribution to the enduring body of . . . knowledge, he has done hardly anything. His true position is that of a potent-but-sterile intellectual rake, who leaves in his merry path a long train of ravished maidens but no viable scientific offspring (p. 114).

It is my hope that the need for Meehl's pessimism will be falsified by future generations of *homo scientus*.

REFERENCES

14, 15, 16, 18, 19, 25, 31, 32, 33, 34, 42, 45, 61, 62, 70, 71, 82, 83, 130, 136, 137, 159, 175, 176, 199, 219, 224, 234, 245, 249, 250, 252, 262, 263, 298, 316, 323, 344, 348, 350, 352, 354, 355, 356, 396, 398, 421, 437, 447, 448, 466, 467, 468, 469, 478, 480, 481, 492.

It is the peculiar and perpetual error of the human intellect to be more moved and excited by affirmatives than by negatives.

Francis Bacon

Men who have excessive faith in their theories are not only ill prepared for making discoveries; they also make very poor observations.

Claude Bernard

People don't usually do research the way people who write books about research say that people do research.

Arthur J. Bachrach

Omissions, no less than commissions, are often times branches of injustice.

Antoninus

The great tragedy of science is the slaying of a beautiful hypothesis by an ugly fact.

Thomas H. Huxley

All theories are born refuted: none will agree with all the facts that are potentially available. Granting that all theories are "lies," some are "blacker" than others, and our problem is to pick, and to attempt to improve, the least black lie from the alternatives available.

Walter B. Weimer

We (men of science) like to be thought devotees of truth uninfluenced by prejudice, as open-minded and serene students of nature, free from presuppositions and welcoming every fact that comes within our ken. Yet ... history has testified against us. ... In the past we see the supporters of new doctrines, the detectors of unwelcome facts ... snuffed out or else browbeaten and ridiculed by the High Priests of Science.

Oliver Lodge

Chapter 8

Reason and Research: The
Truth Conspiracy

Recall that the storybook image of the scientist portrays
him as a paragon of reason. In addition to his superior
intelligence, he purportedly evidences impressive problem
solving skills and a rigorous fidelity to logic. His conclusions are drawn
only when the data so warrant—otherwise he suspends judgment—and
the conclusions he draws are conservative and logical. Likewise, we
are told that *homo scientus* is an accurate data collector who pains-
takingly insures that his observations are objective.

By now, you should be suspecting what I may have to say. Nevertheless, I shall say it. Let us divide our discussion into two broad and
overlapping categories. First, I shall address the critical reasoning
skills of the scientist in both the conduct and interpretation of research. This will also include *which* data are considered relevant for
inquiry. Later, we will survey the issue of data collection and the
scientist's precision as an instrument of observation.

THE CRITICAL REASONING SKILLS
OF THE SCIENTIST

We need not here repeat what was strongly suggested in chapter 7—
that a large percentage of contemporary scientists engage in conventional research methods which are blatantly illogical. But, you
might say, perhaps this is because of our institutions and traditions.
Graduate education and journal publication policies may force the
scientist into justificational endeavors. While I would concede these
influences, understanding the sources of unreason does not thereby

defend its continuation. More to the point, if *homo scientus* were in fact such a logical grand master, he would have long ago recognized the irrationality of many conventional practices. Those who *did* recognize it but failed to adjust their research accordingly are even more culpable (on their own rationality standard).

My point here is that the prevalence of irrationality in contemporary science is attributable not only to institutional (social) processes, but also to the logical fallibilities of individual scientists. On what do I base that assertion? Unfortunately, there has been precious little research on the rationality and problem solving skills of *homo scientus*. It has apparently been assumed that the average scientist is logically skillful—after all, he has to be, doesn't he? Historians of science often laud the reasoning abilities of great scientists, frequently neglecting the multitude of discoveries which have derived from "wrong" reasons and chance occurrences. Indeed, I think one could make a strong case for the argument that serendipity has been a close competitor to logic in rendering scientific innovations (see R. Taton).

Given that many graduate apprenticeships in science fail to include training in logic, it is even more surprising that we so confidently presume superior reasoning skills in the scientist. Is logic an inborn attribute or one which was acquired prior to graduate school? Have we assumed that intelligence and logic are equivalent?

To partially redress our neglect of the scientist's critical reasoning skills, my colleagues and I have conducted several studies in this area (see appendix). In the survey study with Terry Kimper, 77 physicists, biologists, sociologists, and psychologists were asked to rate the validity of four forms of implication. Although most of these scientists recognized the validity of *modus ponens*, over half of them failed to appreciate the validity of *modus tollens* (disconfirmation)! Twenty-eight percent of the social scientists thought that denying the antecedent was logically valid and ten percent thought likewise of affirming the consequent. To further test their reasoning ability, we included an analog task patterned after one employed by Peter Wason. Scientists were asked which of four simple experiments were either crucial or irrelevant to an hypothesis. Fewer than eight percent were able to identify the logically irrelevant experiments and fewer than ten percent were able to specify the only two experiments which had the critical potential of falsification.

In another study with Bob DeMonbreun, the critical reasoning skills of psychologists and physical scientists were compared to those of relatively uneducated Protestant ministers. Our task was again borrowed from Peter Wason, primarily because of its direct assessment of logical abilities. In a series of ingenious studies Wason and his colleagues have shown that many individuals seem to prefer confirmatory rather than disconfirmatory reasoning. As we have already seen, this pattern is a logically dangerous one in science, since confirmation here is always a disguised form of affirming the consequent. The task employed was as follows. Subjects were given a triad of numbers (2, 4, 6) and told that these numbers conformed to a simple mathematical rule. Their task was to discover this rule by generating (testing) other triads of numbers and then deducing the rule. Each time they announced an experimental triad, they were told whether it conformed to the rule. Subjects were told to announce their hypothesis about the rule only when they were very confident of its correctness.

If you are like most subjects (both scientist and non-scientist), our reasoning would probably go somewhat as follows.

Let's see, now—2, 4, 6. Maybe it is increasing by 2s. I'll try a test—does 8, 10, 12 conform? (Experimenter says "yes"). Good, how about 14, 16, 18? (Experimenter says "yes"). Fine, then the rule is "numbers increasing by 2s." (Experimenter says "no").

No? Huh, let's see—2, 4, 6. Well, the second number (4) is twice as large the first, and the third (6) is three times as large. Maybe that's it. Does 10, 20, 30 conform? (Experimenter says "yes"). How about 7, 14, 21? (Experimenter says "yes"). Good, then the rule is "multiply the first number by two to get the second and by three to get the third." (Experimenter says "no").

The above strategy was not uncommon. Incidentally, the correct rule was "any three numbers in increasing order of magnitude." However, notice that this rule would have been difficult to discover if one only employed confirmatory logic. Because the true rule subsumed most of the sub-rules suspected by subjects, their experiments were predominantly confirmatory and very misleading. A single falsifying test (e.g., "2, 8, 12") would have eliminated the "increasing by 2s" hypothesis, and another (e.g., "6, 5, 1") would have suggested that the critical factor was direction of change rather than specific ratios.

How did our subjects fare? In a word, poorly. Most of them did not solve the problem. Of those who did, only two were errorless—both were ministers. Consistent with the argument that disconfirmation is a more efficient reasoning strategy, those subjects who used falsifying experiments were substantially more successful. Unfortunately, as with Wason's undergraduate subjects, neither our scientists nor the nonscientists were very prone to using disconfirmation. Over 85 percent of their self-generated experiments were confirmatory.

Up until this point, it appears that our scientist subjects cannot be differentiated from the non-scientists on the basis of logic. Both were equally poor. But apparent differences did emerge on several other measures of reasoning and conservativeness. Contrary to the story-book image, scientists showed a tendency to be more speculative than non-scientists—generating more hypotheses, more quickly, and with fewer experiments per hypothesis! Likewise, they were apparently more tenacious, as reflected by their differential tendency to return to already falsified hypotheses. The data from this study are summarized below.

Variable	Psychologists (n = 15)	Physical Scientists (n = 15)	Ministers (n = 15)
1. Announced correct hypothesis.	47%	27%	40%
2. Disconfirmed (at least once)	40%	40%	33%
3. Disconfirmatory trials	9%	12%	19%
4. Hypotheses generated ($\bar{x}$)	3.07	3.33	2.00
5. Experiments generated ($\bar{x}$)	7.53	7.60	8.33
6. Experiments per hypothesis	3.03	2.01	6.22
7. Experiments before first hypothesis	1.93	1.07	5.40
8. Latency (seconds) to first hypothesis	35.4	37.7	132.9
9. Returned to previously falsified hypothesis	93%	93%	53%

But this, of course, is only one study, and it has its share of limitations. Are its implications falsified by other existing data? Let us take a brief scan.

I have already mentioned the prevalence of *hypothophilia* in the context of the priority race and the rush to publication. It should be noted, however, that this quick-fire penchant is probably not characteristic of all scientists. In fact, it may lie at one end of a continuum, the other end of which could be termed *speculophobia*. (Notice how a technical term connotes legitimation.) The speculophobic is a scientist who shows profuse sweating at the hint of any ventures beyond the data. He is the personification of the hard-nosed empiricist, conscientiously churning out data and ever-faithful that they will fall into neat principles on their own. The relative merits of hypothophilia and speculophobia present an interesting controversy regarding the role of data in scientific advancement and the necessity of some form of theory as a prerequisite to all data collection. The history of science strongly suggests that data play a secondary (but not unimportant) role in revolutions. While they may be facilitating, anomalous data are neither necessary nor sufficient for the rejection of theories. In fact, much of the evidence which has been given credit for launching or stimulating revolutions was collected only *after* a theory had been proposed. There are numerous instances where data were not considered valid until after they had been "explained" by a later paradigm. Consider evidence suggesting a relationship between activities on the surface of the sun and weather changes in the midwestern United States. These data were generally discredited as artifactual until some very recent speculations on the interaction of electromagnetic fields made them more credible. The data haven't changed, but now that someone has offered a mechanism to explain them, they are suddenly retrieved from banishment. In one sense at least, in the absence of an explanation the data are not really data. This is repeatedly illustrated in resistance to discoveries. The positron data were discredited or ignored for almost a decade, and veritable mounds of evidence in astronomy were in existence for years before being accepted. The scientist does not welcome data *qua* data. They become acceptable only when they are shown to make (theoretical) sense. Thus, evidence of gravitational anomalies, magnetic pole reversals, and strange distributions of animal and plant life—these were de-emphasized until the very recent revolution in geoscience. After half a century of resistance, Alfred Wegener's speculations on "continental drift" are "making sense" of these observations. *Now* it seems obvious to everyone that the earth's continents are resting on constantly moving subterranean plates, that much of the eastern United States was originally part of Africa and Europe, that the earth's magnetic poles have switched their direction every million years, and so on. We might here speculate on other suspect data which would be "legitimated" by an acceptable theory. For example, what would happen if someone were to discover electrical activities in the human brain which approximated radio wave forms? Would ESP then be so alien to science?

Another observation has been that scientists are often relatively tenacious in clinging to beliefs which are blatantly contradicted by data. Why did Copernicus stubbornly maintain his theory when the available evidence was quite contrary? Why was Kelvin so dogmatically closed to the discovery of X rays and the electronic composition of the atom? Edwin G. Boring has commented on this tenacity as a reflection of "egoism":

> A theory which has built up its author's image of himself has become part of him. To abandon it would be suicidal, or at least an act of self-mutilation (p. 682).

It is noteworthy that Mitroff found that differences in tenacity among scientists may be related to their position on the hyptho-philia/speculophobia continuum. His most theoretical subjects were more tenacious than the experimentalists. Interestingly, they were also the most eminent of his sample. In fact, one of the more consistent findings across studies has been the valuation and respect held for theoreticians. The truth spinners are considered the most important of the species *homo scientus.* They are the pioneers and trail blazers in our infinite frontier of knowledge. The task of cultivation is left to the settlers—the experimentalists. And yet, we are told, it is the truth spinner who is most resistant to change. He does not like to be told that he has blazed the wrong path.[a]

Mitroff points out that some degree of theoretical commitment is necessary for the conduct of science. This is conceded by several other workers, although the importance of Kuhn's "normal" (committed) science remains an issue of controversy. To avoid complete, immobilizing skepticism, the scientist must act upon some convictions—even in the comprehensively critical systems forwarded by Bartley and Weimer. The question seems to be one of degree. Can the scientist maintain that delicate and sometimes uncomfortable balance between irrational commitment (the endless defensive retreat) and the impotence of being opinionless? A tentative conviction would seem optimal—one which enables and encourages the conduct of research without simultaneously demanding an irreversible leap of faith. Judging from the annals of science, this feat of conceptual balance has been rarely performed. The veritable absence of suspended judgment in science has, in fact, recently spawned the American Tentative Society, whose sole purpose is to promote skeptical attitudes.[b]

Related to the issue of tenacity and intolerance, of course, is that of selective attention. It should come as no surprise that scientists tend to look for and accept data which support their viewpoints, and to ignore or discredit those which do not. One seldom reads journals

---

[a]Some of Mitroff's scientists stated that their more dogmatic peers could not be persuaded by *any* data. It is noteworthy that—although NASA spent nearly a half billion dollars per pound for its first shipment of lunar soil—one-third of the geoscientists felt that the samples were not collected from the best sites. It would be interesting to examine whether those who complained about unrepresentative samples were also the ones whose prior hypotheses were challenged by the reported data.

[b]I should mention that one possible factor in the maintenance of dogmatic opinions on the part of scientists is the social pressure to be "consistent." In a recent book, for example, I announced a change of opinion regarding some previously published hypotheses. Although in the minority, I received several letters and direct communications that my change in position was bothersome to my readers.

which are known to be opposed to one's own views. This explicit practice of isolationism was recently documented by David Krantz in the area of behavioral psychology. It is even more apparent at conventions and in theoretical books. Thus, in his autobiography, B.F. Skinner sounds almost proud of the fact that he never even bothered to *read* the criticisms levied against him by Noam Chomsky and Michael Scriven. The pattern is not an unusual one. Some of Galileo's detractors refused to even *look* through his telescope—an episode which was repeated in the tragedy of Paul Kammerer. When forced to confront a critic, *homo scientus* displays impressive skills at maintaining his position regardless of the attack. His movements are often as follows:

1. Deny the validity of the data (due to artifact, non-replication, poor measurements, methodological inadequacies, distrust of the experimenter's integrity, and so on); or
2. Concede the data but deny that they have serious implications for your theory (i.e., reinterpret them as irrelevant, peripheral, etc.); or
3. Assume an eschatological stance—i.e., admit the data and their apparent challenge to your theory, but argue that "in the end"—when all the data are in—the problem will evaporate and your theory will prove true.

This pattern of defensiveness, selective discrediting, and continual "system saving" is well documented in Imre Lakatos' chapter on the problems of falsificationism. There are no "critical experiments" precisely because of the scientist's skillful retreats. Such crucial tests as the Michelson-Morley experiment have proven unanimously unconvincing to their opponents. Indeed, Richard Westfall has recently shown that Isaac Newton was an expert at system saving—and perhaps the father of the "fudge factor."[c]

Further illustration of this pattern is found in a second study conducted by Bob DeMonbreun and myself (see appendix). Using undergraduate subjects and an hypothesis testing task, we not only found substantial tenacity—but also selective credibility. Subjects had been told that twenty percent of their experimental outcomes would be invalid. When one group was asked to rate which outcomes were valid and which were invalid, they showed a striking confirmatory bias. Positive data were considered valid almost four times more

---

[c]One way I have tried to redress this pattern has been to require myself and my students to interpret all possible outcomes of a study before we conduct it. If all potential data could yield the same conclusions, we need to evaluate either our tenacity or our design.

often than negative. This may bear on the phenomenon in which a scientist conducts several studies until one produces the "desired" outcome, and then feels no pangs of conscience when he writes that one up for publication and discards the others. Subjectively, it may be easier to convince himself that the successful experiment was valid, particularly in light of current publication policies.

But confirmatory bias and selective credibility are only two of the patterns discriminable in the perception and reasoning of *homo scientus*. He is also an expedient logician. He is (or tries to be) logical only when he has to be, and even then it is prejudicial. Thus, he criticizes a weak methdology when it has yielded negative results, but the same procedures are more leniently treated when their offspring are confirmatory. The absence of data are viewed as synonymous with negative data when they apply to a competitor's theory. When they apply to one's own they simply reflect the newness of the area and its empirical "promise." Phenomena are defined out of existence in question-begging fashion. "Symptom substitution" in psychotherapy, for example, was recently challenged on the basis of there being no such entities as "symptoms." This is reminiscent of an incident related by my friend Don Meichenbaum in which early British scientists had meteorites removed from museums and declared their existence impossible on the grounds that there was no heaven, and therefore there could be no heavenly bodies. Other illustrations of expedient reasoning include the logic of replication. If a repeated procedure yields replicative results, then it is thought to reflect a valid generalization. If the results are not replicated, however, the scientist often attributes them to "nonspecific" differences.

Memory dysfunction is still another phenomenon which plagues *homo scientus*. Robert Merton, for example, has documented the prevalence of "cryptomnesia" (unconscious plagiarism) in scientists. A more frequent illustration, however, and one for which I have no data, has to do with extemporaneous discussions. As Neil Agnew and Sandra Pyke put it:

> We tend to forget those things which don't fit well with our established biases and preferences, and remember those things which do. . . . In addition, time can distort the memory of observations (p. 59).

To test that, ask an unsuspecting colleague to estimate certain quantifiable data in which he has some vested interest—the mean scores in his dissertation, the number of studies supporting his theory, or whatever. A check against the original sources will often reveal some memory bias. This is particularly apparent in lectures and at conventions when the speaker has not had time to refresh his memory of specifics. In retrospect, the gaps get filled in with even better data or procedures.

If the rules of logic are universal and scientists are very logical organisms, then it follows that they should draw the same conclusions from the same set of observations. But this is patently not the case. In discipline after discipline we see wide discrepancies in the interpretation of the same data. Lunar scientists continue to argue over the *implications* of the Apollo evidence, and—as documented by Leon Kamin—the question of racial differences in intelligence has seen more politics than logic. The naturalist and the environmentalist view the same data, and then each draw their own foregone conclusions. This pattern may be more prevalent in the social sciences, where the data are much more amenable to being bent for Procrustean purposes.

But, perhaps I have already belabored long enough. The scientist is not a paragon of reason. In fact, he may often be expediently illogical and prejudicially confirmatory. Like many other contemporary revelations, this one was noted well over three centuries ago by Francis Bacon:

> The human understanding, when any proposition has been once laid down . . . forces everything else to add fresh support and confirmation: and although most cogent and abundant instances may exist to the contrary, yet either does not observe, or despises them, or it gets rid of and rejects them by some distinction, with violent and injurious prejudice rather than sacrifice the authority of its first conclusions (p. 46).

DISTORTING THE DATA

I have already argued that the progress of science is neither won nor lost in the laboratory. The fact that it is ideas, arguments, and persons who wage the battles of revolution does not imply that the data are therefore superfluous. While Lakatos and others have shown that theories may emerge, survive, or fall regardless of the data, one must not overlook the distinction between *psychological* and *epistemological* data functions. Data are usually sought to defend a belief, not to form one. More important, the scientist *believes* that data are the means to knowledge and the proper medium of professional exchange.

My point here is a cautionary one. Up until now, I have been emphasizing the fact that—for better or for worse—the history of science grants less credit to data than to argument. I have reiterated that point several times because it is so foreign to conventional beliefs among scientists.[d] My note of caution is simply this: do not infer from this that data are (or should be) irrelevant to the conduct of science. When preceded or accompanied by a convincing theoretical model, the data may become very influential in effecting scientific revolutions. Although they are not sufficient, neither are they irrelevant. Moreover, from a psychological perspective, anomalies may be critically important factors in shaking one's conceptual foundations and encouraging innovative speculation. When the data are strong enough to break their way through one's theory-imposed perceptual prejudices, they may stimulate some very valuable soul searching in the scientist. How skillful is the scientist in collecting these important entities?

First of all, we should lay to rest the most extreme notion of naive realism (the doctrine of Immaculate Perception). No organism, including *homo scientus*, is an infallible perceiver of reality. The reasons for this border on some rather esoteric themes in philosophy of knowledge. Let me just say in passing that one has no rational defense in claiming the veracity of one's sense data. The *tu quoque* argument here forces you to either question beg (by invoking sense data "tests" as their own defense) or to fall back upon faith.

Let us therefore move on to the relativistic position which is probably held by the majority of scientists. Basically, this position belies a relative faith in one's sense data—not as being perfect reflections of reality, but rather as crude approximations. This perspective is certainly more reasonable, although I doubt whether many scientists (including myself) really appreciate the crudity of those approximations. Consider only three illustrations. First, there is general consensus in the field of perception that the human being has a very limited capacity for processing information. Out of the wide array of continually impinging stimuli, it selectively filters only a few. This selectivity is then supplemented by processes of constructive perception. Basically, this refers to the fact that we are active participants in the process of perception. We help to *construct* our perceptions to fit previous (and perhaps some inborn) molds or schemata. Stimuli do not passively register, but rather "check in" to our biochemical computer in crude disarray. Each of us bends reality in a Procrustean fashion, taking a little off here and adding some elsewhere. This inherent distortion is exacerbated by a third factor in humans—namely, the impact of a symbol system (language) on categories of perception. We tend to focus on sensations which can be

[d]Indeed, my reasons for avoiding encyclopedic documentation and point-by-point references should now be more obvious.

squeezed into one of our symbols, so that our sense data are filtered on the basis of their symbol fit. In a way, we are unwitting conspirators in a plot to pre-package reality.

Now then, how does all of this bear on the scientist? First, it suggests that he is unavoidably imperfect as an instrument of observation. Even more important, it points to the potential role of his symbol systems (theories, paradigms) in determining what he can and does perceive. I have already cited Kuhn's documentation of data which were totally overlooked because they did not fit into the prevailing paradigm. After each revolution, scientists often find "new" data in their old stomping grounds—data they had stared through in their preoccupation with another model. The same data are seen very differently depending on one's preconceived notions and expectancies.

Illustrations of this kind of observational bias are numerous. Reviews by Robert Rosenthal, B.L. Kintz, Theodore X. Barber and others document their pervasiveness in both human and animal experiments. Observers tend to "see" what they expect to see, and to overlook other data. This was dramatically illustrated in an early experiment by Bruner and Postman in which subjects failed to notice a discrepancy in stimulus materials until they had been exposed to them for quite some time. Other research has also documented that even trained observers tend to make recording errors, and that these are usually in the direction of supporting their hypothesis. While these errors may be somewhat more prevalent in the social sciences (where human instruments prevail), they are certainly not absent in the physics laboratory. The spurious observation of "N-rays" by numerous physicists is probably one of the most startling embarrassments of this century, and Langmuir describes hundreds of papers in physics which reported nonexistent phenomena. Indeed, lest the physicist think he is exempt, he should read *The Confessions of a Psychic* by Uriah Fuller. This informative satire describes some of the tricks used by such "psychics" as Uri Geller in duping scientists into endorsing his authenticity. Fuller recommends that the young aspirant "Get to top physicists—they're the easiest of all scientists to fool."

Reports of systematic errors in data perception and/or recording are not hard to find, as indicated in the previously cited reviews. To these errors must be added the distortion produced by other scientist behaviors. The Heisenberg principle of indeterminacy is just as valid in the social sciences as it is in nuclear physics. Scientific measurements often change the phenomenon they are supposed to measure. This "reactivity" of instruments is multiplied by a variety of experimenter effects. For example, a series of studies by Robert Rosenthal and his colleagues have shown that experimenters often behave in ways which (a) convey their hypotheses to human subjects, and (b) increase the likelihood that they will obtain data congruent with those hypotheses. As if this weren't enough, Theodore Barber has cited several instances in which data analyses were in error (always in a "supportive" direction).

So far, I have avoided mentioning a topic which probably represents the most heinous crime in science—faking one's data. This phenomenon is considered rare by most scientists, and cries of alarm are sounded when such scandals are revealed. Unfortunately, the scandals keep appearing and one has to wonder how pervasive such practices are. They may be more readily detected in the physical sciences (where replication and precision are greater), but they still go on. Such tragedies as William T. Summerlin's fabrication of data at the Sloan-Kettering Center bear sad testimonial to the institutional and personal pressures which encourage such frauds. And the annals of science suggest that such pressures have been with us for a long time. Thus, Richard Westfall shows how the peerless Newton did more than a little "doctoring" to make the data fit his hypotheses, and I. Bernard Cohen informs us of the likelihood that Galileo faked some of his data in defending his theory of gravity. As early as 1830, Charles Babbage had written an inventory of frauds in science. Likewise, the noted statistician Ronald Fisher presents a convincing argument that, short of supernatural intervention, Gregor Mendel probably fabricated some of the data for his theory of genetic inheritance. The data were so perfect that the "aid" of statistical inference was hardly needed. To these may be added the great Piltdown forgery, the fabrications by T.D. Lysenko, Johann Beringer's "figured stones," the faked claims of Frederick Cook, and Paul Kammerer's altered specimen. In his excellent review, Theodore Barber cites almost a dozen other instances of known fabrication, and still more are noted by Andreski, Hagstrom, and others. In my recent travels, I have been informed of eight different instances of fabrication.[e] The survey study conducted by Terry Kimper and myself (see appendix) found that 42 percent of the participating scientists knew of at least one instance of data fabrication in their field. Some of these instances

---

[e]In one of these involving a doctoral student at a British University, the fabrication was detected very late in his education. After a full confession, he was given a "colonial Ph.D." (the implication being that he should not return to England). Interestingly, his fabricated data had to do with his adviser's theory and, although aware of their illegitimacy, the adviser continues to cite them as support for his views.

may have been well known in that the 42 percent figure is substantially higher than their estimate that only two percent of their colleagues had ever fabricated data.

I should note that many of the above instances of fabrication allegedly involved research assistants. While the data remain specious, this may at least protect what I hope to be a warranted belief— namely, that the average scientist values integrity more than publication or fame. Even if most of the guilt were laid on technical assistants, however, this does not alleviate the scientist's responsibilities to guard the accuracy of his research. In the social sciences, such practices as double blind experimentation and independent data analyses may be two ways of approaching that goal.

While outright fabrication may be rare, another form of data distortion, selective reporting, is not. Particularly in the social sciences, individuals are likely to write up only those studies which are successful. This is due to the aforementioned publication biases and the prejudice against negative results. Moreover, our survey data suggest that misrepresentation of methodologies may not be uncommon in some fields. Several researchers have discussed the subjectivity and expedience which may enter into experimentation after the data have been collected. Some of the data points can be thrown out in a non-random fashion. Entire studies may be buried in a filing cabinet or discarded. The data will be picked over, transformed, and polished —as will the alleged methodology. When an article is finally published, it may present a very distorted view of both the process and the product of investigation. This speculation is illustrated in Wolin's recent efforts to obtain copies of raw data from scientists. Of 37 subjects, 32 responded—two-thirds of them said that their raw data had been inadvertently lost or destroyed. Out of the seven data analyses Wolin was able to compute, three revealed gross miscalculations which would have forced substantial changes in the conclusions reported!

My intent in this chapter has not been to destroy the rationality of the scientist or to undermine his ability to make accurate observations. Both of these would be gross overgeneralizations. On the premise that awareness may encourage change, however, I think it is important to recognize some of the logical and procedural pitfalls which may entrap *homo scientus*. He must remain apprized of his human fallibility, if only to help reduce its epistemological costs. Neither logic nor perceptual objectivity come inborn. Whatever approximations can be made to these two must be made under the constant surveillance of self-scrutiny and external checks.

It may now be somewhat clearer as to why the policies of (a) outcome-free evaluation, and (b) independent replication are so important to the advancement of scientific knowledge.[f] Given the fallibility of our conduct and the unique epistemological power of falsification, we should be encouraging the publication of studies which are relevant to the question at hand and which address that question in a methodologically adequate fashion. In fact, were it not for the possibility that it would encourage yet another form of selective data reporting, one might argue that our journals should give preferential coverage to studies which report negative results. This policy would undoubtedly foster its own variety of biases in the conduct and reporting of research, however, as well as incurring some justificational problems (chapter 7), so that we may be better off to publish all relevant inquiries and to then weigh their outcomes according to whether they are maximally informative (disconfirmatory).

REFERENCES

12, 13, 17, 19, 28, 30, 54, 55, 58, 63, 64, 69, 72, 75, 76, 91, 93, 94, 95, 102, 112, 113, 117, 118, 123, 124, 128, 130, 131, 136, 138, 141, 142, 144, 147, 148, 152, 154, 162, 167, 168, 171, 175, 176, 177, 181, 182, 184, 185, 192, 204, 206, 207, 214, 215, 216, 223, 224, 227, 235, 238, 239, 240, 241, 242, 244, 249, 253, 258, 259, 273, 274, 275, 277, 287, 288, 289, 290, 291, 297, 301, 307, 312, 315, 316, 317, 319, 322, 326, 335, 336, 339, 342, 343, 345, 354, 355, 356, 362, 364, 379, 380, 381, 384, 385, 386, 387, 388, 389, 391, 392, 395, 398, 403, 413, 416, 417, 420, 421, 423, 424, 427, 432, 440, 448, 450, 451, 453, 454, 455, 456, 457, 458, 459, 472, 474, 485, 486, 487, 488, 493.

[f]One should bear in mind that the merits of replication lie in its assessment of the veracity and generalizability of previous findings. Unfortunately, it is very easy to slip into confirmatory reasoning in the interpretation of replications. A "well-replicated" finding assumes the status of a "well-demonstrated" one, and its repeated observations become elements of inductive accretion. This illicit reasoning must be guarded against, if only by reminding oneself that the crux of replication is disconfirmatory survival. A phenomenon is tentatively considered veridical so long as it can survive replicative tests. From a purely logical perspective, the sheer number of survivals (successful replications) should *not* enhance one's confidence in the veracity of the phenomenon. The number of failures to replicate, on the other hand, can logically demand reappraisal. While a few non-replications may be tentatively attributed to measurement or artifactual errors, repeated non-replication has much stronger epistemological import. Recall that confirmatory outcomes convey less information than disconfirmatory ones. One should not be weighing these two against one another as if they were equivalent. Finally, it should be obvious that replication is an asset but not an essential ingredient in data collection. Phenomena can be scientifically meaningful without being potentially repeatable.

In science the word criticism is not a synonym for disparagement; criticizing means looking for truth.

Claude Bernard

Doubt is not a pleasant condition, but certainty is an absurd one.

Voltaire

If you wish to strive for peace of soul and pleasure, then believe; if you wish to be a devotee of truth, then inquire.

Nietzsche

Maturity is the capacity to endure uncertainty.

John Finley

We must have robust faith and not believe.

Claude Bernard

He that is unaware of his ignorance will be misled by his knowledge.

Whately

There lives more faith in honest doubt,
  Believe me, than in half the creeds.

Alfred Lord Tennyson

Wise men cause arguments; fools decide them.

Anacharsis

The greater the scientist, the more he is impressed with his ignorance of reality, and the more he realizes that his laws and labels, descriptions and definitions, are the products of his own thought.

Alan W. Watts

What peculiar privilege has this little agitation of the brain which we call thought, that we must thus make it the model of the whole universe?

David Hume

Chapter 9

Postscript

The preceding chapters have, I think, documented that many of our popular notions about science and the scientist are sorely misguided. In marked contrast to the storybook image, we have seen that *homo scientus* is a very fallible creature. His research findings—the "raw data of knowledge"—are often contaminated by personal biases and distortions. He is often a dogmatic creature—intolerant of contrary views, resistant to unsavory data, and more faithful to his theories than to anything else. His reasoning skills may be both modest and expedient. Indeed, many of the most popular practices in contemporary science are demonstrably irrational on their own criteria. Instead of being a dispassionate purveyor of knowledge, the scientist is more often an energetic merchant of truth. His emotional involvement is frequently intense and—contrary to his credo of communal sharing and personal humility—his frenzied search is marked by secrecy, paranoia, and fierce competition. Rather than cautiously suspending judgment, he often races to speculation—staking claim on ideas and forcing the data into neat theoretical packages.

Where does all of this leave us? Is science therefore a futile enterprise carried out by irrational dogmatists? Should we abandon the empirical approach to knowledge? After all, I have argued that we are locked into a reality which is at least partially molded by our ideas—preconceptions and theories selectively construct and filter the data which "confirm" them. Is not science then an unending succession of shared delusions, each embellished by its own perceptual bigotry? Is it worth devoting one's life to a pursuit in which there is no "security" or stability—where today's paradigms are tomorrow's history? Can the knowledge seeker derive any satisfaction from an endeavor whose only assurance is change—whose only certainty is perpetual uncertainty?

I obviously hope that at least some of the themes in this book will have an impact on conventional notions of science. For some, this reading may have imposed a kind of paradigm crisis, replete with shaken beliefs, feelings of confusion, and so on.[a] And yet, you may recall, I have repeatedly voiced my continued endorsement of science as a worthwhile endeavor. In fact, I endorse it strongly enough to recommend that it be applied to itself in a retroactive fashion.

On what do I base my optimism and my continued fidelity to science? After all, I have just completed a rather comprehensive polemic highlighting the shortcomings of both science and *homo scientus*. Do I harbor some magical solution—some plan of reform—which will salvage science from its embarrassments and raise the pedigree of its practitioners? Not quite. There are no reforms which can transform science into an absolute avenue of truth, and there are no means of breeding or training *homo scientus* such that he will be totally objective, rational, and so on. Our scientific knowledge will always be incomplete, fallible, and relative—rough approximations whose crudeness can never be conclusively measured. *Homo scientus* will always be imperfect as a knowledge seeker; it is simply a question of degrees. And herein, perhaps, lies the kernel of my optimism. If we abandon the naive and idealistic notions that science is an ultimately perfect (and "justified") avenue to Truth—and that the scientist is (or should be) an impeccable paragon of inquiry—then we can go about the business of assessing and reducing their limitations. So long as we see science as unproblematic and the scientist as accurately portrayed by the storybook image, however, we are unlikely to undertake reforms.

Neither science nor the scientist are currently infallible. More important, neither are *potentially* infallible. This does not imply that they are therefore futile or worthless. My survey has emphasized the problems of science rather than its strengths, and this may have encouraged the illogical dichotomization that either science is justified (good, efficient, rational, etc.) *or* it is a total bust. If, by science, we mean an attempt to describe orderly relationships in experience—to condense or abridge perceived reality via some economical system—then one can hardly argue that science hasn't been

[a]In all honesty, I must confess that I think this reaction to be less likely than one of awe at my incompetence or irrelevance. Since my critics may care little about my conclusions, I have geared my ensuing remarks toward the shifters rather than the shiftless.

impressively successful. Today's world is much more accurately described (predicted, explained) than it was even a century ago. Despite the fallibilities I have documented, science is a robust and powerful approach to knowledge. It may be distorted, but it is not totally delusional.

While the pessimist may be depressed over the necessary imperfections of science, the optimist will see this as fertile ground. After all, no one is claiming that *all* of science is wrong or that *homo scientus* is *never* logical, objective, etc. The contention is simply that we are handicapped with an imperfect system and an imperfect practitioner. Both will always remain imperfect—but this does not mean that they cannot *improve.* Once we accept our compromised goals of relativisms rather than absolutes, confident assertions rather than known facts, then we can launch some more realistic programs of action.

There is, I think, a stimulating challenge inherent in the fallibility of science. Change becomes inevitable, and mutability is recognized as the process—not the plague—of science. In both the content and method of knowing, movement is the byword. We are never stagnated by the belief that a certain, immutable truth has been won, for we know that such truths cannot be ascertained. There is another ironic asset in appreciating the fallibilities of both science and the scientist. Namely, this appreciation may encourage an intellectual humility and flexibility which are impossible in justificationistic science. By recognizing his biases and limitations, the scientist may be more responsive to change and less deceived by his theoretical convictions. He may even adopt the critically self-scrutinizing perspective herein encouraged. In doing so he will, I think, come to appreciate some of the more subtle beauties of his profession. He may ponder, for example, that—like life itself—science is a journey rather than a destination. The fact that one will never "arrive" need not preclude one's traveling hopefully, nor should it prevent one from enjoying the feeling of movement.

RETROSPECT AND REFORM

My meta-strategy, which seems much clearer in hindsight, has been to accomplish three goals:

1. *recognition* of the pervasive fallibilities and limitations of both science and scientists,
2. *acceptance* of the necessity of some of those fallibilities (thereby rejecting such unattainable ideals as justificational epistemologies and the storybook image), and

3. *reform*—the optimization of our inquiry process within the constraints of its own fallibility.

The final goal—reform—is one which can neither be completely outlined nor fully realized at any point in time. That is, I am adopting a comprehensively critical stance in the sense of encouraging that the reforms take a critical self-appraising form. My recommendations for change in the preceding chapters should be viewed as admittedly fallible suggestions which warrant critical scrutiny. The merit of reform does not accrue from any specific procedural changes, but from the metatheoretical stance that all reforms (or potential reforms) are to be critically evaluated—including the notion that one should critically evaluate all reforms.

Let us take a moment here to review some of the major themes which merit reform consideration. I have argued that we know very little about the behavior patterns of scientists. Even though the patterns I have described are (hopefully) representative of the data available, much of that data must be classified as weak—secondary sources, biographies, self-reports, and so on. At this point, we know more about planaria and gibbons than we do about *homo scientus*. If we wish to better understand the scientist, we must redress our neglect of him as an experimental subject. Controlled studies of scientist behavior are direly needed. Under what conditions are scientists most likely to suppress, distort, or fabricate data? How representative are some of the generalizations I have presented? What are the best means for refining the scientist's reasoning skills? What are the processes of "conversion" to a new paradigm? To be useful, of course, this science of science must be recognized as relevant to the daily conduct of inquiry. It must talk to scientists, not philosophers, and it must offer them practical information on such things as pitfalls and assets in scientific investigation.

This first reform priority shades into a second which has already been voiced by such writers as Kuhn, Weimer, and Mitroff—that psychology must be considered an invaluable and essential foundation for the analysis of both science and scientists. The processes and parameters of "knowing" are an integral part of scientific endeavors. While their understanding of this phenomenon remains crude, psychologists can at least offer some relevant analogues and paradigms which may shed light on the biochemical circuitry of *homo scientus*. Studies in human learning, memory, emotion, information processing, belief and attitude change, problem solving—all have obvious relevance for the understanding of the scientist.

A third area cannot be logically separated from the first two—that science is an inherently social phenomenon. It is imbued with institutions and codes of conduct, rites of passage and communication media. As we have seen, the processes which characterize scientific revolution are more psychosocial than epistemological. Theories are accepted or rejected on the basis of rhetorical arguments and other social phenomena. While sociologists of science have made valuable contributions to the study of these institutions and processes, their efforts have borne little fruit in reform. Certain institutional policies and codes of conduct continue to be potentially detrimental to optimal scientific behavior (e.g., contemporary graduate training, the professional reward system, and so on). Likewise, interdisciplinary differences may partially account for discrepancies in the rate and quality of knowledge growth among various fields (e.g., their publication policies, methods of inference, and so on). As yet, there have been no studies on the effects of policy changes such as the valuation of replication, publication based on methodological adequacy versus outcome, and the revocation of tenure. These kinds of studies would, of course, require ambitious longitudinal investments, but their impact on science cannot be otherwise determined.

A final broad category which merits reform consideration has to do with the interface between metatheory and scientific practice. In some ways, this may be the most overriding issue in that such perspectives as Weimer's include a metatheory (theory of theories) which encompasses the epistemology, psychology, and sociology of science. Thus, developments such as comprehensively critical rationalism—which has dramatic relevance for the conduct of science—must be allotted visibility and consideration. The aversion to (and ignorance of) philosophy which is shared by so many scientists must be redressed by reforms in graduate training and interdisciplinary stimulation.

My belief and general comments on reform suggest two broad strategies of investigation:

1. *Descriptive research*, which will tell us more about processes, correlates, patterns, and parameters in both the individual scientist and in his social institutions; and
2. *Evaluative research*, which will allow us to (fallibly) judge the efficiency of various patterns (or reforms) in attaining specified scientific goals.

To stimulate these research ventures, I have been intentionally polemical. Whether it derives from curiosity or defensiveness, research on the processes of science is sorely needed. If this book enjoys any degree of visibility and assimilation, I do not doubt that there will be very vocal critics of some of its molar and molecular points. These I welcome—for reasons that should now be obvious. The prospect of being shown to have been wrong is even a welcome one in that it presupposes that my speculations have at least stimulated some research in the area. In fact, as an additional heuristic offering, I am including an abbreviated theory of belief ("The Costs of Commitment"—see appendix) as a further target of scrutiny. Finally, as I have already mentioned, all of the royalties from this book are being contributed to a non-profit research foundation which will encourage further investigations in the area.

REFLECTIONS: A CRITICAL SELF-APPRAISAL

Some of you may have detected the perplexing fact that my suggested reforms presuppose scientific research, and yet I have argued the fallibility of that research. Can science be expected to pull itself up by its own culpable bootstraps? For example, my invocation of psychology as a useful supplement to the understanding of science may appear to be self-contradictory in the sense that it presupposes the validity of the former. This paradox is, I think, an illusory one in that I do not presuppose the validity of any one science in understanding the entire enterprise. There is no logical necessity for a perfect tool in the measurement or repair of a faulty one. Although we are unquestionably handicapped in our bootstrapping operations, we are not prohibited. We may never get out of Plato's cave, but we may at least refine our perceptions of the shadows.

A second seeming paradox is a bit more subtle. In the preceding chapters I have argued that the scientist is a very fallible collector and processor of information—that he selectively attends to confirmatory data and ignores or rejects contradictory evidence. In expounding his theories and hypotheses, he often falls prey to expedient reasoning and distortion. Now then, it has hopefully occurred to you that, if this is true—if the theory I present in "The Costs of Commitment" (see appendix) is valid—then I too must have been selective, confirmatory, distortional, and so on! Otherwise, I would be a falsifying instance for my own theory. Although my awareness of scientist fallibilities has probably helped me to detect and correct some misrepresentations in earlier drafts of this work, I think it is reasonable to assert that a critic could go back over my arguments and/or data and show more than a few instances of dubious logic or misrepresentation. I do not know of those instances at the moment, but I am confident they are there—and it is that confidence which insures a lingering and (I think) adaptive self-scrutiny.

CONCLUDING REMARKS

Homo scientus that I am, it should come as no surprise that I hope some of my remarks will have been persuasive enough to at least warrant further consideration and empirical scrutiny. I suspect that—if my hope is realized—the persons who respond to my conjectures will probably be among my younger and more flexible colleagues. I do not intend this to sound evaluative—only predictive. Given that they are more likely to be receptive to my speculations and recommendations, my closing comments are primarily directed toward them.

If this endeavor called "science" is indeed the noble one I consider it to be, then its continued growth and refinement is literally in *your* hands. It should be obvious from the preceding chapters that I have few illusions regarding either the epistemological or psychological purities of our profession. It is a thoroughly fallible and inherently limited endeavor. Both its powers and its impotence are strikingly apparent in contemporary life. This book has focused on some of the possible sources of its dysfunction—ranging from the professional reward system to some of the absurdities in scientist training and communication.

If changes are in order—and I obviously think they are—you are their means. You may now (or soon) be in the position to exert significant impact on graduate training practices, journal publication policies, and—perhaps most critically—research priorities. With your technical skills and professional integrity, we may hope to see changes which will revolutionize both the *direction* and the *process* of science. With your sensitivity to the inequities and inhumanities which abound both inside and outside the science game, we may look toward a future of more relevant research—a future in which humanistic priorities are served by a more sensitive science. And finally, with your attitude of continual self-scrutiny and critical tentativeness, we may hopefully look forward to an era in which scientific inquiry is seen in the cautiously optimistic light of its fitting role—as a thoroughly human journey rather than some sacrosanct destination. Its challenge lies partly in its fallibility, its infinite room for refinement. Your dedicated pursuit of that endeavor has my most intense respect and encouragement. May you travel hopefully.

REFERENCES

5, 31, 32, 33, 70, 93, 114, 137, 172, 226, 229, 263, 273, 296, 300, 311, 314, 316, 326, 328, 331, 353, 414, 460, 466, 467, 468, 469.

One person with a belief is equal to a force of ninety-nine who have only interests.

John Stuart Mill

Every man, wherever he goes, is encompassed by a cloud of comforting convictions, which move with him like flies on a summer day.

Bertrand Russell

I believe, in the first instance, that it is necessary to believe something.

Julian Huxley

The Devil can quote scripture for his purpose.

Shakespeare

By false desires and false thoughts man has built up for himself a false universe: as a mollusc, by the deliberate and persistent absorption of lime and rejection of all else, can build up for itself a hard shell which shuts it from the external world, and only represents in a distorted and unrecognizable form the ocean from which it was obtained. This hard and wholly unnutritious shell, this one-sided secretion of the surface-consciousness, makes as it were a little cave of illusion for each separate soul.

Evelyn Underhill

In human memory the testimony of a positive case always overshadows the negative one. One gain easily outweighs several losses. Thus the instances which affirm . . . always loom far more conspicuously than those which deny.

Bronislaw Malinowski

The search for order, regularity and meaning is a general characteristic of human thought processes. It is one of our salient modes of adaptation to an ever-changing world.

Gustav Jahoda

If given the chance, true believers can become genuine menaces to the advancement of human knowledge.

D. Cohen

Appendix

The Effect of Data Return
Patterns on Confidence
in an Hypothesis

BOBBY G. DeMONBREUN AND
MICHAEL J. MAHONEY

Recent research in the psychology of problem solving and hypothesis testing has suggested that the human organism is primarily confirmatory in its approach to problems. That is, it appears to selectively emphasize events which support rather than challenge already held beliefs. This bias has been shown to exist in a variety of both subjects and tasks—ranging from laboratory problem solving to clinical disorders. Once subjects have become "committed" to an hypothesis, they are generally slow to discard it when faced with contradictory evidence. The processes underlying this tenacity have received very little experimental attention. One hypothesis has been that of "primacy"—that individuals form a belief based on early information and then distort subsequent data to fit that belief. Some support for this analysis has been offered by Peterson and DuCharme.

The present investigation was designed to extend these earlier inquiries into confirmatory bias and to further explore the role of temporal parameters. Subjects were given a mathematical problem similar to that employed in previous studies by Wason and his colleagues. They were asked to form an hypothesis regarding its solution. This was followed by twenty trials in which the subject used his hypothesis to predict the outcome of twenty analogous problems. These predictions were followed by one of three prearranged sequences of accuracy feedback: (1) early positive, (2) early negative, or (3) random. For one group of subjects, the first ten predictions were met with seventy percent success. In the second group, seventy percent of these early predictions were announced as incorrect. A third group received a standard random sequence of accuracy feedback. Subjects were told that twenty percent of the feedback they received was actually invalid. All three groups completed the twenty trials with the same final accuracy rate (50 percent). Thus, in one group, the early "data returns" were predominantly positive and later ones were negative. The reverse of this pattern was experienced in group two and a random pattern of feedback was employed in the third group. After receiving feedback on the accuracy of their prediction after each trial, subjects were asked to rate their current confidence in their hypothesis. This design facilitated examination of the trial-by-trial impact of experimental outcome on confidence in an hypothesis. It likewise assessed the influence of different patterns of data returns.

Experiment I

Subjects were volunteers from an introductory psychology course at The Pennsylvania State University ($N = 30$). They were divided by sex and randomly assigned to three experimental groups: (1) Early Positive Feedback, (2) Early Negative Feedback, and (3) Random Feedback.[a] Upon arriving for the experiment, subjects were instructed as follows:

"This study deals with human problem solving and some of its subjective aspects. Let me begin by showing you this card. As you can see, it has three pairs of numbers on it—5, 10; 8, 16; and 21, 42. Each of these pairs has a feature in common with the other two. As a matter of fact, they were all generated by the same mathematical rule. The rule here is that the second number in each pair is twice as large as the first. Once you have discovered that rule, you can easily predict whether other pairs of numbers would fit it or not. For example, if I asked you whether 7, 12 fits the rule, you would say "no" since 12 is not twice as large as seven. This is basically the way that science works. The researcher formulates a rule or hypothesis and then makes predictions based upon it.

"This is exactly what I would like you to do today. I am going to show you another card which has three groups of numbers on it. To make things a bit more difficult, each group will contain three numbers instead of just two. What I would like you to do is formulate a rule or hypothesis

[a]Due to an early clerical error, two extra subjects were assigned to the first group, so that their respective n's were 12, 10, and 8. While unfortunate, this accidental deviation from true "randomness" was not considered devastating to the internal validity of the experiment.

about the numbers. Okay, here is the card. The numbers are: 2, 4, 6; 10, 12, 14; and 68, 70, 72. You can take a couple of minutes if you need them. What I want you to do is write down your rule on this card. Do you understand what you are supposed to do? Let me know when you have formed your hypothesis. (Maximum pause = 120 seconds)

"Okay, now you have a rule by which you can make predictions. We can now go on to the next phase of the experiment. First, tell me your current confidence in the accuracy of your rule. One hundred percent confident means that you are certain it is correct; zero percent means you are certain it is wrong.

"Theoretically, if your rule is the same as the correct rule, you and I should always agree. However, scientific research is seldom that simple or clearcut. Many experiments yield results which are misleading. To duplicate that situation, we have programmed this experiment so that twenty percent of my feedback to you is incorrect. That is, on twenty percent of the trials, the feedback I give you will be invalid."

A practice trial was then given and subjects were reminded that twenty percent of their feedback would be invalid. They were told that a total of twenty trials would be run. On each trial the subject was shown a card containing a new triad of numbers and was asked to make his or her prediction about whether that specific triad also conformed to the general rule. They received accuracy feedback in a prearranged manner (i.e., irrespective of their prediction) based on a schedule appropriate to their assigned condition. Although all subjects ended the twenty trials with a success rate of fifty percent, the distribution of their successes and failures was varied. In the Early Positive group, subjects were told that their predictions were correct on seven of the first ten trials and only three of the final ten. For these subjects, the following trials brought positive results: 1, 2, 3, 4, 6, 8, 9, 13, 16, 19. The opposite pattern was employed in the Early Negative group—i.e., each of the trials enumerated above brought negative results. Accuracy rates in the Random group were determined by a random number series which yielded forty percent success in the first ten trials and sixty percent in the second half of the experiment (trials 1, 3, 5, 8, 12, 13, 14, 16, 18, and 20 were positive).

Results

The three groups did not appear to differ in their pre-experimental confidence regarding their hypotheses. As reflected in figure A-1, their confidence ratings were slightly differentiated at trial ten, but were again indistinguishable at the completion of the experiment. An interesting and unanticipated finding was the marked tenacity in confidence shown by subjects in all three groups. Despite the fact that

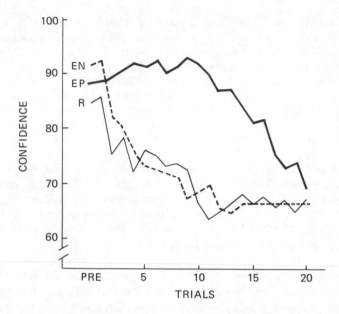

Figure A-1. Mean confidence ratings per trial when data return patterns were early positive (EP), early negative (EN), or random (R).

fifty percent of their predictions had been pronounced as wrong, forty percent of the subjects remained virtually certain of the veracity of their hypothesis at the end of the experiment (confidence rating ≥ 98%). Moreover, an analysis of individual changes in confidence suggested that subjects may have been relatively insensitive to accuracy feedback. Despite the fact that each subject had twenty opportunities to change his or her confidence rating, shifts in confidence were relatively rare. On seventy-five percent of the trials, subjects displayed no change in confidence from the previous trial. This tenacity suggested a corollary experiment.

Experiment II

Twelve additional subjects from the same pool were run in the same manner as Random Feedback subjects in Experiment I. In the present study, however, they were asked to rate each trial as to whether they thought the feedback given by the experimenter was valid or invalid.

Results

Consistent with the findings of Experiment I, subjects were frequently tenacious in their confidence. Three individuals completed the twenty trials still certain of the veracity of their hypothesis. Moreover, subjects were again relatively static in their confidence ratings— there was no change in this rating on 71 percent of the trials. Most interesting, perhaps, was the finding that subjects tended to believe experimenter feedback when the feedback was positive, but to disregard it as invalid when it was negative. Even though success/failure feedback was evenly split at fifty percent, subjects rated ninety-four percent of their successes as being "valid" as compared with only twenty-five percent of their failures. Congruent with the confirmatory bias demonstrated in previous studies, subjects thus showed a preference for accepting positive results and rejecting negative ones. Eight individuals (67%) thought that *all* of their successful outcomes were valid, and three of these subjects were totally dichotomous in the sense that they rated all successes as valid and all failures as invalid.

Discussion

Data from individual subjects are presented in table A-1. Taken together, the results of these two experiments suggest further ev-

Table A-1. Confidence Ratings By Trial[b]

Group 1 (Early Positive)
S-1 (P-20) 100; *S-2* (P-20) 100; *S-3* (P-20) 100; *S-4* (P-20) 100; *S-5*; (P-6) 95, (7-8) 90, (9-11) 95, (12-13) 90, (14-17) 80, (18) 75, (19-20) 80; *S-6* (P-16) 100, (17-20) 95, *S-7* (P) 85, (1-2) 90, (3) 95, (4) 97, (5-8) 90, (9-10) 95, (11) 90, (12) 80, (13-14) 85, (15) 75, (16) 80, (17) 75, (18) 60, (19) 65, (20) 40; *S-8* (P-1) 75, (2) 80, (3) 85, (4-5) 90, (6) 95, (7) 90, (8-9) 95, (10) 90, (11) 85, (12-14) 75, (15-16) 70, (17-19) 60, (20) 40; *S-9* (P-1) 10, (2) 12, (3) 15, (4-5) 25, (6-7) 30, (8) 40, (9) 50, (10) 45, (11) 40, (12-13) 30, (14) 25, (15-16) 20, (17) 15, (18-19) 10, (20) 9; *S-10* (P-6) 100, (7-10) 90, (11-13) 80, (12-16) 50, (17-20) 0; *S-11* (P-19) 100, (20) 90; *S-12* (P-6) 95, (7-11) 93, (12-14) 90, (15-16) 85, (17) 83, (18-19) 80, (20) 75.

Group 2 (Early Negative)
S-1 (P) 95, (1-20) 100; *S-2* (P-20) 100; *S-3* (P-1) 100, (2-4) 50, (5-11) 30, (12-20) 0; *S-4* (P-3) 100, (4-8) 80, (5-20) 60; *S-5* (P-1) 50, (2) 45, (3-5) 40, (6-20) 35; *S-6* (P-1) 100; (2-3) 99, (4-20) 100; *S-7* (P-2) 99, (3) 97, (4) 95, (5-7) 99, (8) 96, (9) 98, (10-12) 99, (13) 97, (14-15) 99, (16) 98, (17-18) 99, (19) 97, (20) 99; *S-8* (P-1) 95, (2-3) 80, (4) 75, (5-7) 65, (8-14) 60, (15-20) 55; *S-9* (P-1) 100, (2) 80, (3) 60, (4-6) 50, (7-8) 40, (9-11) 30, (12-20) 20; *S-10* (P-1) 80, (2-3) 75, (4-5) 70, (6) 61, (7) 72, (8) 70, (9) 64, (10) 75, (11) 85, (12) 86, (13) 80, (14) 90, (15-18) 98, (19) 95, (20) 99.

Group 3 (Random)
S-1 (P-20) 100; *S-2* (P) 70, (1) 80, (2) 70, (3-8) 80, (9-14) 70, (15-20) 80; *S-3* (P-1) 90, (2) 80, (3) 90, (4-9) 50, (10-13) 40, (14-18) 50, (19-20) 40; *S-4* (P-1) 60, (2-10) 10, (11-20) 0; *S-5* (P-1) 75, (2-4) 60, (5-6) 85, (7-9) 75, (10) 50, (11-14) 40; (15-20) 30; *S-6* (P-1) 100, (2-4) 98, (5-20) 99; *S-7* (P-2) 90, (3) 92, (4) 85, (5) 90, (6) 85, (7-9) 80, (10-12) 75, (13) 85, (14) 90, (15) 80, (16) 85, (17) 75, (18) 80, (19) 75, (20) 90; *S-8* (P-7) 95, (8-9) 97, (10) 90, (11) 85, (12-13) 95, (14) 97, (15) 95, (16) 97, (17) 95, (18-19) 97, (20) 98.

Table A-1 continued

Corollary Group (Experiment II)
S-1 (P-20) 100 (1, 3-5, 8, 12-14, 16, 18, 20); *S-2* (P-4) 100, (5-20) 80 (1, 3-5, 8, 12-14, 16, 18, 20); *S-3* (P-20) 100 (1, 3, 5, 8, 12-14, 16, 18, 20); *S-4* (P-20) 100 (1, 3, 5, 8, 12-14, 16, 18, 20); *S-5* (P-2) 75, (3) 77, (4-5) 75, (6-9) 70, (10-12) 60, (13-15) 65, (16) 70, (17-18) 60, (19) 55, (20) 60 (1, 3, 5, 6, 8, 10-14, 16, 18-20); *S-6* (P-2) 50, (3) 60, (4-6) 50, (7-8) 40, (9) 20, (10-20) 0 (1, 3-5, 8-13, 15-16, 19-20); *S-7* (P-1) 99, (2) 50, (3-4) 75, (5) 80, (6) 50, (7) 0, (8-9) 25, (10) 10, (11-20) 0 (1-3, 5, 7-8, 11-13, 15, 17, 19-20); *S-8* (P-1) 99, (2-11) 50, (12-20) 0 (1-3, 8, 12-14, 16, 18, 20); *S-9* (P-1) 100, (2-6) 90, (7-10) 80, (11-17) 60, (18) 40, (19-20) 30 (1-5, 7-8, 11-13, 16, 18, 20); *S-10* (P-6) 100, (7) 80, (8-12) 50, (13-14) 75, (15-20) 50 (1, 3, 5, 8, 12-14, 16, 18, 20); *S-11* (P-9) 100, (10-20) 95 (1, 3, 5, 8, 12-16, 18-20); *S-12* (P-1) 100, (2-10) 99, (11-14) 95, (15-16) 80, (17) 30, (18) 20, (19-20) 5 (1-3, 5, 8, 11-20).

---

[b]Numbers in parentheses refer to trials; "P" represents their "pre" ratings. In the Corollary Group, the final set of parentheses contains those trials which a subject rated as "valid."

idence for confirmatory bias and marked tenacity on the part of human problem solvers. Although the first study failed to show any differential lasting effects resulting from the pattern of early versus late data returns, it did suggest that subjects were often quite confident in the veracity of their hypotheses despite strong evidence of their invalidity. One possible source of this tenacity was explored in the second experiment, which suggested that individuals show a strong tendency to "believe" (rate as valid) those outcomes which support their hypothesis and to disbelieve (view as invalid) those which do not. The observed tenacity may have also been related to the fact that subjects were not allowed to *change* their hypothesis during the course of the experiment. Had they had that option, more variability might have been encountered.

REFERENCES

11, 63, 238, 239, 273, 274, 275, 342, 362, 453, 454, 455, 456, 458, 459.

From Ethics to Logic: A Survey of Scientists

MICHAEL J. MAHONEY AND
TERRENCE P. KIMPER

This survey was designed to obtain information about con-temporary policies and patterns in the conduct of scientific research. Four general topics were addressed via questionnaire: (1) Negative Results, (2) Publication Policies, (3) Professional Ethics, and (4) Logical Reasoning Skills. The responses of scientists in four different fields were then scored and analyzed.

Method

A questionnaire was constructed to provide information on four broad areas of scientific conduct. This questionnaire is reproduced in table A-2. Scientist subjects were randomly selected from four disciplines: (1) physics, (2) biology, (3) psychology, and (4) sociology. Sample populations consisted of those names contained in the most recent professional directories available in each field.[a] A random numbers table was used to select 100 physicists, 100 biologists, 100 psychologists, and 100 sociologists. These subjects were sent the questionnaire along with a cover letter briefly describing the purposes of the survey.

[a]The 1973-74 Directory of Physics and Astronomy Faculties, the 1973-74 Directory of Members of the Federation of American Societies for Experimental Biology, the 1974 Directory of the American Psychological Association, and the 1973-74 Directory of Members of the American Sociological Association.

Table A–2

Name _____

Position or Academic Rank_____   Your Field of Science _____

1. NEGATIVE RESULTS

Let us define "negative results" as research data which fail to support an experimental hypothesis or which are not congruent with some generally accepted relationship.

a. What percentage of your total research has yielded negative results? _____

b. In the long run, are you *more* likely to continue a line of research which is yielding positive or negative results? _____ positive _____ negative

c. Which of the following emotions comes closest to describing your usual reaction to negative results? _____ disappointment _____ neutrality _____ happiness

d. When you do obtain negative results, what is the probability that you will write them up for publication? (0 to 1.0) _____

e. What is the probability of a negative results manuscript being accepted? _____

2. PUBLICATION POLICIES

a. On the average, how many manuscripts do you submit per year? _____

b. What percentage of your manuscripts are accepted by the first journal to which they are submitted (include acceptances which request some revision)? _____

c. When an article is rejected, how often do you re-submit it to another journal? _____ almost never _____ occasionally _____ frequently _____ almost always

d. Which of the following reasons have been offered in rejecting your articles? (Check all that apply) _____ negative results _____ inadequate methodology _____ no reason given _____ improper data reporting or analysis _____ lack of originality _____ irrelevance of the problem _____ your interpretation of the data

e. What percentage (if any) of your rejecting reviews have been abusive in content? _____

3. PROFESSIONAL ETHICS

a. Do you know of any instances in which an individual in your field has attempted to suppress or discard data contrary to his/her viewpoint? _____ none _____ 1 person _____ 2 persons _____ 3 or more persons

b. Directly or indirectly, do you know of any individuals in your discipline who have fabricated or faked some data? _____ none _____ 1 person _____ 2 persons _____ ⩾ 3

c. To what extent do political rivalries and/or "personality clashes" influence chances for publication or granting in your field? _____ almost never _____ occasionally _____ frequently _____ almost always

Table A-2 continued

---

d. Estimate what percentage (if any) of the individuals in your discipline have *ever* engaged in each of the following: _____ data fabrication _____ data suppression or omission _____ plagiarism of ideas _____ plagiarism of actual written matter _____ misrepresentation of methodology _____ criticism of a colleague's character

4. PHILOSOPHY OF RESEARCH

a. Assume that the four boxes which are presented below are actually cards which each have a *letter* on one side and a *number* on the other side. You are asked to test the hypothesis that—for these 4 cards—if a vowel appears on one side, then an even number will appear on the other side. Your "testing," of course, will involve turning one or more cards over.

I	II	III	IV
e	m	8	7

Are any of the cards irrelevant to the hypothesis? (Circle)   I II III IV No
Are any of the cards critical to the hypothesis? (Circle)   I II III IV No
Which card(s) would you turn over to test the hypothesis? I II III IV

b. Many experiments in science rely on a type of logic called material implication. This is symbolized $p \rightarrow q$, which can be read "if p, then q" or "p entails (implies) q." Adopting this logical form, rate each of the following on the validity of their conclusion.

rule	observation	conclusion	valid? (mark "yes" or "no")
$p \rightarrow q$	p	q	_____
$p \rightarrow q$	not-p	not-q	_____
$p \rightarrow q$	q	p	_____
$p \rightarrow q$	not-q	not-p	_____

Results and Discussion

From the initial sample of 400 subjects, 82 questionnaires were returned.[b] Five of these had to be eliminated because of insufficient information. Data from the remaining subjects were scored in a standardized fashion by an independent rater. Descriptive statistics from the four groups are presented in Table A-3. Within the constraints of the procedures and sample employed, the following tentative conclusions are suggested:

1. *Negative Results.* Although "negative" results were reported to

[b]This relatively low rate of return may have been due to a variety of factors (e.g., the absence of a postpaid return envelope, conduct of the survey during the summer months, resistance by scientists to this kind of research, etc.). Whatever the causes, the small sample places serious limitations on the generalizability of the obtained results. Nonetheless, the data are valuable in offering at least a tentative sketch of the issues addressed. More sophisticated and representative surveys will hopefully refine this sketch into a much clearer portrait.

Table A–3

	Physi-cists	Biolo-gists	Psycholo-gists	Sociolo-gists
NEGATIVE RESULTS				
1. Mean percentage of research which has yielded negative results.	24.1	34.7	39.1	33.5
2. Percent who said they were more likely to follow up on negative results.	16.7	21.4	20.0	16.7
3. Percent who reported "disappointment" as their reaction to negative results.	50.0	53.8	69.6	30.4
4. Mean probability that they would write up negative results for publication.	0.44	0.30	0.38	0.48
5. Mean probability of a negative results manuscript getting published.	0.51	0.30	0.18	0.26
PUBLICATION POLICIES				
6. Mean number of manuscripts submitted per year.	2.23	4.33	3.52	2.76
7. Mean percentage of manuscripts accepted by the first journal.	90.8	81.3	60.7	55.0
8. Percent who "frequently" or "almost always" resubmitted rejected manuscripts to another journal.	66.7	71.4	86.4	79.2
9. Mean percent of rejecting reviews which were abusive.	5.6	4.8	13.3	14.7
PROFESSIONAL ETHICS				
10. Percentage who knew of at least one incident of someone suppressing or discarding "negative" data in their field.	23.1	46.7	56.5	56.0
11. Percent who knew of at least one incident of someone fabricating data in their field.	30.8	57.1	40.9	38.5
12. Percent who said political rivalries or personality clashes influenced chances of publication				

Table A-3 continued

PROFESSIONAL ETHICS (continued)

or granting at least occasionally.	76.9	86.7	90.5	86.4
13. Mean estimated percent of individuals in the field who had suppressed data.	3.33	1.58	25.62	14.27
14. Mean estimated percent of individuals in the field who had faked data.	0.50	0.40	2.94	3.64
15. Mean estimated percent of individuals in the field who had plagiarized other's ideas.	12.22	2.60	23.35	17.60
16. Mean estimated percent of individuals in the field who had plagiarized other people's writings.	2.00	1.00	2.19	8.00
17. Mean estimated percent of individuals in the field who had misrepresented their methodology.	2.83	1.60	8.13	21.50
18. Mean estimated percent of individuals in the field who had criticized a colleague's character.	10.00	15.45	33.53	34.00

LOGICAL REASONING
SKILLS

19. Percent who correctly identified both irrelevant cards (II & III).	0.0	6.7	17.4	4.2
20. Percent who correctly identified the "critical" (potentially falsifying) cards (I & IV).	0.0	6.7	17.4	12.0
21. Percent who correctly rated *modus ponens* as logically valid.	100.0	100.0	87.0	91.7
22. Percent who correctly rated *modus tollens* as logically valid.	61.5	33.3	39.1	39.1
23. Percent who correctly rated *denying the antecedent* as logically invalid.	100.0	86.7	78.3	63.6
24. Percent who correctly rated *affirming the consequent* as logically invalid.	100.0	86.7	91.3	87.5

be relatively common, they were rated as less likely to be pursued in further research. About half of the scientists reported an emotional reaction of "disappointment" to negative results. The probability of writing up such results was about 0.40, and the mean estimated probability of publication varied across disciplines with a high of 0.51 in physics and a low of 0.18 in psychology.

2. *Publication Policies.* Scientists in the various disciplines appeared to differ in their mean number of manuscripts per year, with biologists and physicists being most and least prolific, respectively. Manuscripts were apparently better received in the physical (versus social) sciences, but the "perseverance to print" (resubmission of rejected manuscripts) was apparent in all four disciplines. Abusive rejecting reviews were reported as occurring approximately one-tenth of the time, with a somewhat higher frequency in the social sciences.

3. *Professional Ethics.* Almost half of the scientists reported knowing of at least one instance of data suppression in their field. This phenomenon was less prevalent among physicists. Over 40 percent knew of at least one instance of data fabrication in their field.[c] Political rivalries and personality clashes were frequently rated as at least occasional factors of influence in the four disciplines. Estimates of the prevalence of data suppression were lower in the physical sciences. The social scientists estimated that about 20 percent of their colleagues had engaged in this behavior. Data fabrication was estimated as rare in all four disciplines, with a slightly higher frequency in the social sciences. Plagiarism of ideas was rated as least prevalent in biology and most prevalent in psychology. The theft of written material was rated as rare in all four fields. Misrepresentation of procedures was alleged to be more common in the social sciences, particularly sociology. Subjects estimated that approximately one-fourth of their peers had criticized a colleague's character.

4. *Logical Reasoning Skills.* Fewer than eight percent of the scientists were able to identify the irrelevant "experiments" in the analogue hypothesis-testing task. Fewer than ten percent correctly selected the experiments which had the critical potential of falsifying the sample hypothesis. Likewise, although the vast majority of subjects were able to recognize the validity of *modus ponens*

---

[c]These data cannot be interpreted as estimates of prevalence since the scientists might have been aware of some well-known scandal in their field. This is corroborated by their much lower estimates of prevalence for these behaviors (items 13 and 14).

(confirmation) and the invalidity of affirming the consequent, almost 30 percent of the social scientists incorrectly rated denying the antecedent as a valid form of reasoning. Most interesting, perhaps, is the finding that over half the scientists did not recognize *modus tollens* (disconfirmation) as being logically valid.

These conclusions must be underlined as *tentative* because of the limitations of the survey and the need for further research. Until such refinements and extensions are made, however, the present data stand as a crude start in the direction of this sorely needed inquiry.

The Costs of Commitment

MICHAEL J. MAHONEY

The present treatise is a brief attempt to sketch a theory of thought and belief. As such, it joins an already large family of predecessors—all of which are marked by the distinction that they are unanimously viewed as inadequate. I have no delusions about the likelihood that the present theory can escape such a consistent trend, nor do I harbor any notions of originality. As far as I can tell, everything that I have to say has already been said in one form or another. My delusions (or aspirations) of contribution therefore lie in a different realm—that of integration and heuristics. Specifically, I am attempting the modest task of assimilating some interdisciplinary parallels and complementarities which (I think) are becoming more and more apparent. The fields from which I shall borrow include cognitive psychology and information processing, cybernetics, epistemology, social psychology and attitude change, belief systems, sociology, genetics, paleoneurology, anthropology, psychotherapy, superstition, psychopathology, and the psychology of religion. It should be obvious that the temptation to undertake such a task may be a better reflection of my ignorance than my knowledge. But since academicians seldom allow ignorance to stifle their verbiage, there is at least precedent for my actions.

Before I begin, I should share two relevant points. First, in case you are asking yourself why this treatise is presented in a book about scientists, let me offer (with slight trepidation) the promissory note that—should the theory make sense to you—its relevance for *homo scientus* will be very clear. (Should it not make sense, it probably doesn't matter). My second point is more of a confession. What follows is a very condensed version of a theory (or perspective) which has been emerging for several years. It is the product of many variegated themes in my background. Ideas and "data" have been borrowed from such strange bedfellows as axiology and computer science, Ulric Neisser and B.F. Skinner, philosophy of religion and nuclear physics. In fact, when I first conceived of this book, its tentative title was "The Costs of Commitment" and its theme was the content of this single appendix. I had intended to outline a theory of "belief" and to illustrate it via three divergent exemplars —religion, science, and psychopathology. It was (and is) my contention that some striking parallels can be drawn across these and many other phenomena (e.g., politics, astrology, etc.). I have included some of the major illustrations of my contention in the bibliography for this treatise. However, after extensive reconnaissance and rumination, I decided that the book was better devoted to scientists and that the theory should merit only meek exposition in an appendix. My reasons for that decision were multiple. Even if I had restricted my illustrations to religion, science, and psychopathology, this undertaking would have assumed an almost prohibitive bulk. Those of you who are familiar with the vast literatures on religion and pathology will, I think, be particularly grateful for my restraint.

A second reason was my appreciation of the inadequacies of the theory in its present form. Like its predecessors, its fallibilities are almost as salient as its strengths. Some of my opinions regarding "belief" are undergoing revision even as I am writing these words. Given that I am not yet comfortable with the model—particularly in its details rather than in generalizations—I decided not to seal its immediate demise in a lengthy list of half-baked speculations and ambivalent assertions. The broad generalities which remain in the sketch to follow are, I think, the least black of the lies inherent in the theory. They, too, will ultimately (and perhaps soon) fall prey to revision and rejection—a prospect which I welcome. Any model which stimulates inquiry in either its defense or destruction is contributory, not from a naive cumulation (accretion) perspective, but from the perspective of heuristic criticism. Until it is proferred in at least a crude form, however, the model has little chance of stimulating such criticism. The undeceived theorist realizes that his goal is suicidal—that the main contribution of his theory may well lie in its inevitable self-destruction (via the powerful machinery of normal science) and its ultimate concession to its successor.

My main reason for devoting a book to scientists and an appendix to belief systems, however, was my somewhat belated realization that our understanding of the latter are critically dependent upon our confidence in the former. Our "knowledge" about almost all phenomena—including religiosity and psychopathology—is unavoidably limited by the precision and skills of the persons to whom we entrust the noble goal of knowledge gathering—i.e., *homo scientus*. Given this epistemological dependence, the scientist might well be viewed as the most critical link in our chain of knowing. There may have been other factors in my decision—such as the relative neglect of *homo scientus* and perhaps some dim hopes that, as an organism committed to inquiry, he might be more receptive to my sermons on self-scrutiny—but the main one was the pivotal role of scientists in most other forms of public knowledge.

Having thus bared my teleological soul, let us hasten my act of theoretical suicide. Where my points appear vague, poorly articulated, or neglected, you should not presume that I could always remedy these faults in a more exhaustive presentation. More often than not, they are probably reflections of ignorance, agnosticism, or myopia.

The Evolution of Memory and Thought

If one grants the admittedly equivocal premise that progressive evolutionary developments have generally enhanced rather than endangered the survival of their bearers, then one can ask whether there are any commonalities or trends in these "adaptive" features. (This strategy is obviously correlational in its rationale, but I shall soon argue that most forms of adaptation have been equally correlational). Now then, what are some of the features which seem to correlate with ascension up the evolutionary ladder? As a start we might list the following:

1. increased complexity (at both the cellular and systemic levels),
2. increased response options (i.e., a broader range of survival-relevant actions), and
3. increased sensory capacities (as reflected in the emergence of specialized receptor systems).

This partial list (which is simplistic at best) fails to include, however, what I think may well be the most critical feature in successful adaptation. Namely:

4. increased ability to utilize information from past experience to guide present and future performance.

This last feature, which might be roughly equated with "memory" and "reasoning," is (I think) the basic ingredient in "learning." Put most simply, *learning is the ability to relationalize*—i.e., the ability to relate (connect) past and present experiences in an ostensibly adaptive fashion. The paradigm for studying learning is one in which the organism's performance is compared to its prior history of performance or to the continuing performances of some comparison group. If, after the intercession of some experience (e.g., "training"), the organism's performance reflects some minimally enduring change congruent with the information contained in that experience, then "learning" is said to have occurred.[a]

Let me back up for a moment to clarify my assertion about *relationalizing*. From a phenomenological perspective, all sensate organisms probably experience an ongoing flux of perceptions, the "raw data" of their experiential world. In organisms with some minimal degree of sensory differentiation, these perceptions are marked by at least three primary characteristics:

1. *simultaneity*—many of them are concurrent,
2. *succession*—they may also be described as a sequence (which, at least in humans, gives rise to the concept of "time"), and
3. *correlation*—certain perceptions (or categories of perceptions) tend to show regular or repetitive patterns.

Now then, the process of relationalizing is one in which the organism has developed certain abilities which may enhance its discovery and utilization of those patterns. Research in information processing suggests that relationalizing may require such sub-skills as *discrimination* (the ability to differentiate perceptions and patterns of perception), *selective attention* (the ability to select "relevant" perceptions from among a complex simultaneous array), and *retention* (the ability to codify or "store" information about past perceptions and correlations). To these I would add the feature of *selective connection* (the ability to identify relevant correlations in experience).

---

[a]It is interesting to note that not *any* change in performance will be deemed as indicative of learning. The observed change must "make sense" from the experimenter's perspective, otherwise it is termed superstition, artifact, etc. Likewise, not all experiences qualify as being capable of inducing learning. Surgery, for example, may be followed by more dramatic performance changes than many other experiences, but it is not considered eligible of being "instructive." Suicide is another example of dramatic performance change (i.e., to "dead behavior") but no attribution of learning. The learning theorist is obviously making some tacit assumptions here.

This latter capacity is clearly illustrated in some of the recent research on "preparedness" and inheritable selectivities in conditioning.

The *codification* of experiential information is probably adaptive for a variety of reasons. First, by facilitating information storage, it allows the organism to bridge spatio-temporal gaps. Second, by forcing experience into codified categories, it produces a degree of consistency which may facilitate learning. Finally, as a result of these two, codification may enhance the organism's ability to anticipate, prepare for, or control given events. These advantages, of course, take their toll in that the codified abridgments of reality are necessarily distortional. This is always the case with simplification. Moreover, coding processes often impose restrictions on *potential* experience. Sensory events are forced into available categories or are overlooked. This means that organisms may frequently force round sensations into square holes. Expansion of the coding system may occasionally take place to accommodate new categories of experience, but these expansions cannot be infinite without jeopardizing the purpose of condensation. All of which implies that *all codifying organisms may be biologically predisposed toward confirmation* (i.e., the registration or processing of events which "fit" expected categories of experience). This confirmatory bias is overcome only with extensive counter-experience. In organisms which rely extensively on codification, adaptation to the environment becomes critically related to (a) the accuracy of codified information, and (b) the flexibility (mutability) of the codification system. As the paleoneurologist Jerison has pointed out, biological intelligence is generally attributed only to organisms which are *flexible* in their adaptation and not to those in whom survival rules are rigidly inborn.

But what is this thing called *information* and how is it stored? Some of the problems in this perspective are addressed by cognitive psychologists (see references) and are noted briefly in my previous book, *Cognition and Behavior Modification*. Suffice it that the mechanisms of information storage remain poorly understood. At the risk of misrepresenting the continuing divergence of opinion in the field, let me extrapolate those points on which there seems to be general consensus:

1. Information storage requires some form of *codification* which (at least at the present time) is presumed to be biochemical in nature;
2. Information storage abilities have increased with certain evolutionary developments, particularly in the nervous system (e.g.,

the emergence of neurons from the ectoderm, the development of myelinization, synaptic complexities and increasing concentrations of certain chemical "transmitter substances," etc.); and

3. The codification of information can be functionally differentiated into at least three code forms:

   a. referential codes (what I shall term *ontocodes*), which are representations of experiences (either as elements or as complexes). In a sense, these are one's filing system for reality. They include *sensocodes* (those referring to sensory experience) and *ideocodes* (those which represent "conceptual" experiences—thoughts, images, symbols);

   b. correlational codes (which I shall term *implicodes*), which relate other code forms with one another. These are the "if/then's" of experience, stored in the form of codified implications. They include genetic varieties (e.g., "instincts," "reflexes") which may be distinguished on the basis of their independence from experience, and acquired (learned) correlations; and

   c. directive codes (which I shall call *actocodes*), which contain information about the components of action (from simple to complex).

Note that I have said nothing about these codes being "symbolic" or language-based. We will see in a moment that—although a symbol system may dramatically facilitate codification and other processes in learning—language is not essential for either "memory" or "reasoning." Animals can "remember" in the sense of profiting from past experience and they may even "think" if, by this, we mean that they can anticipate the consequences of some actions.[b]

The most rudimentary form of memory is that of *recognition* which, in its simplest form, may be diagrammed as follows:

Time	Experience	Example
T	A is followed by B	Storm clouds are followed by rain.
T + 1	actions patterns associated with (or preparatory to) B are observed in the presence of A alone	Rain-relevant behavior is observed to correlate with the appearance of rain clouds.

[b]This assertion may appear anthropomorphic or unparsimonious to some of you, but I would argue that both logic and the history of science place greater emphasis on compatibility with (rather than proximity to) the data. *All asser-*

The mechanisms of learning here are still energetically debated, although thousands of studies have begun to offer some consensus on important parameters (frequency, primacy/recency, survival relevance, and so on). It is noteworthy that the evidence for learning belies an *expectancy* or anticipation. From past experiential correlations, the organism is expected to expect similar patterns in its future. When its performance belies that expectancy, it is said to have "learned."

Recognition memory probably evolved before that of *recall*, if such a distinction is feasible. Recall memory is usually reserved for humans and, as far as I can tell, has little to differentiate it from recognition other than the fact that the original event need not be repeated.[c] In recall, the organism displays B-relevant actions in the absence of A. This is usually attributed to a symbolic representation of A or some spontaneous covert experience of A. The emergence of recall is probably reflected in the evolutionary development of dreaming, which has now been shown to correlate with several measures of learning and memory (see *Cognition and Behavior Modification*). When an animal is dreaming, it is probably experiencing some form of codified retrieval of past events. In both animals and man, this form of retrieval is typically disorganized and inaccurate—the dream may portray impossible correlations and never-experienced connections. With the development of a symbol system, man acquired some ability to control his recall memory and to utilize it more efficiently in preparing for future experience.

As yet, I have discussed memory as if it were the prime element in cognitive processes. But this would lead us to the ancient problem of creativity—how an organism can ever develop innovative solutions or preparations. Let me offer three comments. First, I can find little to distinguish a memory from a thought. If these two neurochemical entities are different, it is most probably in the realm of their previous history of having been experienced or in their use of symbolic codes. In humans, at least, thoughts are usually deemed relatively original and language-dependent, but I think one could cogently argue that few thoughts are without personal precedent and that many are independent of language. My second contention is that creativity stems

---

tions *involve inferences* (i.e., those which presume the veracity of one's data, the validity of one's logic, and the validity of the assertion itself). The issue is therefore not one of purism (whether to infer) but rather pragmatics (when to infer). When an entity or process is inferred as a necessary (logical) implication of the data, one can ask whether the inference increases one's precision or breadth in identifying lawful relationships. If it does, then it has paid its admission.

[c]Since it is technically impossible to have an identical repetition of any event (if only because the passage of time introduces a new element), I would argue that all instances of recognition are actually forms of recall.

(in part) from a variability which may be inherent to all living creatures. Evolution presupposes variation, and that variation is very
prevalent in all sciences. We may cling to our ideal of complete and
utter determinism, but we must do so in the face of overwhelming
evidence to the contrary. Our imprecise instruments may bear some
of the guilt, but I think it is naive to assume that all variance is error
variance. The entire field of statistics was established to deal with the
inescapable variability encountered in all phenomena. Indeed, the
primary purpose of science has been to reduce that variability. I
would argue that we at least consider the possibility that—given the
impossible requirements of a crucial test—we would find some events
and some organisms to be "erratic" in the sense of occasionally vio-
lating some norm or law. This deviance could be inherent rather than
attributable to "measurement error" or uncontrolled variables.[d]

My third comment is simply that innovation may further stem
from symbolic experience—the manipulation of codified symbols.
This capability is best developed in humans, and the cultural encouragement of creativity is quite conducive to unprecedented symbol
arrangements.

The Emergence of Symbols and "Beliefs"

Humans were apparently among the first to develop socially communicable symbol systems. Notice, however, that symbols are a
sophisticated form of codification. *Homo sapiens* had long since
developed memorial and relationalizing abilities. With the emergence of symbols, however, his personally codified reality was predominantly (but not totally) supplanted by a social reality—i.e., one
which could be shared. This development brought unmistakable
advantages in the coordination of interpersonal activity and the trans-
mission of knowledge to future generations. It also facilitated the
codification and retrieval of information, as well as the ability to
substitute symbolic experiments ("reasoning") as preparatory tests
of experience. But again, the new arrival brought problems. In some
ways, symbolic codification was more rigid than its predecessor in

---

[d]One must, of course, be careful here not to conjure up teleological sources
of variability such as "free will" or an evolutionary deviance demon. In animals,
at least, occasional instances of indeterminism may stem from biological limitations which favor approximations over exact replications. In any case, I see
indeterminism as being infrequent relative to broad and molar instances of determinism, so that my invitation to reconsider total determinism should not be
construed as a challenge to the aspirations of science. For those who are interested in some of the evidence and argumentation on the role of intracellular
indeterminism in biology and evolution, I suggest perusal of Jacques Monod's
classic *Chance and Necessity*.

that it required social consensus rather than allowing personal idiosyncrasies. This rigidity may have further enhanced the perceived consistency of the real world, but not without distortion. As the symbol system became more and more important, it grew to dominate much of the organism's adaptation. Naive realism was replaced by *naive symbolism*, and *homo sapiens* began to pay more homage to its symbolically-filtered world than to the rawer version of his ancestors. He did not have a choice in this deception, however, since his symbols had come to govern most of his percepts. With the advent of language, man lost his already tenuous grasp of "raw experience."

Symbols brought more assets than liabilities, however. They increased capacities for information storage and expanded the capacity to overcome spatio-temporal gaps. In addition, they opened up a realm which had heretofore been restricted to observation—namely, that of vicarious learning. Through their shared language, humans were able to educate one another regarding experiential correlations. When their shared experiences implied a consensus, the correlations were labeled "knowledge, truth, reality." When their assertions were met with only partial consensus, they were termed "attitudes, opinions." Propositions which were truly idiosyncratic were labeled "deviant, insane, strange."

In its most basic form, a symbolically expressed correlation is simply a *description* of associated events ("Storm clouds are followed by rain"). Since these correlations were used to guide future behavior, however, they soon took the form of inductive *predictions* ("Storm clouds will be followed by rain"). More interestingly, perhaps, they came to assume the role of *explanations* for past events ("It rained because there were storm clouds"). Thus, depending on whether it preceded or followed the events in question, a correlational description might serve either predictive or explanatory purposes. Indeed, I think that all forms of prediction, explanation, and even evaluation can be reduced (at some level) to a description. In the case of evaluation, to say that some action is "good" or "bad" is to predict its consequences, such prediction being a description of presumed correlations.

With the emergence of the symbol system came the concept of "belief." Unfortunately, this is a term which has yet to receive an unequivocal definition. Not being one to violate tradition, I shall add still another equivocal contender. Let me first state, however, that our understanding of the concept might be better served by studying the conditions in which it is invoked (by a *labeler*) rather than the attributes of its owner (the *labelee*). Bearing that in mind, I shall venture that *a belief is a propositional rule which is attributed to an organism*. These inferred propositions are usually (a) restricted to humans, (b) given primary residence in the central nervous system (albeit with behavioral and emotional correlates), (c) considered capable of influencing action, and (d) deemed relatively immutable. The attribution of belief usually serves either a predictive or an explanatory function. The primary criterion for attributing belief is behavioral performance. Unless there are extenuating or conspicuous circumstances to account for their discrepancy, the inconsistency of a behavior and an attributed belief will usually result in re-labeling of the belief.

The foregoing comments should not be misconstrued as meaning that "beliefs are in the eye of the beholder." Based in part on my own phenomenology, I do believe in beliefs. That is, I consider it probable that human actions are influenced by propositional rules (some of which are communicable in a shared symbol system). Most individuals are probably not aware of *all* of their beliefs, nor do many realize that they attribute beliefs to themselves based on their self-observed performances. Thus, we cannot restrict our attention to external labelers. The concept of belief invokes a cyclic complexity in which belief and behavior interact in infinite regress and ongoing intimacy. In textbooks and novels, sermons and songs, we symbolize our self-attributions and recommend them to our peers. They are our explanations for deviance, our descriptions of the universe, and our avenues to immortality. We train professionals to inculcate them in our children. Our individual sets of beliefs distinguish us from animals . . . and savages . . . and holy rollers . . . and Republicans. They are our excuses for war and our justifications for suffering.

When beliefs are organized into thematic *systems* and inculcated as comprehensive ways of approaching reality, their adaptive and mal-adaptive functions become most apparent. Institutionalized belief systems share at least four common features: (1) knowledge claims, (2) performance recommendations, (3) value directives (affective elements), and (4) maintenance features (such as isolationism and proselytization). The marketing of belief systems—whether they be in politics, religion, science, or wherever—offers an interesting documentary on the psychology of dogmatism and persuasion. It also raises ethical issues in that proselytization is a value-laden endeavor. The promotion and marketing of a belief system is tantamount to claiming its superiority and value over competing systems, and yet few systems outside of science (and sometimes even there) stand "accountable" for their claims. Converts are expected to accept the system on faith, and they often have little else to go on. Each belief system makes its own claims to justification, whatever its source (reason, authority, evidence, emotional satisfaction, etc.). And, if we view each system as a paradigm, each is selectively distortional in accounting its assets and ignoring its liabilities. But the liabilities remain, regardless of the belief system.

The Costs of Commitment

It has been my argument that all codifications are distortional in the sense that they condense reality at the cost of oversimplification. In addition, they encourage a perceptual incest by favoring the processing of experiences which already fit its categories. From here, it is a short leap to say that *all belief systems are costly*. This assertion rests somewhat precariously on an assumption which might be called "adaptive correspondence." This is the assumption that the organism's survival or adaptation is enhanced by accurate constructions of reality. Notice that the relative costs of a belief system are herein evaluated in terms of its "survival value"—an admittedly troublesome and arbitrary concept. Let me attempt to clarify what I mean by survival-relevant costs.

Cognitively, a belief system is deemed more or less costly than other belief systems on the basis of its knowledge claims (propositional *contents*) and its epistemology (knowledge-relevant *processes*). A belief system is generally considered more costly when:

1. its propositional contents are extensively contradicted by contemporary evidence;
2. it distorts, precludes, or otherwise impairs the collection of optimally (albeit imperfectly) "accurate" data relevant to the belief system or its competitors;
3. it tolerates, encourages, or exacerbates the "erroneous" processing of data relevant to that system; or
4. it promotes its own rigidity by prohibiting or discouraging critical examination, evaluation, or revision of the system.

We could at this point, spend quite a bit of time destroying the above criteria on both epistemological and terminological grounds. I will be the first to confess their technical inadequacy. On the other hand, I think they are communicative and potentially useful; I shall therefore retreat into the role of a lexicographer and continue with my attempted clarification of the "costs" of belief.

Behaviorally, a belief system is deemed more costly when—relative to alternative thematic belief systems—it dictates, encourages, or condones:

1. behaviors which are *apparently* at variance with "veridical" survival contingencies;
2. behaviors which—although not directly survival-threatening— are nevertheless superfluous expenditures of effort (and whose only "real" consequences are endemic to the belief system); or
3. behaviors which effectively restrict exposure to experiences which might have relevance for the critical evaluation of the current belief system.

Emotionally, a belief system is deemed more costly when—relative to alternative thematic belief systems—it encourages or condones:

1. static, universal, absolutistic, or dichotomous values;
2. closure-inducing contentment; or
3. intolerance of criticism, anomaly, or competing belief systems.

Sounds nice and neat, doesn't it? Unfortunately—as I mentioned after the discussion of cognitive costs—the criteria outlined above are plagued with a multitude of terminological and epistemological problems and assumptions. Their examination might interest those of you with a penchant for systems analysis, but I would rather forego that timely and tortuous tangent at the present time. Suffice it that I think (believe?) that the problems are not entirely insurmountable and, furthermore, that they are no more extensive than those encountered in several pragmatically useful psychological theories.

Less apparent in the foregoing criteria are some value biases which deserve at least brief mention. First, I have already referred to the arbitrary choice of survival as the ultimate criterion of adaptiveness. A second evaluative assumption is that regarding "superfluous expenditures of effort." This may sound like a disguised endorsement of the Protestant ethic. It should not, however, be interpreted as devaluing esthetics, recreation, or similar pursuits. The denigration of extraneous performances refers only to performances which are inaccurately perceived and pursued as survival-enhancing. As finite and probably mortal organisms, we have a very limited sojourn on our planet. Because of our limitations, our pursuit of some activities precludes the pursuit of others. My value-laden assertion is that— when an organism engages in a behavior pattern (which is often sacrificial or effortful) *because* he erroneously believes it to be survival-relevant—then the belief system which has proferred that belief (and its associated performance) is relatively costly.

A third evaluative assumption deals with my apparent glorification of skepticism, critical examination, and synthesis. This emphasis derives in part from epistemological considerations which should now be obvious.

Now then, the relative costs of a belief system are influenced by three interdependent features: (1) the survival relevant contents of the system, (2) its openness to revision, and (3) the individual's degree of commitment to it. A system may be potentially costly (in terms of its ontology and epistemology) but relatively harmless unless it is faithfully obeyed. *Commitment* refers to the degree to which an individual (a) accepts its knowledge claims (the probability-certainty continuum), (b) abides by its performance directives (relativistic versus ritualistic obedience), and (c) experiences strong emotional responses to its maintenance, expansion, or attack.

Up until this point, my contentions may be summarized as follows:

1. The process of learning is one in which past experience is codified in a manner which makes it relevant for future performance;
2. Codification is necessarily distortional in the sense that it reduces variance by simplification and imposes some restrictions on categories of likely (or potential) experience;
3. As forms of codification, beliefs are also costly;[e]
4. The costs of a belief system are related to the contents of the system, its flexibility, and the individual's degree of commitment to it.

These relatively broad statements are sufficiently vague to insulate them from any critical data, but this may be less of a crime than we had once thought. Having now read the book, it should be clear that rhetoric and conceptual parameters may be more active ingredients than data. Nevertheless, I would like to reduce my ambiguities by spelling out more specific features of commitment to a costly belief system. Bear in mind that the caricature which follows is somewhat exaggerated in that it portrays patterns which would be found only when an individual were strongly committed to a costly and inflexible belief system. Since most individuals and systems lie at less ex-

[e]There is, in fact, some reason to believe that there may well be differences in the costs imposed by symbolic (versus non-symbolic) codification. Language-imposed *perceptual* constraints are discussed by Benjamin Whorf, and its *conceptual* liabilities are suggested by P.C. Wason's finding that humans have difficulty dealing with negative reasoning.

treme points on the continuum, the portrait here may be dimmer than average. In addition, the costs of commitment to a belief system must be measured relative to the individual's performance (reasoning, emotions) in other neutral spheres. Thus, when his baseline skills are minimal to begin with, the difference between a person's "committed" and "uncommitted" reasoning should be less discriminable. I shall divide my discussion of costs into three spheres: cognitive, behavioral, and emotional.

Cognitive Correlates

Data Collection Deficits. The arbitrary distinction between data "collection" and data "processing" may or may not be a useful one. For the time being, I am entertaining it. Thus, under the present subdivision are included several patterns which relate to the "sampling" here referring primarily to the perceptual realm. Borrowing from Eric Hoffer, let me hereafter use the term "true believer" to denote the committed individual.

a. *Selective Attention and Inattention.* The true believer tends to attend to and perceive data which are congruent with his belief system and to simultaneously ignore or deemphasize contradictory data. There are relatively rare exceptions to this generality, such as (i) when the incongruity is frequent and/or extreme, or (ii) situational exigencies force him to at least acknowledge the data (e.g., in an argument or when asked to role play an opponent). In these instances, the incongruous data are often discredited through data processing (to be discussed shortly). Note that it is *not* being contended that the individual is literally and universally "blind" to unsupportive data. Analogous to experiments on parallel (simultaneous) information processing, the person *could* discriminate disconfirmatory events. In the absence of extreme anomaly or situational exigencies, however, confirmatory data have a higher likelihood of perceptual selection, credibility assignment, and further processing.

b. *Data Distortion and Creation.* When belief-relevant data are relatively vague or ambiguous, the true believer will tend to categorize them more frequently as supportive than non-supportive. Thus, in a laboratory belief task involving ostensibly dichotomous feedback (e.g., a tone of frequency X signifies "yes" and a tone of frequency Y signifies "no"), when the feedback are near perceptual threshhold or ambiguous (e.g., a tone of frequency $(X+Y)/2$), the true believer will be more likely to categorize it as confirmatory. The depressive, for example, should be more likely to interpret feedback as negative.

The creation aspect of the present sub-proposition stems from the concept of constructive perception in information processing. In instances where the datum is incomplete (i.e., partial), this tendency should be most apparent. That is, the true believer will be more likely to fill in missing parts of a datum in a way which is congruent with the belief system. In a laboratory task in which a subject was told that belief-relevant feedback would be presented (e.g., flashed on a screen), the act of flashing blank or nonsense images will probably result in the true believer interpreting such events more frequently as supportive.

Data Processing Errors. Once the data have "registered," their subsequent analysis will be differentially affected by their relevance for and bearing upon the belief system. Although it will soon become more apparent, bear in mind that the "data" referred to throughout our discussion include "internal" events (memories, current sensations, etc.). Also, the fine line between "perceptual" and "conceptual" processes will soon appear very tenuous.

a. *Confirmatory Set.* Given any set of belief-relevant data, the true believer is more likely to interpret (analyze, process) them as supportive rather than non-supportive. This, of course, is moderated to some extent by the data, with the more "equivocal" being affected more than data whose implications are more clear-cut. This proposition complements that of selective attention, contributing to an overall tendency for the person to confirm rather than disconfirm his beliefs. A third related proposition, which shall be discussed under behavioral correlates, contends that the true believer tends to act in ways which increase the likelihood of confirmatory experience (e.g., through the "experiments" he conducts, the social groups and mass media to which he subscribes, etc.).

In sum, then, the gist of the current sub-proposition is that the true believer is more likely to select, emphasize, and process those data points which confirm rather than disconfirm his beliefs.

b. *Discreditory Defensiveness.* In a confrontation with ostensibly anomalous data, the true believer is more likely to minimize or deny the incongruity. This defensiveness often takes one of the following strategic forms:

(i) discredit the content of the anomaly (e.g., challenge the validity of the data, the representativeness of the data, the representativeness of the sample, experimental methodology (where appropriate), the adequacy of the logic, the nature of the premises, etc.);

(ii) discredit the source of the anomaly (e.g., the credibility of the observer—even, in some cases, oneself);

(iii) deny or minimize the relevance of the data (e.g., by admitting their possible validity but challenging their interpretation as relevant or threatening to the belief; alternatively, one may challenge whether this type of data (or, in some cases, any type of "data") have any bearing on the belief); or

(iv) assume an eschatological stance (i.e., that the present experience may, in fact, be anomalous but—relative to past confirmations of the belief and one's expectation of future confirmation—they pose no meaningful threat to the *ultimate* veracity of the belief.

c. *Expedient Reasoning.* In a committed belief system, the true believer is likely to apply differential criteria of reason and experience depending on whether the argument or data in question are (i) in favor of or opposed to the preferred belief system, or (ii) in favor of or opposed to competing (unpreferred) belief systems. In general, the individual will impose less stringent criteria for evidence supportive of his beliefs or critical of competing beliefs. For example, in scientific pursuits, experimental methodology is seldom challenged unless the obtained results contradict expectation. Likewise, the more divergent the claim (from one's anchor belief), the more stringent the criteria imposed upon it. ESP researchers must demonstrate phenomenal significance levels (and—even then —their data are discredited).

In the realm of logical inference, the true believer will condone or commit more frequent or extensive logical errors when defending his preferred belief. On the other hand (and granting minimal critical thinking skills), he can often legitimately devastate the logic employed by proponents of alternative belief systems. Although this expedience of reasoning probably derives from errors in both (i) premises and (ii) inferences, the former are probably more frequent culprits. That is, in dialectics, the true believer is more prone to be critical of the premises of his opponents than of his own.

d. *Certainty and Closure.* The true believer tends to hold the knowledge claims of his belief system (both ontological and epistemological) with a greater degree of certainty and finality. In Rokeach's terms, he is often not "open" to examining the foundations of his beliefs or to synthesizing new data or beliefs into the system. This propensity is often expressed in the form of *dichotomous, absolute*, and *universal* propositions. Those beliefs which are least amenable to experimental tests are often held with greatest certainty.

e. *Memory Dysfunction.* The strongly committed adherent of a belief system tends to selectively store material which is congruent with or supportive of that system. Even when anomalous experiences are perceived and acknowledged as inconsistent with the system, they tend to show a lower probability of recall from long term memory. Whether this selective recall is attributable to encoding or rehearsal deficiencies, motivated forgetting (repression), instructed forgetting, or some other process is open to speculation. An additional cognitive correlate, however, is *reconstruction*. There is some consensus in contemporary theories of memory that at least some items in long term store are actively and sometimes elaborately reconstructed rather than passively recalled. The analogy might be that—instead of going to a hypothetical filing system and retrieving the requested material—the individual often retrieves only small segments of the actual event and, under certain circumstances, constructs the "recall" report around those items. For the true believer, this reconstruction process is particularly relevant. He often "recalls" events as being much more congruent with his belief system than was actually the case. Marginal experiences (those which were initially neither confirmatory nor disconfirmatory) trend in reconstruction toward confirmation. Supportive material often becomes more dramatically supportive with time, and formerly anomalous experience becomes less anomalous. Thus, the individual who believes himself to have been quite the high school lover will often differentially recall his "successful" experiences, often with elaborate confabulation. This reconstructive embellishment is often tacit, and its pervasiveness may be most apparent when memories are compared at class reunions.

f. *Pervasive Exemplars and Tacit Submergence.* The true believer will frequently "find" pervasive illustrations of the validity, adaptiveness, or superiority of his belief system. The depressed client will often report a multitude of daily experiences which document (and confirm) his worthlessness or ineptitude. The sociologist will see the relevance of his knowledge in cocktail parties and car pools. The devout theist will find pervasive exemplars of the world's need for religion, the power of faith, and the perils of irreligion. The pervasive exemplar set is also frequently illustrated in an increased disposition to infer *causality* regarding belief-relevant events. For the health food enthusiast, every physical ache and pain may be attributed to impurities and additives in his diet.

More intriguing, perhaps, is the pattern of "tacit submergence," which denotes the trend for a belief system to become almost axiomatic. What were formerly considered fundamental propositions—with due awareness and frequent communication—often evolve into primitive truths which are seldom acknowledged unless challenged. Although their influence is still pervasive, their momentary consciousness (symbolic representation?) to the believer becomes infrequent. This submergence of the belief system is sometimes accompanied by a symbolic shorthand which facilitates rapid processing but defies interpersonal communication. An illustration of this is when the person is asked to "come out of" an engrossing train of thought and—when asked to describe what he was thinking—can *now* place semantic labels on the process but recognizes that language was *not* a part of his meditative ramblings (nor was imagery).

On this topic of tacit submergence, I might insert the qualifier that it is probably *less* frequent in those individuals responsible for the inculcation of the belief system (call it proselytization, marketing, or education—their job is to deliver the system unto the unbelievers). Because their pedagogical role forces them to present (and sometimes defend) the basics of the system, they usually do not show the same degree of submergence as the non-proselytizing believer.

g. *System Saving.* Finally, we have a cognitive correlate which overlaps with several of those mentioned above. Briefly (and metaphorically), it deals with the true believer's tendency to continually "patch up" and "remodel" the old belief system rather than move into a new one. When the belief system is seriously threatened (by data, social trends or whatever), the tendency is to "salvage and re-tool" rather than abandon. This pattern is particularly clear in contemporary Christianity, in which steadfast dogmas are being shed faster than nuns' habits (re: folk masses, secularity, youth groups, the liberal clergy, fish on Friday, legalized divorce, poetic—rather than literal—interpretations of Genesis, etc.).

Behavioral Correlates of Commitment

This section deals with activities of the somatic or skeletal nervous system. As you will discover, it is much less elaborate than the preceding, but not necessarily less significant.

Performance Blueprints. Most belief systems endorse specific performance-directing propositions, which are often phrased in "how to" formats (how to . . . attract girls, make love, conduct research, know God, get rich, etc.). Their formality may range from that of the Ten Commandments to the more tacit "life philosophies" of the therapy client. They can usually be translated into some form of a means-end relationship. Some of them bear relevance not only for the individual's successful pursuit of specified ends, but also deal with the maintenance of the system itself.

Maintenance Engineering. It should come as no shock that most belief systems of the costlier variety contain inherent maintenance features. These, of course, overlap extensively with the confirmatory features of the cognitive correlates. At the risk of simplification, I would suggest that the following are representative illustrations of maintenance engineering:

a. *Endemic Ritual.* These are performances which can serve a range of functions in the maintenance of the belief system. They are often public in nature and express the believer's acceptance of and commitment to the system (note the significance of vicarious processes). Although frequently defended as means toward some specified ends, their apparent role in the system often emphasizes *contribution*. This may be financial, spiritual, or epistemological (although I have yet to find many large scale belief systems which don't include the financial aspect). The term *sacrifice* is sometimes aired and there is a frequent valuation of goals which (theoretically, at least) transcend individuals' interests in favor of group or worldly ideals. In formal religious systems, the rituals often range from attendance at services to tithings and participation in special endeavors. For the scientist, conventions, specialized societies, and contributions to the literature" are frequent rituals. The political believer will most certainly be asked to render financial support for the advancement of the system (as well as voting a particular way, littering his auto bumper, and so on). In the less socially cohesive belief systems, the rituals are more frequently private and place more direct and candid emphasis on individual interests (e.g., in health food faddism, astrology, etc.).
b. *Structured Rehearsal.* A salient element in some of the more populous belief systems is their emphasis on memorization and rehearsal. The true believer is often evaluated by his peers on the basis of his knowledge of system particulars (history, ontological

propositions, subtleties, etc.). Formal religions usually encourage both public and private "exercises" which serve to maintain or expand the individual's familiarity with (and perhaps acceptance of) system dogma. Prayer, Bible reading, and sermons (gospels) are illustrative. The professional specialist (physician, scientist, educator, etc.) is also expected to "stay on top of his field" by means of private exercise (journal reading, etc.) and participation in occasional public sermons (conventions, workshops, etc.).

c. *Physical and Social Engineering.* Most believers, and particularly the true believer, usually place themselves predominantly in environments which are at least consistent with, and often supportive of, their belief system. The scientist executes experiments which are conventional and primarily biased toward confirmation of his beliefs. The behavior therapist seldom asks about dreams (or nutrition, heredity, zodiac sign, etc.) and the psychoanalyst rarely considers such variables as social reinforcement patterns. Opponents to euthanasia and abortion spend little time on the hospital back wards filled with vegetative retardates; and adherents of these practices demonstrate little exposure to the cases of "personal success" in congenitally malformed individuals. One might add that most fish spend very little time out of water.

Media engineering is another significant pattern in true belief. The committed individual tends to expose himself almost exclusively to those media which are most congruent with his belief system (Newspapers, professional journals, movies, television, etc.). In the more populous systems, however, *social* engineering is by far the most elaborate (and perhaps powerful) maintenance strategy. Informally, most individuals socialize predominantly with persons whose beliefs are generally congruent with their own. In those rare instances where belief incongruities are present, there is often an explicit or implicit agreement to avoid the contested ground (politics, religion, childrearing, health food, etc.). Social exigencies also account for some apparent exceptions to the social maintenance pattern (e.g., forced socialization via employment or familial obligations). Formalized social engineering is also a frequent aspect of the more populous belief systems. Church meetings, professional conventions and political rallies are cases in point. It may seem all too obvious, but it is worth noting that one rarely hears of an adherent of Belief System A attending the social gatherings of Belief System B (except in Ireland, where such attendance serves the function of demolition). On second thought, I think a recent Democratic convention was attended by a few select Republicans.

In the more formalized strategies of social engineering, an intriguing *stratification* can be observed. Recognized *authorities* are usually established, with frequent division of labor into specialized responsibilities (e.g., history, public relations, proselytization and expansion, finance management, etc.). Most revered of these authorities, however, are the *truth keepers*, who range from Biblical scholars and historians to society officers and journal editors. Their primary responsibilities usually include the maintenance of tradition, defense, expansion, or refinement of the system, and proselytization. In the maintenance function of social engineering, authority figures often play a more influential role than peer reinforcement and modeling.

d. *Personalization/Proselytization.* In belief systems which claim a relevance for relatively broad aspects of human functioning, the individual adherent is often expected to "market" the system to his peers. This is frequently done via formal social engineering channels (church services, religious publications, professional journals and meetings, etc.). As a matter of fact, I would speculate that when an individual attends a meeting (or contributes to a journal) which is not congruent with his own beliefs, it is often due to a proselytic intention (via debate, a critique, etc.). The greatest emphasis on marketing, however, appears to be placed on the younger candidates for a belief system (children, college students, etc.). There is probably more than a "service" function associated with the high density of religious institutes and congregations which characterize university towns. This marketing function was made explicit by early leaders of the Mormon church, who candidly planned to facilitate the expansion of their religion by locating institutes near major educational institutions.

Regardless of whether or not his belief system explicitly encourages proselytization, the true believer often introduces such behaviors into formal and informal social interactions. With a few moderating situational variables, he often markets his own beliefs in very subtle ways. The scientist conveys his confidence in empiricism; the theist introduces religious topics and relevancies, and so on. These patterns are particularly apparent when they are placed in the role of an educator or parent.

Personal belief systems, on the other hand, claim relevance only for their "owner" and proselytization is not a characteristic pattern in their maintenance. As a matter of fact, their lack of communication can often be said to contribute to their maintenance. Personal beliefs are seldom changed in the absence of some form of relevant social feedback. When the true (personal) believer keeps his propositional rules to himself, he effectively reduces the likelihood of their social evaluation and possible alteration. Thus, for example, the fact that American presidential assassins have predominantly been "loners" who held deviant beliefs has been interpreted as illustrating the possible importance of social feedback in "non-deviant" belief. Clinical illustrations of this same point are not hard to provide. Clients often dilvulge (sometimes with great reluctance) personal beliefs which appear to be very incongruent with reality but which have been seldom, if ever, exposed to social feedback.

The Emotional Correlates of Commitment

Although the following comments pertain primarily to the automatic nervous system, the arbitrariness of their classification will often be apparent. Because of their extensive interdependence, it is difficult (if not impossible) to exclusively separate central, somatic, and autonomic correlates.

Elite Knowledge: The Security of Truth. Phenomenologically, the true believer often displays an apparent "contentment" regarding the adequacy or superiority of the beliefs in question. Although this feeling is occasionally self-reported, it is more frequently reflected in other indexes of assurance and complacency.

Evaluative Dichotomies. Implicitly or explicitly, all belief systems condone or presume dichotomies of value. The following series of term pairs may illustrate what I mean: "right/wrong," "good/bad," "sacred/profane," "scientific/unscientific," "strong/weak," "virtuous/evil," "healthy/unhealthy," "adaptive/maladaptive," "righteous/sinful," "positive/negative," "replicable/unreplicable," "valid/invalid," "significant/insignificant," etc. (the list could be expanded considerably). These evaluations are usually applied to both means and ends. They dictate the "should's" and "should not's" of religion, science, personal hygiene, education, etc.

The Agonies of Anomaly. In those rare instances in which a belief system has predicted relatively explicit relational observations (if X, then Y), the opportunity arises for straightforward disconfirmatory trials. When these occur, the true believer will often experience frustration, anger, and occasionally even guilt. This latter emotion stems from the fact that, particularly in the true believer, initial anomalies are often attributed to the individual's incompetence (unworthiness, ineptitude, etc.). When personal responsibility is not attributed, initial anomalies are often discredited (as measurement or sampling error, etc.). For the true believer, these first incongruities are more likely to be fallacious or invalid when they are either slight or extreme in their violation of the belief system. That is, slight anomalies are readily discarded as irrelevant and the most blatant incongruities are—at least initially—rejected outright (often on the grounds of their deviance from what is "known" to be true). As the frequency and magnitude of anomalous experiences increases, the true believer's emotional distress does likewise until some degree of resolution is achieved (through discrediting of the experiences, accelerated confirmatory experiences, or modifications in the belief system).

Sensitivity to Attack. An individual's commitment to a belief system is often illustrated emotionally in his response to (i) attacks upon that system, and (ii) defenses of competing or incompatible systems. Unfortunately (for the theorist, at least), the parameters of his emotional responding are quite complicated. For example, each of the following is probably important in predicting the true believer's tolerance/intolerance:

a. *Nature of the attack.* Direct attacks on one's current system usually elicit more emotional arousal and intolerance than invitations to or defenses of an alternative system.
b. *Focus of the attack.* Does it address "integral" (central aspects) of the belief system or peripheral subtleties? I must confess to ignorance as to the direction of the probable relationship here (if one exists). Although attacks on central premises might appear to be most threatening, attacks on central premises are also more likely to be totally disregarded as too deviant to be meaningful.
c. *Source of the attack.* Challenges from prestigious sources and authority figures often evoke more autonomic arousal than those emanating from relative pawns. When the authorities come from competing belief systems, they are particularly ill received. When they come from *within* the belief system attacked, the response is often dichotomous (sometimes resulting in pluralistic branching of "schools" of belief).
d. *Strength of the attack.* "Strength" refers to the "backing" behind the attack, which may be measured in logic, data, and—most often —social variables (number and prestige of detractors). In the true believer (as opposed, in this case, to the "faltering" believer), weak attacks are often met with patronizing pity and complacency. Strong attacks, on the other hand, elicit extreme arousal and intol-

erance, often resulting in active counterattacks and a cohesive rallying of true believers.

An individual's emotional commitment to a belief system is probably reflected most accurately in his response to its attack (rather than its expansion). For some individuals at least, the emotional correlates of a belief system are apparent *only* when the system encounters anomaly or direct attack.

Conversion and Dogmatism

It need hardly be pointed out that fidelity to a belief system is more prevalent than defection. The true believer usually remains true, and instances of conversion are relatively rare. This is probably due to the myriad features which facilitate belief maintenance—confirmatory bias, isolation, and so on. We have already seen that at least some forms of belief tenacity may be culturally contributory. Kuhn and others have argued that the dogmas of normal science are necessary for revolution and progress. Without some degree of commitment, a belief system would have little chance of performing its valuable function in the cyclic competition of models. Even in the patently skeptical stance of comprehensively critical rationalism, conviction and tentative confidence are deemed prerequisites for pragmatic action.

Does all of this mean that tenacity and dogmatism are "good"? That probably depends on one's definition of "good" and the degree of dogmatism involved. Tentative conviction seems to be an essential prerequisite to the evaluation and potential refinement of a belief system. Unless it is adopted, its adaptiveness can hardly be assessed. If the system precludes its own criticism, however, it begins on very maladaptive footing. Thus, we must conclude that a delicate balance may be optimal—one which allows sufficient conviction for pragmatic (and evaluative) action without simultaneously removing the system from susceptibility to reform.

I should mention that we have now stumbled into the thorny issue of choice criteria. Given that one may choose from among several different belief systems (in science, religion, politics, etc.), what are the "best" criteria? This question has been hotly debated for several centuries. The most popular criteria have been: reason and evidence, authority, ethics, and emotional satisfaction. Generally, such writers as Hume, Russell, Clifford, and Huxley have held logic supreme, while Plato, Marx, and others have invoked the value of "noble lies" which could serve as palliative beliefs. In his classic paper, "The Will To Believe," William James argued for emotional satisfaction as a legitimate consideration when reason is insufficient. James' remarks were primarily directed at Clifford who had outspokenly claimed that "It is wrong always, everywhere, and for anyone, to believe anything on insufficient evidence."

The legitimate criteria for belief will probably evade agreement for some (if not all) time to come. Likewise, they may turn out to be functionally variable. That is, some beliefs may serve different functions than others, thereby requiring different criteria. It is not my intention here to resolve the issue of belief criteria. However, it is interesting to note that—with the exception of comprehensively critical rationalism—all institutionalized belief systems have presupposed the legitimacy of their own criteria, marketing themselves as "the" road to salvation, truth, or political reform. Proselytization, or the marketing of belief systems, is an intriguing phenomenon in itself and one which could consume several volumes of discussion. Since this treatise is already too lengthy, I shall condense my comments.

First of all, despite centuries of frenzied practice, the act of proselytization is still one which is seldom effective. That is, conversion is rare relative to continued fidelity. When it does occur, its mechanisms are poorly understood. Consider, for example, the following partial list of questions which surround the phenomenon of belief conversion:

1. To what extent is it affected by age, intelligence, and prior familiarity with the new belief system?
2. Are certain features of the old system conducive to conversion (e.g., rigidity)?
3. Does resistance to conversion increase with such factors as length of fidelity to the system?
4. Is "doubt" a prerequisite?
5. Are indirect (Socratic) approaches more successful than authoritarian ones?
6. If a belief system is temporarily doubted but retained, is it thereafter more resistant to conversion?
7. Does the destruction of early childhood belief systems (e.g., Santa Claus) have any impact on later belief flexibility?

To date, the only two relatively clear seeds of wisdom regarding conversion are that (a) a belief system is seldom rejected in the absence of an alternative system, and (b) in at least some individuals, emotional arousal may facilitate a "conversion experience." Aside from these, the art of proselytization remains almost where Aristotle left it in his *Rhetoric*. Since I have already voiced some of my own speculations on possible factors in belief change (see *Cognition and Behavior Modification*), I shall forego their expansion here.

Conclusion

In admittedly crude form, I have tried to offer a theory of belief which will hopefully serve heuristic functions (if only in its rejection). It should be obvious that the true believer takes many forms and that his convictions cover a wide range of human experience. It is the parallels in those forms which I have tried to convey. As I mentioned at the end of the book, however, there is no escaping fallibilism. Knowledge of the costs of commitment does not thereby produce immunity. As I have outlined, tentativity . . . skepticism . . . self-disconfirmation—these are all "unnatural" acts which require constant attention and effort. While I have labored to remain self-scrutinizing, I have no illusions that my beliefs about beliefs are not distorted, selectively reasoned, and so on. The theory pronounces its own culpability. As a scientist, I can hope for no more than that it will have encouraged a more adequate model to take its place.

REFERENCES

1, 8, 9, 11, 27, 30, 35, 40, 44, 56, 57, 66, 67, 68, 74, 77, 79, 80, 89, 125, 129, 132, 133, 139, 140, 141, 146, 154, 161, 189, 191, 198, 201, 202, 207, 209, 211, 212, 221, 225, 257, 258, 260, 261, 263, 264, 272, 273, 277, 285, 289, 290, 291, 308, 310, 312, 318, 319, 344, 352, 363, 370, 372, 379, 380, 384, 397, 404, 405, 406, 410, 419, 426, 436, 445, 453, 454, 455, 456, 458, 459, 475, 478, 490.

References

1. Abelson, R.P. Modes of resolution of belief dilemmas. *Conflict Resolution*, 1959, *3*, 343–352.

2. Abramson, J. *The invisible woman: Discrimination in the academic profession*. San Francisco: Jossey-Bass, 1975.

3. Agassi, J. Towards an historiography of science. *History and theory*. Beiheft 2, Wesleyan University Press, 1963.

4. Agnew, N.M., & Pyke, S.W. *The science game*. Englewood Cliffs, N.J.: Prentice-Hall, 1969.

5. Anderson, J.R., & Bower, G.H. *Human associative memory*. Washington, D.C.: Winston & Sons, 1973.

6. Andrade, E.N. da Robert Hooke. In *Lives in science*. New York: Simon and Schuster, 1957. Pp. 31–44.

7. Andreski, S. *Social sciences as sorcery*. New York: St. Martin's Press, 1972.

8. Argyle, M. *Religious behaviour*. London: Routledge & Kegan Paul, 1958.

9. Aristotle. *The rhetoric of Aristotle*. (L. Cooper, transl.) New York: Appleton-Century-Crofts, 1932.

10. Armour, R. *The academic bestiary*. New York: William Morrow & Co., 1974.

11. Asch, S.E. Forming impressions of personality. *Journal of Abnormal and Social Psychology*, 1946, *41*, 258–290.

12. Asher, J. Can parapsychology weather the Levy affair? *American Psychological Association Monitor*, 1974, *5* (11), 4.

13. Asher, J. Uri Geller—Is he a medicine show hype or a challenge to science? *American Psychological Association Monitor*, 1974, *5* (2), 4.

14. Ayer, A.J. *Language, truth, and logic*. New York: Dover, 1936.

15. Ayer, A.J. *The problem of knowledge*. Baltimore: Penguin, 1956.

16. Ayer, A.J. (Ed.), *Logical positivism*. Glencoe, Ill.: Free Press, 1959.

17. Azrin, N.H., Holz, W., Ulrich, R., & Goldiamond, I. The control of conversation through reinforcement. *Journal of the Experimental Analysis of Behavior*, 1961, *4*, 25-30.

18. Bachrach, A.J. *Psychological research*. (2nd ed.) New York: Random House, 1965.

19. Bacon, F. *Novum organum*. (original 1621) New York: Bobbs-Merrill, 1960.

20. Bakan, D. *On method*. San Francisco: Jossey-Bass, 1973.

21. Bandura, A. *Principles of behavior modification*. New York: Holt, Rinehart & Winston, 1969.

22. Bandura, A. (Ed.), *Psychological modeling: Conflicting theories*. Chicago: Aldine-Atherton, 1971.

23. Bannister, D. Psychology as an exercise in paradox. *Bulletin of the British Psychological Society*, 1966, *19*, 21-26.

24. Barber, B. *Science and the social order*. New York: Collier, 1952.

25. Barber, B. Resistance by scientists to scientific discovery. *Science*, 1961, *134*, 596-602.

26. Barber, B., & Hirsch, W. (Eds.), *The sociology of science*. New York: Free Press, 1962.

27. Barber, T.X. Death by suggestion: A critical note. *Psychosomatic Medicine*, 1961, *23*, 153-155.

28. Barber, T.X. Pitfalls in research: Nine investigator and experimenter effects. In R.M.W. Travers (Ed.), *Second handbook of research on teaching*. Chicago: Rand McNally, 1973. Pp. 382-404.

29. Barnes, B. (Ed.), *Sociology of science: Selected readings*. Baltimore: Penguin, 1972.

30. Bartlett, F.C. *Remembering*. Cambridge: Cambridge University Press, 1932.

31. Bartley, W.W. *The retreat to commitment*. New York: Alfred A. Knopf, 1962.

32. Bartley, W.W. Rationality versus the theory of rationality. In M. Bunge (Ed.), *The critical approach to science and philosophy*. New York: Free Press, 1964. Pp. 3-31.

33. Bartley, W.W. Theories of demarcation between science and metaphysics. In I. Lakatos and A. Musgrave (Eds.), *Problems in the philosophy of science*. Amsterdam: North Holland Publishing Company, 1968. Pp. 40-64.

34. Barzun, J. *Science: The glorious entertainment*. New York: Harper & Row, 1964.

35. Batson, C.D. Rational processing or rationalization?: The effect of disconfirming information on a stated religious belief. *Journal of Personality and Social Psychology*, 1975, *32*, 176-184.

36. Baxter, J.P. *Scientists against time*. Cambridge, Mass.: MIT Press, 1968.

37. Bayer, A.E., & Folger, J. Some correlates of a citation measure of productivity in science. *Sociology of Education*, 1966, *39*, 381-390.

38. Beardslee, D.C., & O'Dowd, D.D. The college-student image of the scientist. *Science*, 1961, *133*, 997-1001.

39. Bell, E.T. *Men of mathematics*. New York: Simon & Schuster, 1937.

40. Bem, D.L. *Beliefs, attitudes, and human affairs*. Monterey, Calif.: Brooks/Cole, 1970.

41. Ben-David, J. *The scientist's role in society: A comparative study*. Englewood Cliffs, N.J.: Prentice-Hall, 1971.

42. Benjamin, A.C. *Operationism*. Springfield, Ill.: Charles C. Thomas, 1955.

43. Berelson, B. *Graduate education in the United States*. New York: McGraw-Hill, 1960.

44. Berger, P.L. *The sacred canopy*. Garden City, N.Y.: Doubleday, 1967.

45. Berger, P.L., & Luckman, T. *The social construction of reality: A treatise in the sociology of knowledge*. Garden City, N.Y.: Anchor, 1967.

46. Berkner, L.V. Secrecy and scientific progress. *Science*, 1956, *123*, 783-786.

47. Bernal, J.D. *The social function of science*. Cambridge, Mass.: MIT Press, 1967.

48. Bernard, C. *An introduction to the study of experimental medicine*. (original 1865) New York: Dover, 1957.

49. Beveridge, W.I.B. *The art of scientific investigation*. New York: W.W. Norton, 1957.

50. Blashfield, R.K. Graduate admissions: A case study of a department of psychology. *JSAS Catalog of Selected Documents in Psychology*, 1975, *5*, 225.

51. Blissett, M. *Politics in science*. Boston: Little, Brown, 1972.

52. Blume, S.S. *Toward a political sociology of science*. New York: Free Press, 1974.

53. Boalt, G. *The sociology of research*. Carbondale, Ill.: Southern Illinois University Press, 1969.

54. Bok, B.J. A critical look at astrology. *Humanist*, 1975, *35*, 6-9.

55. Bok, B.J., Jerome, L.E., & Kurtz, P. Objections to astrology: A statement by 186 leading scientists. *Humanist*, 1975, *35*, 4-6.

56. Bolles, R.C. Reinforcement, expectancy, and learning. *Psychological Review*, 1972, *79*, 394-409.

57. Bonhoeffer, D. *The cost of discipleship*. New York: Macmillan, 1959.

58. Boring, E.G. Cognitive dissonance: Its use in science. *Science*, 1964, *145*, 680-685.

59. Bourne, C.P. *The world's technical journal literature*. Menlo Park, Calif.: Stanford Research Institute, 1961.

60. Bowen, D.D., Perloff, R., & Jacoby, J. Improving manuscript evaluation procedures. *American Psychologist*, 1972, *27*, 221-225.

61. Bridgman, P.W. *The logic of modern physics*. New York: Macmillan, 1927.

62. Bridgman, P.W. Remarks on the present state of operationism. *Scientific Monthly*, 1954, *79*, 224-226.

63. Brody, N. The effect of commitment to correct and incorrect decisions on confidence in a sequential decision-task. *American Journal of Psychology*, 1965, *78*, 251-256.

64. Brogden, W.J. The experimenter as a factor in animal conditioning. *Psychological Reports*, 1962, *11*, 239-242.

65. Brown, D.G. *The mobile professors.* Washington, D.C.: American Council on Education, 1967.

66. Brown, L.B. A study of religious belief. *British Journal of Psychology*, 1962, *53*, 259-272.

67. Brown, L.B. (Ed.), *Psychology and religion.* Baltimore: Penguin, 1973.

68. Brown, R., & McNeill, D. The "tip of the tongue" phenomenon. *Journal of Verbal Learning and Verbal Behavior*, 1966, *5*, 325-337.

69. Bruner, J.S., & Postman, L. On the perception of incongruity: A paradigm. *Journal of Personality*, 1949, *18*, 206-223.

70. Brush, S.G. Should the history of science be rated X? *Science*, 1974, *183*, 1164-1172.

71. Bunge, M. (Ed.), *The critical approach to science and philosophy.* New York: Free Press, 1964.

72. Cahoon, D.D. Symptom substitution and the behavior therapies: A reappraisal. *Psychological Bulletin*, 1968, *69*, 149-156.

73. Calvert, J.G. Pitts, J.N., & Dorion, G.H. *Graduate school in the sciences.* New York: Wiley, 1972.

74. Campbell, B.A., & Spear, N.E. Ontogeny of memory. *Psychological Review*, 1972, *79*, 215-236.

75. Campbell, D.T. Systematic error on the part of human links in communication systems. *Information and Control*, 1958, *1*, 334-369.

76. Campbell, D.T. Systematic errors to be expected of the social scientist on the basis of a general psychology of cognitive bias. Paper presented to the American Psychological Association, Cincinnati, September, 1959.

77. Campbell, D.T. On the conflicts between biological and social evolution and between psychology and moral tradition. *American Psychologist*, 1975, *30*, 1103-1126.

78. Campbell, D.T., & Stanley, J.C. *Experimental and quasi-experimental designs for research.* Chicago: Rand McNally, 1963.

79. Cannon, W.B. "Voodoo" death. *American Anthropologist*, 1942, *44*, 169-181.

80. Cannon, W.B. "Voodoo" death. *Psychosomatic Medicine*, 1957, *19*, 182-190.

81. Caplow, T., & McGee, R.J. *The academic marketplace.* New York: Basic Books, 1958.

82. Carnap, R. *The logical syntax of language.* London: Kegan Paul, 1937.

83. Carnap, R. Truth and confirmation. In H. Feigl & W. Sellars (Eds.), *Readings in philosophical analysis.* New York: Appleton-Century-Crofts, 1949.

84. Cartter, A.M. *An assessment of quality in graduate education.* Washington, D.C.: American Council on Education, 1966.

85. Castaneda, C. *A separate reality: Further conversations with Don Juan.* New York: Simon and Schuster, 1971.

86. Cattell, R.B., & Butcher, H.J. *The prediction of achievement and creativity.* New York: Bobbs-Merrill, 1968.

87. Cattell, R.B., & Drevdahl, J.E. A comparison of the personality profile (16P.F.) of eminent researchers with that of eminent teachers and administrators and of the general population. *British Journal of Psychology*, 1955, *46*, 248.

88. Chase, J.M. Normative criteria for scientific publication. *American Sociologist*, 1970, *5*, 262-265.

89. Chesen, E.S. *Religion may be hazardous to your health*. New York: Collier, 1972.

90. Christiansen, D. Judging the judges. *Institute of Electrical and Electronics Engineers Spectrum*, 1975, *12*, 29.

91. Churchman, C.W. Perception and deception. *Science*, 1966, *153*, 1088-1090.

92. Clarke, B.L. Multiple authorship trends in scientific papers. *Science*, 1964, *143*, 822-824.

93. Cofer, C.N. Constructive processes in memory. *American Scientist*, 1973, *61*, 537-543.

94. Cohen, D. *Myths of the space age*. New York: Dodd, Mead, 1965.

95. Cohen, I.B. Galileo. In *Lives in science*. New York: Simon and Schuster, 1957, Pp. 3-20.

96. Cohen, I.B. Isaac Newton. In *Lives in science*. New York: Simon and Schuster, 1957. Pp. 21-30.

97. Colburn, R. *Way of the scientist*. New York: Simon and Schuster, 1967.

98. Cole, J.R., & Cole, S. *Social stratification in science*. Chicago: University of Chicago Press, 1973.

99. Cole, S. Professional standing and the reception of scientific discoveries. *American Journal of Sociology*, 1970, *76*, 286-306.

100. Cole, S., & Cole, J.R. Scientific output and recognition: A study in the operation of the reward system in science. *American Sociological Review*, 1967, *32*, 377-390.

101. Consolazio, W.V. *The dynamics of academic science*. Washington, D.C.: National Science Foundation, 1967.

102. Cordaro, L., & Ison, J.R. Psychology of the scientist: X. Observer bias in classical conditioning of the planarian. *Psychological Reports*, 1963, *13*, 787-789.

103. Cornford, F.M. *Microcosmographia academia: A guide for the young academic politician*. Arlington, Va.: Beatty, 1908.

104. Cotgrove, S., & Box, S. *Science, industry and society: Studies in the sociology of science*. London: Allen and Unwin, 1970.

105. Cowan, T.A. The game of science. Paper presented to the American Association for the Advancement of Science, Berkeley, December, 1965.

106. Cox, M. *Genetic studies of genius, II: The early mental traits of three hundred geniuses*. Stanford, Calif.: Stanford University Press, 1926.

107. Crane, D. Scientists at major and minor universities: A study of productivity and recognition. *American Sociological Review*, 1965, *30*, 699-714.

108. Crane, D. The gatekeepers of science: Some factors affecting the selection of articles for scientific journals. *American Sociologist*, 1967, *2*, 195-201.

109. Crane, D. Social structure in a group of scientists: A test of the "invisible college" hypothesis. *American Sociological Review*, 1969, *34*, 335-352.

110. Crane, D. *Invisible colleges: Diffusion of knowledge in scientific communities*. Chicago: University of Chicago Press, 1972.

111. Crowder, T. Scientific publishing. *Science*, 1964, *144*, 633-637.

112. Culliton, B.J. The Sloan-Kettering affair: A story without a hero. *Science*, 1974, *184*, 644-650.

113. Culliton, B.J. The Sloan-Kettering affair (II): An uneasy resolution. *Science*, 1974, *184*, 1154-1157.

114. Davis, G.A. *Psychology of human problem solving.* New York: Basic Books, 1973.

115. Dawes, R.M. A case study of graduate admissions: Application of three principles of human decision making. *American Psychologist*, 1971, *26*, 180-188.

116. Dawes, R.M. Graduate admission variables and future success. *Science*, 1975, *187*, 721-723.

117. de Grazia, A. (Ed.), The politics of science and Dr. Velikovsky. *The American Behavioral Scientist*, 1963, 7, 3-68.

118. de Grazia, A. The scientific reception system and Dr. Velikovsky. *The American Behavioral Scientisl* 1963, 7, 45-68.

119. De Gré, G. *Science as a social institution.* New York: Doubleday, 1955.

120. Dement, W.C. *Some must watch while some must sleep.* Stanford, Calif.: Stanford University Press, 1972.

121. Diederich, P.B. Components of the scientific attitude. *Science Teacher*, 1967, *34*, 23-24.

122. Dixon, B. *What is science for?* New York: Harper and Row, 1973.

123. DuShane, G., Krauskopf, K.B., Lerner, E.M., Morse, P.M., Stenbach, H.B., Straus, W.L., & Tatus, E.L. An unfortunate event. *Science*, 1961, *134*, 945-946.

124. Dunnette, M.D. Fads, fashions, and folderol in psychology. *American Psychologist*, 1966, *21*, 343-352.

125. Ehrlich, H.J., & Lee, D. Dogmatism, learning, and resistance to change: A review and a new paradigm. *Psychological Bulletin*, 1969, *71*, 249-260.

126. Eiduson, B.T. *Scientists: Their psychological world.* New York: Basic Books, 1962.

127. Einstein, A. *Ideas and opinions.* New York: Bonanza Books, 1954.

128. Enloe, C.F. It ain't necessarily so! *Nutrition Today*, 1974, *9*, 16.

129. Evans, C. *Cults of unreason.* New York: Dell, 1973.

130. Falmagne, R.J. (Ed.), *Reasoning: Representation and process.* Hillsdale, N.J.: Lawrence Erlbaum Associates, 1975.

131. Farrer, J.A. *Literary forgeries.* London: Longmans Green, 1907.

132. Feather, N.T. Acceptance and rejection of arguments in relation to attitude strength, critical ability, and intolerance of inconsistency. *Journal of Abnormal and Social Psychology*, 1964, *69*, 127-136.

133. Festinger, L., Riecken, H.W., & Schachter, S. *When prophecy fails.* Minneapolis: University of Minnesota Press, 1956.

134. Feuer, L.S. *The scientific intellectual.* New York: Basic Books, 1963.

135. Feyerabend, P.K. How to be a good empiricist—A plea for tolerance in matters epistemological. In B. Baumrin (Ed.), *Philosophy of science: The Delaware seminar.* Vol. 2. New York: Wiley, 1963.

136. Feyerabend, P.K. Against method: Outline of an anarchistic theory of knowledge. *Minnesota studies in the philosophy of science.* Vol. 4. Minneapolis: University of Minnesota Press, 1970. Pp. 17-130.

137. Feyerabend, P.K. Consolations for the specialist. In I. Lakatos and A.

Musgrave (Eds.), *Criticism and the growth of knowledge*. Cambridge: Cambridge University Press, 1970. Pp. 197-230.

138. Fisher, R.A. Has Mendel's work been rediscovered? *Annals of Science*, 1936, *1*, 115-137.

139. Frank, J.D. *Persuasion and healing*. Baltimore: Johns Hopkins Press, 1961.

140. Frankl, V.E. *Man's search for meaning*. New York: Washington Square Press, 1959.

141. Freedman, J.L., & Sears, D. Selective exposure. In L. Berkowitz (Ed.), *Advances in experimental social psychology*. New York: Academic Press, 1965. Pp. 59-98.

142. Friedlander, F. Type I and Type II bias. *American Psychologist*, 1964, *19*, 198-199.

143. Frost, R. Kitty Hawk. From *In the clearing*. New York: Rinehart & Winston, 1942.

144. Fuller, U. *Confessions of a psychic*. Published by Karl Fulves, Box 433, Teaneck, N.J.: 1975.

145. Galileo. *Discoveries and opinions of Galileo*. (S. Drake, transl.) New York: Doubleday, 1957.

146. Galton, F. Statistical inquiries into the efficacy of prayer. *Fortnightly Review*, 1872, *12*, 125-135. Reprinted in *Humanist*, 1974, *34*, 31-33.

147. Gardner, M. *Fads and fallacies in the name of science*. New York: Dover, 1957.

148. Gardner, M. Paranonsense. *The New York Review*, Oct. 30, 1975, 14-15.

149. Gaston, J. Secretiveness and competition for priority of discovery in physics. *Minerva*, 1971, *9*, 472-492.

150. Gaston, J. Social processes in science. *New Scientist*, 1972, *56*, 581-583.

151. Gaston, J. *Originality and competition in science*. Chicago: University of Chicago Press, 1973.

152. Gephart, W.J., & Antonoplos, D.P. The effects of expectancy and other research-biasing factors. *Phi Delta Kappan*, 1969, *50*, 579-583.

153. Gillispie, C.C. *The edge of objectivity: An essay in the history of scientific ideas*. Princeton: Princeton University Press, 1960.

154. Gilson, C., & Abelson, R.P. The subjective use of inductive evidence. *Journal of Personality and Social Psychology*, 1965, *2*, 301-310.

155. Glaser, B.G. Variations in the importance of recognition in scientists' careers. *Social Problems*, 1963, *10*, 268-276.

156. Glaser, B.G. Comparative failure in science. *Science*, 1964, *143*, 1012-1014.

157. Glaser, B.G. *Organizational scientists*. New York: Bobbs-Merrill, 1964.

158. Glass, B. The academic scientist 1940-1960. *Science*, 1960, *132*, 598-603.

159. Gödel, K. *On formally undecidable propositions of Principia Mathematica and related systems*. (B. Meltzer, transl.) London: Oliver Boyd, 1962.

160. Goldsmith, M., & Mackay, A. (Eds.), *The science of science*. New York: Simon and Schuster, 1965.

161. Gonzalez-Wippler, M. *Santeria: African magic in Latin America*. New York: Julian Press, 1973.

162. Good, I.J., Mayne, A.J., & Smith, J.M. (Eds.), *The scientist speculates: An anthology of partly-baked ideas.* New York: Basic Books, 1962.

163. Graham, C.D. A glossary for research reports. *Metal Progress*, 1957, *71*, 75. Reprinted in R.L. Weber (Ed.), *A random walk in science.* New York: Crane, Russak & Co., 1973.

164. Grant, D.A. Testing the null hypothesis and the strategy and tactics of investigating theoretical models. *Psychological Review*, 1962, *69*, 54-61.

165. Greenberg, D. *The politics of pure science.* New York: New American Library, 1967.

166. Greenberg, D. *The politics of American science.* Baltimore: Penguin, 1969.

167. Greenwald, A.G. Consequences of prejudice against the null hypothesis. *Psychological Bulletin*, 1975, *82*, 1-20.

168. Guest, L. A study of interviewer competence. *International Journal of Opinion and Attitude Research*, 1947, *1*, 17-30.

169. Haberer, J. *Politics and the community of science,* New York: Van Nostrand Reinhold, 1969.

170. Haberer, J. Politicalization in science. *Science*, 1972, *178*, 713-724.

171. Hagstrom. W.O. *The scientific community.* New York: Basic Books, 1965.

172. Hall, J.F. *Verbal learning and attention.* Philadelphia: J.B. Lippincott, 1971.

173. Halmos, P.R. "Nicolas Bourbaki." *Scientific American*, 1957, *196*, 88-99.

174. Halmos, P. (Ed.), The sociology of science. *The Sociological Review*, 1972, Monograph No. 18.

175. Hanson, N.R. *Patterns of discovery.* Cambridge: Cambridge University Press, 1958.

176. Hanson, N.R. Scientists and logicians: A confrontation. *Science*, 1962, *138*, 1311-1313.

177. Harding, T.S. *The degradation of science.* New York: Farrar and Rinehart, 1931.

178. Hargens, L., & Hagstrom, W.O. Sponsored and contest mobility of American academic scientists. *Sociology of Education*, 1967, *40*, 24-38.

179. Harmon, L.R. The high school backgrounds of science doctorates. *Science*, 1961, *133*, 679.

180. Hart, I.B. *The world of Leonardo Da Vinci.* London: MacDonald, 1961.

181. Hartmann, D.P., & Atkinson, C. Having your cake and eating it too: A note on some apparent contradictions between therapeutic achievements and design requirements in N = 1 studies. *Behavior Therapy*, 1973, *4*, 589-591.

182. Hayek, F.A. *The counter revolution of science: Studies on the abuse of reason.* New York: Free Press, 1955.

183. Hearst, E. The behavior of Skinnerians. *Contemporary Psychology*, 1967, *12*, 402-403.

184. Hebb, D.O. Science and the world of imagination. *Canadian Psychological Review*, 1975, *16*, 4-11.

185. Henle, M. On the relation between logic and thinking. *Psychological Review*, 1962, *69*, 366-378.

186. Hill, K. (Ed.), *Management of scientists.* Boston: Beacon Press, 1963.

187. Hillman, H., & Ararbanel, K. *The art of winning foundation grants.* New York: Vanguard Press, 1976.

188. Hirsch, W. *Scientists in American society.* New York: Random House, 1968.

189. Hoffer, E. *The true believer.* New York: Harper & Bros., 1951.

190. Holland, J.L. Undergraduate origins of American scientists. *Science,* 1957, *126,* 433-437.

191. Holt, W.C. Death by suggestion. *Canadian Psychiatric Association Journal,* 1969, *14,* 81-82.

192. Holton, G. On the role of themata in scientific thought. *Science,* 1975, *188,* 328-334.

193. Hoyt, D.P. College grades and adult achievement: A review of the literature. *The Educational Record,* 1966, *47,* 70-75.

194. Hudson, J. *A case of need.* New York: New American Library, 1968.

195. Hudson, L. *Contrary imaginations.* New York: Schocken, 1966.

196. Hudson, L. *The cult of the fact.* New York: Harper & Row, 1972.

197. Huff, D. *How to lie with statistics.* New York: W.W. Norton, 1954.

198. Hume, D. *Dialogues concerning natural religion.* (original 1779) New York: Bobbs-Merrill, 1947.

199. Hume, D. *Enquiry concerning the human understanding.* (original 1777) Oxford: Clarendon Press, 1902.

200. Humphreys, W.C. *Anomalies and scientific theories.* San Francisco: Freeman, Cooper, 1968.

201. Huxley, F. *The invisibles.* New York: McGraw-Hill, 1969.

202. Huxley, J. *Religion without revelation.* New York: New American Library, 1957.

203. Huxley, L. *Life and letters of Thomas Henry Huxley.* London: Macmillan, 1900.

204. Hyman, H.H. *Interviewing in social research.* Chicago: University of Chicago Press, 1954.

205. Hyman, S.R. The Miller Analogies Test and University of Pittsburgh PhD's in psychology. *American Psychologist,* 1957, *12,* 35-36.

206. Jahn, M.E., & Woolf, D.J. *The lying stones of Dr. Johann Bartholomew Adam Beringer.* Berkeley: University of California Press, 1963.

207. Jahoda, G. *The psychology of superstition.* Baltimore: Penguin, 1969.

208. James, W. *Principles of psychology.* Vols. 1 and 2. New York: Henry Holt and Co., 1890.

209. James, W. *The will to believe.* (original 1896) New York: Longmans, Green, 1912.

210. James, W. *Memories and studies.* New York: Longmans, Green, 1912.

211. Jerison, H.J. *Evolution of the brain and intelligence.* New York: Wiley, 1973.

212. Jerison, H.J. Paleoneurology and the evolution of mind. *Scientific American,* 1976, *234,* 90-101.

213. Jevons, F.R. *Science observed: Science as a social and intellectual activity.* London: Allen and Unwin, 1973.

214. Johnson, R.W., & Adair, J.G. The effects of systematic recording error

vs. experimenter bias on latency of word association. *Journal of Experimental Research in Personality*, 1970, *4*, 270-275.

215. Juergens, R.E. Minds in chaos: A recital of the Velikovsky story. *The American Behavioral Scientist*, 1963, *7*, 4-18.

216. Kamin, L.J. *The science and politics of IQ*. Hillsdale, N.J.: Lawrence Erlbaum Associates, 1974.

217. Kaplan, A. *The conduct of inquiry*. Scranton: Chandler, 1964.

218. Kaplan, N. (Ed.), *Science and society*. Chicago: Rand McNally, 1965.

219. Kant, I. *Critique of pure reason*. (original 1768, N. Kemp Smith, transl.) London: Macmillan, 1963.

220. Kay, H. Should refs sign name. *American Psychological Association Monitor*, 1974, *5*, 12.

221. Kelly, G.A. *The psychology of personal constructs*. Vols. 1 and 2. New York: W.W. Norton, 1955.

222. Kent, L.M., & Springer, G.P. (Eds.), *Graduate education today and tomorrow*. Albuquerque: University of New Mexico Press, 1972.

223. Kent, R.N., O'Leary, K.D., Diament, C., & Dietz, A. Expectation biases in observational evaluation of therapeutic change. *Journal of Consulting and Clinical Psychology*, 1974, *42*, 774-780.

224. Kessel, F. S. The philosophy of science as proclaimed and science as practiced: "identify" or "dualism"? *American Psychologist*, 1969, *24*, 999-1005.

225. Kiesler, C.A. *The psychology of commitment: Experiments linking behavior to belief*. New York: Academic Press, 1971.

226. Kintsch, W. *Learning, memory, and conceptual processes*. New York: Wiley, 1970.

227. Kintz, B.L., Delprato, D.J., Mettee, D.R., Persons, C.E., & Schappe, R.H. The experimenter effect. *Psychological Bulletin*, 1965, *63*, 223-232.

228. Klaw, S. *The new brahmins: Scientific life in America*. New York: William Morrow and Co., 1968.

229. Kleinmuntz, B. (Ed.), *Problem solving: Research, method, and theory*. New York: Wiley, 1966.

230. Knapp, R.H., & Goodrich, H.B. *Origins of American scientists*. Chicago: University of Chicago Press, 1952.

231. Knapp, R.H., & Greenbaum, J.J. *The younger American scholar: His collegiate origins*. Chicago: University of Chicago Press, 1953.

232. Knickerbocker, W.S. *Classics of modern science*. New York: Alfred A. Knopf, 1927.

233. Koestler, A. *The watershed*. Garden City, N.Y.: Doubleday, 1960.

234. Koestler, A. *The sleepwalkers: A history of man's changing vision of the universe*. New York: Macmillan, 1965.

235. Koestler, A. *The case of the midwife toad*. New York: Random House, 1972.

236. Kolstoe, O.P. *College professoring*. Carbondale: Southern Illinois University Press, 1975.

237. Kornhauser, W. *Scientists in industry: Conflict and accommodation*. Berkeley: University of California Press, 1962.

238. Kozielecki, J. Investigation of the strategy of thinking in different probabilistic situations. *Psychologia Wychowawcza*, 1961, *4*, 458-459.

239. Kozielecki, J. Mechanism samopotwierdzania hipotezy w sytuacji

probabilistycznej. Unpublished doctoral dissertation, University of Warsaw, 1964.

240. Krantz, D.L. The separate worlds of operant and non-operant psychology. *Journal of Applied Behavior Analysis*, 1971, *4*, 61-70.

241. Krause, M.S. Corroborative results and subsequent research commitments. *Journal of General Psychology*, 1971, *84*, 219-227.

242. Kretschmer, E. *The psychology of men of genius*. New York: Harcourt Brace, 1931.

243. Krohn, R.G. *The social shaping of science*. Westport, Conn.: Greenwood Publishing Co., 1971.

244. Kubie, L.S. Some unresolved problems of the scientific career. *American Scientist*, 1954, *42*, 104-112.

245. Kuhn, T.S. *The copernican revolution*. Cambridge, Mass.: Harvard University Press, 1957.

246. Kuhn, T.S. *The structure of scientific revolutions*. Chicago: University of Chicago Press, 1962.

247. Kuhn, T.S. Logic of discovery or psychology of research? In I. Lakatos and A. Musgrave (Eds.), *Criticism and the growth of knowledge*. Cambridge: Cambridge University Press, 1970, Pp. 1-23.

248. Kuhn, T.S. Reflections on my critics. In I. Lakatos and A. Musgrave (Eds.), *Criticism and the growth of knowledge*. Cambridge: Cambridge University Press, 1970. Pp. 231-278.

249. Lakatos, I. Falsification and the methodology of scientific research programmes. In I. Lakatos and A. Musgrave (Eds.), *Criticism and the growth of knowledge*. Cambridge: Cambridge University Press, 1970. Pp. 91-196.

250. Lakatos, I., & Musgrave, A. (Eds.), *Criticism and the growth of knowledge*. Cambridge: Cambridge University Press, 1970.

251. Lamar, R. How physicists discovered two new particles. *The Stanford Observer*, 1975, *9*, (3), 3.

252. Langfeld, H.S. (Ed.), Symposium on operationism. *Psychological Review*, 1945, *52*, 241-294.

253. Langmuir, I. Pathological science. Colloquium at the Knolls Research Laboratory, December 18, 1953. Cited by G. McCain and E.M. Segal, *The game of science*, (2nd ed.) Monterey, Calif.: Brooks/Cole, 1973.

254. Lannholm, G.V. *Review of studies employing GRE scores in predicting success in graduate study 1952-1967*. Princeton, N.J.: Educational Testing Service, 1968.

255. Lannholm, G.V., Marco, G.L., & Schrader, W.B. *Cooperative studies of predicting graduate school success*. Princeton, N.J.: Educational Testing Service, 1968.

256. Lazarsfeld, P.F., & Thielans, W. *The academic mind*. Glencoe, Ill.: Free Press, 1958.

257. Leacock, S., & Leacock, R. *Spirits of the deep: A study of an Afro-Brazilian cult*. New York: Doubleday, 1972.

258. Lefford, A. The influence of emotional subject matter on logical reasoning. *Journal of General Psychology*, 1946, *34*, 127-151.

259. Legrenzi, P. Discovery as a means to understanding. *Quarterly Journal of Experimental Psychology*, 1971, *23*, 417-422.

260. Lehman, A. *Superstition and magic*. Stuttgart: Enke, 1898.

261. Lenski, G. *The religious factor.* Garden City, N.Y.: Doubleday, 1961.

262. Leonard, H.S. *Principles of reasoning.* New York: Dover, 1967.

263. Lesswing, N.J. The implications of contemporary thought in philosophy of science, cognition, and rhetoric for psychotherapy theory, research, and practice. Unpublished doctoral dissertation, Pennsylvania State University, 1976.

264. Lester, D. Voodoo death: Some new thoughts on an old phenomenon. *American Anthropologist,* 1972, *74,* 386–390.

265. Lipkin, H.J. Typical examination questions as a guide to graduate students studying for prelims. *Journal of Irreproducible Results,* 1958, *7,* 12.

266. Lipsey, M.W. Research and relevance: A survey of graduate students and faculty in psychology. *American Psychologist,* 1974, *29,* 541–553.

267. Livesey, H. *The professors.* New York: Charterhouse, 1975.

268. Lodahl, J.B. & Gordon, G. The structure of scientific fields and the functioning of university graduate departments. *American Sociological Review,* 1972, *37,* 57–72.

269. Lodge, O. Foreword in R.H. Murray, *Science and scientists in the nineteenth century.* London: The Sheldon Press, 1925.

270. Lotka, A.J. The frequency distribution of scientific productivity. *Journal of the Washington Academy of Sciences,* 1926, *16,* 317.

271. Lykken, D.T. Statistical significance in psychological research. *Psychological Bulletin,* 1968, *70,* 151–159.

272. Lynch, M.D. Avenues for reducing tension produced by attack on belief. *Journalism Quarterly,* 1967, *44,* 267–275.

273. Mahoney, M.J. *Cognition and behavior modification.* Cambridge, Mass.: Ballinger, 1974.

274. Mahoney, M.J. Publication prejudices. Mimeo, Pennsylvania State University, 1975.

275. Mahoney, M.J., & DeMonbreun, B.G. Confirmatory bias in scientists and non-scientists. Mimeo, Pennsylvania State University, 1975.

276. Mahoney, M.J., Kazdin, A.E., & Kenigsberg, M. Getting published: The effects of self-citation and institutional affiliation. Mimeo, Pennsylvania State University, 1975.

277. Malinowski, B. *Magic, science, and religion.* Garden City, N.Y.: Doubleday, 1948.

278. Manis, J.G. Some academic influences upon publication productivity. *Social Forces,* 1951, *29,* 267–272.

279. Marcson, S. *The scientist in American industry.* New York: Harper, 1960.

280. Marston, A.R. It is time to reconsider the Graduate Record Examination. *American Psychologist,* 1971, *26,* 653–655.

281. Marston, A.R. Rejoinder to Weitzman's comments on "It is time to reconsider the GRE." *American Psychologist,* 1972, *27,* 900.

282. Maslow, A.H. *The psychology of science: A reconnaissance.* Chicago: Henry Regnery Company, 1966.

283. Mason, S.D. Oral examination procedure. *Proceedings of the Institute of Radio Engineers,* 1956, May, 696.

284. Masterman, M. The nature of a paradigm. In I. Lakatos and A. Musgrave (Eds.), *Criticism and the growth of knowledge.* Cambridge: Cambridge University Press, 1970. Pp. 59-89.

285. Matson, W.I. *The existence of god.* Ithaca: Cornell University Press, 1965.

286. Maxwell, J.C. Foreword in C.C. Gillespie, *The edge of objectivity.* Princeton, N.J.: Princeton University Press, 1960.

287. McCain, G., & Segal, E.M. *The game of science.* (2nd ed.) Monterey, Calif.: Brooks/Cole, 1969.

288. McGuigan, F.J. The experimenter: A neglected stimulus object. *Psychological Bulletin*, 1963, *60*, 421-428.

289. McGuire, W.J. A syllogistic analysis of cognitive relationships. In C.I. Hovland and M.J. Rosenberg (Eds.), *Attitude organization and change.* New Haven: Yale University Press, 1960. Pp. 65-111.

290. McGuire, W.J. Selective exposure: A summing up. In R.P. Abelson, E. Aronson, W.J. McGuire, T.M. Newcomb, M.J. Rosenberg, and P.H. Tannenbaum (Eds.), *Theories of cognitive consistency: A sourcebook.* Chicago: Rand McNally, 1968. Pp. 797-801.

291. McGuire, W.J. Theory of the structure of human thought. In R.P. Abelson, E. Aronson, W.J. McGuire, T.M. Newcomb, M.J. Rosenberg, and P.H. Tannenbaum (Eds.), *Theories of cognitive consistency: A sourcebook.* Chicago: Rand McNally, 1968. Pp. 140-162.

292. McNemar, Q. At random: Sense and nonsense. *American Psychologist*, 1960, *15*, 295-300.

293. McReynolds, P. Reliability of ratings of research papers. *American Psychologist*, 1971, *26*, 400-401.

294. Mead, M., & Metraux, R. The image of the scientist among high-school students. *Science*, 1957, *126*, 384-390.

295. Meadows, A.J. *Science and controversy.* Cambridge, Mass.: MIT Press, 1972.

296. Medawar, P.B. *Induction and intuition.* Philadelphia: American Philosophical Society, 1969.

297. Medvedev, Z.A. *The rise and fall of T.D. Lysenko.* New York: Columbia University Press, 1969.

298. Meehl, P.E. Theory-testing in psychology and physics: A methodological paradox. *Philosophy of Science*, 1967, *34*, 103-115.

299. Mehrabian, A. Undergraduate ability factors in relationship to graduate performance. *Educational and Psychological Measurement*, 1969, *29*, 409-419.

300. Melton, A.W., & Martin, E. (Eds.), *Coding processes in human memory.* New York: Wiley, 1972.

301. Merton, R.K. The self-fulfilling prophecy. *Antioch Review*, 1948, *8*, 193-210.

302. Merton, R.K. Priorities in scientific discovery: A chapter in the sociology of science. *American Sociological Review*, 1957, *22*, 635-659.

303. Merton, R.K. Resistance to the systematic study of multiple discoveries in science. *European Journal of Sociology*, 1963, *4*, 250-282.

304. Merton, R.K. The Matthew Effect in science. *Science*, 1968, *159*, 56–63.

305. Merton, R.K. *Social theory and social structure.* New York: Free Press, 1968.

306. Merton, R.K. Behavior patterns of scientists. *American Scientist*, 1969, *57*, 1–23.

307. Merton, R.K. *The sociology of science: Theoretical and empirical investigations.* Chicago: University of Chicago Press, 1973.

308. Metraux, A. *Voodoo in Haiti.* (H. Charteris, transl.) New York: Schocken, 1972.

309. Michelson, I. Velikovsky forum. *Science*, 1974, *185*, 207–208.

310. Miller, G.A. The magical number seven, plus or minus two: Some limits on our capacity for processing information. *Psychological Review*, 1956, *63*, 81–97.

311. Miller, G.A., Galanter, E., & Pribram, K. *Plans and the structure of behavior.* New York: Holt, Rinehart & Winston, 1960.

312. Mills, J. Interest in supporting and discrepant information. In R.P. Abelson, E. Aronson, W.J. McGuire, T.M. Newcomb, M.J. Rosenberg, and P.H. Tannenbaum (Eds.), *Theories of cognitive consistency: A sourcebook.* Chicago: Rand McNally, 1968. Pp. 771–776.

313. Mischel, W. *Personality and assessment.* New York: Wiley, 1968.

314. Mitroff, I.I. A Brunswik Lens model of dialectical inquiring systems. *Theory and Decision*, 1974, *5*, 45–67.

315. Mitroff, I.I. Norms and counter-norms in a select group of the Apollo moon scientists: A case study of the ambivalence of scientists. *American Sociological Review*, 1974, *39*, 579–595.

316. Mitroff, I.I. *The subjective side of science.* New York: Elsevier, 1974.

317. Mitroff, I.I., & Featheringham, T.R. On systematic problem solving and the error of the third kind. *Behavioral Science*, 1974, *19*, 383–393.

318. Monod, J. *Chance and necessity.* (A. Wainhouse, transl.) New York: Random House, 1971.

319. Morgan, J.J.B., & Morton, J.T. The distortion of syllogistic reasoning produced by personal convictions. *Journal of Social Psychology*, 1944, *20*, 39–59.

320. Morrison, D.E., & Henkel, R. E. (Eds.), *The significance test controversy.* New York: Aldine, 1970.

321. Mulkay, M. *The social process of innovation: A study in the sociology of science.* New York: Macmillan, 1972.

322. Murray, R.H. *Science and scientists in the nineteenth century.* London: The Sheldon Press, 1925.

323. Nagel, E. *The structure of science.* New York: Harcourt, Brace and World, 1961.

324. Nagi, S.Z., & Corwin, R.G. *The social contexts of research.* New York: Wiley, 1972.

325. Neher, A. Probability pyramiding, research error and the need for independent replication. *Psychological Record*, 1967, *17*, 257–262.

326. Neisser, U. *Cognitive psychology.* New York: Appleton-Century-Crofts, 1967.

327. Nelson, C.E., & Pollock, D.K. (Eds.), *Communication among scientists and engineers.* Lexington, Mass.: Heath, 1970.

328. Newell, A., & Simon, H.A. *Human problem solving.* Englewood Cliffs, N.J.: Prentice-Hall, 1972.

329. Newman, J.R. Laplace. In *Lives in science.* New York: Simon and Schuster, 1957. Pp. 45-58.

330. Newman, R.I. GRE scores as predictors of GPA for psychology graduate students. *Educational and Psychological Measurement,* 1968, *28,* 433-436.

331. Norman, D.A. *Memory and attention.* New York: Wiley, 1969.

332. Nunnally, J. The place of statistics in psychology. *Educational and Psychological Measurement,* 1960, *20,* 641-650.

333. Obler, P.G., & Estria, H.A. (Eds.), *The new scientist.* Garden City, N.Y.: Doubleday, 1962.

334. Ogburn, W.F., & Thomas, D. Are inventions inevitable? *Political Science Quarterly,* 1922, *37,* 83.

335. O'Leary, K.D., Kent, R.N., & Kanowitz, J. Shaping data collection congruent with experimental hypotheses. *Journal of Applied Behavior Analysis,* 1975, *8,* 43-51.

336. Orne, M.T. On the social psychology of the psychological experiment: With particular reference to demand characteristics and their implications. *American Psychologist,* 1962, *17,* 776-783.

337. Ortega y Gasset, J. *The revolt of the masses.* New York: W.W. Norton, 1932.

338. Paisley, W.J. *The flow of (behavioral) science information: A review of the research literature.* Stanford: Stanford Institute for Communication Research, 1965.

339. Panati, C. Fata morgana. *Newsweek,* 1975, *86,* (22) 16.

340. Pelz, D.C., & Andrews, F.M. *Scientists in organizations.* New York: Wiley, 1966.

341. Perry, S.E. *The human nature of science.* New York: Free Press, 1966.

342. Peterson, C.R., & DuCharme, W.M. A primacy effect in subjective probability revision. *Journal of Experimental Psychology,* 1967, *73,* 61-65.

343. Pfungst, O. *Clever Hans.* (C.L. Rahn, transl.) New York: Holt, 1911.

344. Piaget, J. *Psychology and epistemology.* New York: Viking, 1970.

345. Pirsig, R.M. *Zen and the art of motorcycle maintenance.* New York: Bantam, 1974.

346. Planck, M. *Scientific autobiography and other papers.* (F. Gaynor, transl.) New York: Philosophical Library, 1949.

347. Platz, A., McClintock, C., & Katz, D. Undergraduate grades and the Miller Analogies Test as predictors of graduate success. *American Psychologist,* 1959, *14,* 285-289.

348. Plutchik, R. Operationism as methodology. *Behavioral Science,* 1963, *8,* 234-241.

349. Polanyi, M. *Science, faith, and society.* London: Oxford University Press, 1946.

350. Polanyi, M. Passion and controversy in science. *Bulletin of the Atomic Scientists,* 1957, *13,* 114-119.

351. Polanyi, M. *Personal knowledge.* London: Routledge and Kegan Paul, 1958.

352. Polanyi, M. *The tacit dimension.* London: Routledge and Kegan Paul, 1967.

353. Polya, G. *How to solve it.* (2nd ed.) Princeton, N.J.: Princeton University Press, 1957.

354. Popper, K.R. *The logic of scientific discovery.* New York: Harper & Bros., 1959.

355. Popper, K.R. *Conjectures and refutations.* New York: Harper & Bros., 1963.

356. Popper, K.R. *Objective knowledge: An evolutionary approach.* London: Oxford University Press, 1972.

357. Porter, A.L., & Wolfle, D. Utility of the doctoral dissertation. *American Psychologist*, 1975, *30*, 1054-1061.

358. Porter, J.R. Challenges to editors of scientific journals. *Science*, 1963, *141*, 1014-1017.

359. Price, D.J.S. *Science since Babylon.* New Haven: Yale University Press, 1961.

360. Price, D.J.S. *Little science, big science.* New York: Columbia University Press, 1963.

361. Professor X. *This beats working for a living: The dark secrets of a college professor.* New Rochelle, N.Y.: Arlington House, 1973.

362. Pruitt, D.G. Informational requirements in making decisions. *American Journal of Psychology*, 1961, *74*, 433-439.

363. Pruyser, P.W. *Between belief and unbelief.* New York: Harper & Row, 1974.

364. Randi, T.A. *The magic of Uri Geller.* New York: Ballantine, 1975.

365. Ravetz, J.R. *Scientific knowledge and its social problems.* London: Oxford University Press, 1971.

366. Rawls, J.R., Rawls, D.J., & Harrison, C.W. An investigation of success predictors in graduate school in psychology. *The Journal of Psychology*, 1969, *72*, 125-129.

367. Reif, F. The competitive world of the pure scientist. *Science*, 1961, *134*, 1957-1962.

368. Reiser, O.L. Noted in T.S. Harding, *The degradation of science.* New York: Farrar and Rinehart, 1931.

369. Reuck, A., & Knight, J. (Eds.), *Communication in science.* London: Churchill, 1967.

370. Richter, C.P. On the phenomenon of sudden death in animals and men. *Psychosomatic Medicine*, 1957, *19*, 190-198.

371. Richter, M.N. *Science as a cultural process.* Cambridge: Schenkman, 1972.

372. Riopelle, A.J. (Ed.), *Animal problem solving.* Baltimore: Penguin, 1967.

373. Robertson, M., & Hall, E. Predicting success in graduate school. *The Journal of General Psychology*, 1964, *71*, 359-365.

374. Robertson, M., & Nielson, W. The Graduate Record Examination and selection of graduate students. *American Psychologist*, 1961, *16*, 648-650.

375. Roe, A. *The making of a scientist.* New York: Dodd, Mead, 1952.

376. Roe, A. A psychologist examines 64 eminent scientists. *Scientific American,* 1952, *187*, 21-25.

377. Roe, A. The psychology of the scientist. *Science,* 1961, *134*, 456-459.

378. Roe, A. Changes in scientific activities with age. *Science,* 1965, *150*, 313-318.

379. Rokeach, M. *The open and closed mind.* New York: Basic Books, 1960.

380. Rokeach, M. *Beliefs, attitudes, and values.* San Francisco: Jossey-Bass, 1968.

381. Romanczyk, R.G., Kent, R.N., Diament, C., & O'Leary, K.D. Measuring the reliability of observational data: A reactive process. *Journal of Applied Behavior Analysis,* 1973, *6*, 175-184.

382. Roose, K.D., & Anderson, C.J. *A rating of graduate programs.* Washington, D.C.: American Council on Education, 1970.

383. Rose, H., & Rose, S. *Science and society.* Baltimore: Penguin, 1969.

384. Rosen, N.A., & Wyer, R.S. Some further evidence for the "Socratic Effect" using a subjective probability model of cognitive organization. *Journal of Personality and Social Psychology,* 1972, *24*, 420-424.

385. Rosenhan, D.L. On being sane in insane places. *Science,* 1973, *179*, 250-258.

386. Rosenthal, R. Experimenter outcome-orientation and the results of the psychological experiment. *Psychological Bulletin,* 1964, *61*, 405-412.

387. Rosenthal, R. *Experimenter effects in behavioral research.* New York: Appleton-Century-Crofts, 1966.

388. Rosenthal, R. Covert communication in the psychological experiment. *Psychological Bulletin,* 1967, *67*, 356-367.

389. Rosenthal, R., & Rosnow, R.L. (Eds.), *Artifact in behavioral research.* New York: Academic Press, 1969.

390. Roskies, E. Publish and perish. *American Psychologist,* 1975, *30*, 1165-1168.

391. Rostand, J. *Error and deception in science.* New York: Basic Books, 1960.

392. Roth, J.A. Hired hand research. *American Sociologist,* 1966, *1*, 190-196.

393. Rozeboom, W.W. The fallacy of the null-hypothesis significance test. *Psychological Bulletin,* 1960, *57*, 416-428.

394. Rudin, S.A. The art of finding the right graph paper to get a straight line. *Journal of Irreproducible Results,* 1964, *12*, (3).

395. Rusch, F.R., Walker, H.M., & Greenwood, C.R. Experimenter calculation errors: A potential factor affecting interpretation of results. *Journal of Applied Behavior Analysis,* 1975, *8*, 460.

396. Ryle, G. *The concept of mind.* New York: Barnes and Noble, 1949.

397. Sargant, W. *Battle for the mind: A physiology of conversion and brainwashing.* New York: Harper & Bros., 1957.

398. Scheffler, I. *Science and subjectivity.* New York: Bobbs—Merrill, 1967.

399. Russell, B. *The conquest of happiness.* New York: Bantam Books, 1958.

400. Schwartz, G., & Bishop, P.W. (Eds.), *Moments of discovery.* New York: Basic Books, 1958.

401. *Science Citation Index*. Philadelphia: Institute for Scientific Information, 1961 - .

402. Scott, W.A. Interreferee agreement on some characteristics of manuscripts submitted to the *Journal of Personality and Social Psychology*. *American Psychologist*, 1974, *29*, 698-702.

403. Sears, D.O. The paradox of de facto selective exposure without preference for supportive information. In R.P. Abelson, E. Aronson, W.J. McGuire, T.M. Newcomb, M.J. Rosenberg, and P.H. Tannenbaum (Eds.), *Theories of cognitive consistency: A sourcebook*. Chicago: Rand McNally, 1968.

404. Seligman, M.E.P. On the generality of the laws of learning. *Psychological Review*, 1970, *77*, 406-418.

405. Seligman, M.E.P. *Helplessness*. San Francisco: W.H. Freeman, 1975.

406. Seligman, M.E.P., & Hager, J.L. (Eds.), *Biological boundaries of learning*. New York: Appleton-Century-Crofts, 1972.

407. Selye, H. *From dream to discovery: On being a scientist*. New York: McGraw-Hill, 1964.

408. Shapere, D. The structure of scientific revolutions. *Philosophical Review*, 1964, *73*, 383-394.

409. Shapere, D. The paradigm concept. *Science*, 1971, *172*, 706-709.

410. Shapiro, A.K. Placebo effects in medicine, psychotherapy, and psychoanalysis. In A.E. Bergin and S.L. Garfield (Eds.), *Handbook of psychotherapy and behavior change*. New York: Wiley, 1971. Pp. 439-473.

411. Shapiro, S.I., Gregory, J., Allman, T., & Yoshimura, E.K. The psychology and sociology of science: A bibliography. *JSAS Catalog of Selected Documents in Psychology*, 1975, *5*, 178.

412. Shapley, D. Nobelists: Piccioni lawsuit raises questions about the 1959 prize. *Science*, 1972, *176*, 1405-1406.

413. Sheatsley, P.B. Some uses of interviewer report forms. *Public Opinion Quarterly*, 1947, *11*, 601-611.

414. Sheerer, M. Problem solving. *Scientific American*, 1963, *208*, 118-128.

415. Shils, E. *The intellectuals and the powers*. Chicago: University of Chicago Press, 1972.

416. Silverberg, R. *Scientists and scoundrels: A book of hoaxes*. New York: Thomas Y. Crowell Company, 1965.

417. Silverman, I. The effects of experimenter outcome expectancy on latency of word association. *Journal of Clinical Psychology*, 1968, *24*, 60-63.

418. Singer, B.F. Toward a psychology of science. *American Psychologist*, 1971, *26*, 1010-1015.

419. Skinner, B.F. *Contingencies of reinforcement: A theoretical analysis*. New York: Appleton-Century-Crofts, 1969.

420. Skinner, B.F. An autobiography. In P.B. Dews (Ed.), *Festschrift for B.F. Skinner*. New York: Appleton-Century-Crofts, 1970.

421. Smart, R. The importance of negative results in psychological results. *Canadian Psychologist*, 1964, *5a*, 225-232.

422. Smigel, E.O., & Ross, H.L. Factors in the editorial decision. *American Sociologist*, 1970, *5*, 19-21.

423. Sorokin, P.A. *Fads and foibles in modern sociology and related sciences*. Chicago: Henry Regnery, 1956.

424. Staddon, J.E.R., & Simmelhag, V.L. The "superstition" experiment: A reexamination of its implications for the principles of adaptive behavior. *Psychological Review*, 1971, *78*, 3-43.

425. Standen, A. *Science is a sacred cow*. New York: E.P. Dutton, 1950.

426. Stark, R., & Glock, C.Y. *American piety: The nature of religious commitment*. Berkeley: University of California Press, 1968.

427. Stecchini, L.C. The inconstant heavens: Velikovsky in relation to some past cosmic perplexities. *American Behavioral Scientist*, 1963, *7*, 19-43.

428. Sterling, T.D. Publication decisions and their possible effects on inferences drawn from tests of significance—or vice versa. *Journal of the American Statistical Association*, 1959, *54*, 30-34.

429. Stinchcombe, A.L. A structural analysis of sociology. *American Sociologist*, 1975, *10*, 57-64.

430. Storer, N.W. *The social system of science*. New York: Holt, Rinehart & Winston, 1966.

431. Storer, N.W. Introduction in R.K. Merton, *The sociology of science: Theoretical and empirical investigations*. Chicago: University of Chicago Press, 1973.

432. Straus, W.L. The great Piltdown hoax. *Science*, 1954, *119*, 265-269.

433. Strauss, A.L., & Rainwater, L. *The professional scientist*. Chicago: Aldine, 1962.

434. Strutt, R.J. *John William Strutt, Third Baron Rayleigh*. London: Arnold, 1924.

435. Student X. *Professors and other inmates*. New Rochelle, N.Y.: Arlington House, 1974.

436. Stunkard, A. Satiety is a conditioned reflex. *Psychosomatic Medicine*, 1975, *37*, 383-387.

437. Taton, R. *Reason and chance in scientific discovery*. London: Hutchinson Scientific and Technical, 1957.

438. Taylor, C.W., & Barron, F. *Scientific creativity: Its recognition and development*. New York: Wiley, 1963.

439. Taylor, J. *The scientific community*. London: Oxford University Press, 1973.

440. Taylor, J. *Superminds: A scientist looks at the paranormal*. New York: Viking, 1975.

441. Terman, L.M. Scientists and nonscientists in a group of 800 gifted men. *Psychological Monographs*, 1954, *68*, 44.

442. Terman, L.M., & Oden, M.H. *The gifted child grows up*. Stanford, Calif.: Stanford University Press, 1947.

443. Terry, R.L. Expectancy confirmation and affectivity. *British Journal of Social and Clinical Psychology*, 1971, *10*, 228-233.

444. Terry, R.L., & Lindsay, D. Expectancy confirmation and affectivity: A role playing variation. *Psychological Record*, 1974, *24*, 469-475.

445. Trotter, R. Evolution of language: A hatful of theories. *American Psychological Association Monitor*, 1976, *7*, (1), 1-13.

446. Tully, G.E. Screening applicants for graduate study with the aptitude test of the Graduate Record Examinations. *College and University*, 1962, *38*, 51-60.

447. Turner, M.B. *Philosophy and the science of behavior.* New York: Apple-ton-Century-Crofts, 1967.

448. Tversky, A., & Kahneman, D. Judgment under uncertainty: Heuristics and biases. *Science,* 1974, *185,* 1124-1131.

449. Twain, M. The damned human race. (original 1905) In B. DeVoto (Ed.), *Mark Twain: Letters from the earth.* New York: Harper & Row, 1962.

450. Velikovsky, I. *Worlds in collision.* New York: Macmillan, 1950.

451. Velikovsky, I. Some additional examples of correct prognosis. *American Behavioral Scientist,* 1963, *7,* 50-54.

452. Walster, G.W., & Cleary, T.A. A proposal for a new editorial policy in the social sciences. *The American Statistician,* 1970, *24,* 16-19.

453. Wason, P.C. On the failure to eliminate hypotheses in a conceptual task. *Quarterly Journal of Experimental Psychology,* 1960, *12,* 129-140.

454. Wason, P.C. The effect of self-contradiction on fallacious reasoning. *Quarterly Journal of Experimental Psychology,* 1964, *16,* 30-34.

455. Wason, P.C. 'On the failure to eliminate hypotheses . . .'—A second look. In P.C. Wason and P.N. Johnson-Laird (Eds.), *Thinking and reasoning.* Baltimore: Penguin, 1968. Pp. 165-174.

456. Wason, P.C. Problem solving and reasoning. *British Medical Bulletin,* 1971, *27,* 206-210.

457. Wason, P.C., & Golding, E. The language of inconsistency. *British Journal of Psychology,* 1974, *65,* 537-546.

458. Wason, P.C., & Johnson-Laird, P.N. (Eds.), *Thinking and reasoning.* Baltimore: Penguin, 1968.

459. Wason, P.C., & Johnson-Laird, P.N. *Psychology of reasoning.* Cambridge, Mass.: Harvard University Press, 1972.

460. Watts, A.W. *The wisdom of insecurity.* New York: Random House, 1951.

461. Watson, D.L. *Scientists are human.* London: Watts, 1938.

462. Watson, D.L. *The study of human nature.* Antioch, Ohio: Antioch Press, 1953.

463. Watson, J.D. *The double helix.* New York: New American Library, 1969.

464. Weber, M. Science as vocation. In H.H. Gerth and C.W. Mills (Eds.), *From Max Weber.* London: Oxford University Press, 1958.

465. Weber, R.L. (Ed.), *A random walk in science.* New York: Crane, Russak and Co., 1973.

466. Weimer, W.B. The history of psychology and its retrieval from historiography: I. The problematic nature of history. *Science Studies,* 1974, *4,* 235-258. II. Some lessons for the methodology of scientific research. *Science Studies,* 1974, *4,* 367-396.

467. Weimer, W.B. The psychology of inference and expectation: Some preliminary remarks. In G. Maxwell and R.M. Anderson (Eds.), *Induction, probability, and confirmation.* Minneapolis: University of Minnesota Press, 1975. Pp. 430-486.

468. Weimer, W.B. *Psychology and the conceptual foundations of science.* Hillsdale, N.J.: Lawrence Erlbaum Associates, 1976.

469. Weimer, W.B. *Structural analysis and the future of psychology.* Hillsdale, N.J.: Lawrence Erlbaum Associates, 1976.

470. Weimer, W.B., & Palermo, D.S. Paradigms and normal science in psychology. *Science Studies*, 1973, *3*, 211-244.

471. Weinberg, A.M. *Reflections on big science.* Cambridge, Mass.: MIT Press, 1968.

472. Weiner, J.S. *The Piltdown forgery.* London: Oxford University Press, 1955.

473. West, S.S. The ideology of academic scientists. *Institute of Radio Engineers Transactions on Engineering Management*, 1960, June, 54-62.

474. Westfall, R.S. Newton and the fudge factor. *Science*, 1973, *179*, 751-758.

475. White, T.H. *Breach of faith: The fall of Richard Nixon.* New York: Atheneum, 1975.

476. Whitehead, A.N. *The principles of natural knowledge.* Cambridge: Cambridge University Press, 1919.

477. Whitley, R.D. *Social processes of scientific development.* London: Routledge and Kegan Paul, 1974.

478. Whorf, B.L. *Language, truth, and reality.* New York: Wiley, 1956.

479. Willingham, W.W. Predicting success in graduate education. *Science*, 1974, *183*, 273.

480. Wittgenstein, L. *Tractatus logico-philosophicus.* London: Routledge, 1922.

481. Wittgenstein, L. *Philosophical investigations.* (G.E.M. Anscombe, transl.) London: Blackwell, 1953.

482. Wolfe, D. *America's resources of specialized talent.* New York: Harper & Bros., 1954.

483. Wolff, W.M. A study of criteria for journal manuscripts. *American Psychologist*, 1970, *25*, 636-639.

484. Wolff, W.M. Publication problems in psychology and an explicit evaluation scheme for manuscripts. *American Psychologist*, 1973, *28*, 257-261.

485. Wolin, L. Responsibility for raw data. *American Psychologist*, 1962, *17*, 657-658.

486. Wood, R.W. N rays. In R.L. Weber (Ed.), *A random walk in science.* Crane, Russak and Co., 1973. Pp. 77-79.

487. Wyatt, D.F., & Campbell, D.T. A study of interviewer bias as related to interviewers' expectations and own opinions. *International Journal of Opinion and Attitude Research*, 1950, *4*, 77-83.

488. Wyatt, D.F., & Campbell, D.T. On the liability of stereotype or hypothesis. *Journal of Abnormal and Social Psychology*, 1951, *46*, 496-500.

489. Zaltman, G. *Scientific recognition and communication behavior in high energy physics.* New York: American Institute of Physics, 1968.

490. Zangwill, O.L. *Remembering* revisited. *Quarterly Journal of Experimental Psychology*, 1972, *24*, 123-138.

491. Ziman, J. *Public knowledge: The social dimension of science.* Cambridge: Cambridge University Press, 1968.

492. Ziman, J.M. Some pathologies of the scientific life. *Nature*, 1970, *227*, 996-997.

493. Zirkle, C. The citation of fraudulent data. *Science*, 1954, *120*, 189-190.

494. Zubin, J. Vulnerability—A new view of schizophrenia. Paper presented to the American Psychological Association, Chicago, August, 1975.

495. Zuckerman, H.A. Patterns of name ordering among authors of scientific papers: A study of social symbolism and its ambiguity. *American Journal of Sociology*, 1968, *74*, 276-291.

496. Zuckerman, H. Stratification in American science. *Sociological Inquiry*, 1970, *40*, 235-257.

497. Zuckerman, H.A. *Scientific elite: Studies of Nobel laureates in the United States*. Chicago: University of Chicago Press, 1975.

498. Zuckerman, H., & Merton, R.K. Patterns of evaluation in science: Institutionalisation, structure and functions of the referee system. *Minerva*, 1971, *9*, 66-100.

While this book was going to press I learned of several new resources relevant to the topic of the psychology of science. The editors of *Pensée* have published a book titled *Velikovsky Reconsidered* (Doubleday, 1976) and Joseph Hixson has reviewed the Sloan-Kettering tragedy in *The Patchwork Mouse* (Anchor Press, 1976). Additionally, Lionel S. Lewis has documented some of the politics in academic tenure and promotion (*Scaling the Ivory Tower*, Johns Hopkins Press, 1975) and Gerald Holton has offered a recent note on the psychology of scientists (*Annals of the New York Academy of Sciences*, 1976, *265*, 82-101). These contributions are hopefully a sign of increasing interest in redressing our neglect of the scientist as subject.

Index

About the Author

Michael J. Mahoney is an Associate Professor of Psychology at The Pennsylvania State University and a member of the editorial boards of *Behavior Therapy*, *Addictive Behaviors*, and *Biofeedback and Self-Regulation*. He is the author of COGNITION AND BEHAVIOR MODIFICATION; co-author of BEHAVIORAL SELF-CONTROL; PERMANENT WEIGHT CONTROL; and BEHAVIOR MODIFICATION: ISSUES, PRINCIPLES, AND APPLICATIONS; and co-editor of SELF-CONTROL: POWER TO THE PERSON.